Leadership for Rural Schools
Lessons for All Educators

edited by
Donald M. Chalker

A SCARECROWEDUCATION BOOK

The Scarecrow Press, Inc.
Lanham, Maryland, and London
1999
Originally published by
Technomic Publishing Co, Inc.
Lancaster, Pennsylvania

A SCARECROWEDUCATION BOOK

Published in the United States of America
by Scarecrow Press, Inc.
A Member of the Rowman & Littlefield Publishing Group
4720 Boston Way, Lanham, Maryland 20706
www.scarecroweducation.com

4 Pleydell Gardens, Folkestone
Kent CT20 2DN, England

The Technomic edition of this book was catalogued as follows by the Library
of Congress:
Main entry under title:
   Leadership for Rural Schools: Lessons for All Educators
Bibliography: p.
Includes index p. 303
Library of Congress Catalog Card No. 98-87453
ISBN No. 1-56676-695-8
Reprinted by ScarecrowEducation
First paperback edition 2002
ISBN No. 0-8108-4436-2

♾™ The paper used in this publication meets the minimum requirements of
American National Standard for Information Sciences—Permanence of
Paper for Printed Library Materials, ANSI/NISO Z39.48–1992.
Manufactured in the United States of America.

To tomorrow's leaders:
Ashley, Kate, Jessie, and Michael

Table of Contents

Section III: Rural Site-Based Leadership

Foreword

INTEREST in American rural education has an enigmatic history. In the early nineteenth century, the rural schoolhouse was often a community site for social gatherings, civic education, and the teaching of English and protestant "manners." Observers of the American countryside often found much to praise in the existence and practice of these places and suggested that their existence and dynamics demonstrated the vision and vitality of American democracy itself. By the late nineteenth century, however, sentiments and policy had become oppositional to most tenants of rural schooling. Rather than being portrayed as bastions of democracy and civic purpose, they were increasingly castigated as outmoded, inefficient, and unprofessional. City and state educational leaders led this critique.

Mid-twentieth-century policies were also either unkind or ignorant to the possibilities and achievements of rural schools. Advocates of academic excellence in the 1960s targeted rural schools as impossible instructional sites for the proliferation of science and math courses they believed were required for national success. Equal opportunity advocates during the following 2 decades likewise suggested that equal schools often meant bigger and more comprehensive ones. Only with appropriate curricular differentiation available at all times to students of different ability could avenues of upward mobility be attained. Or so the argument went.

As the contributions to *Leadership for Rural Schools: Lessons for All Educators* suggest, however, the historical conviction that rural schools are, by definition, inferior is hotly debated today. In addition, rural school leaders can point to all sorts of scholarship today that underscores the viability and importance of most remaining rural schools. The evidence now is that bigger schools are usually not better schools, that multi-age classrooms more frequent in rural schools can have important instructional advantages over graded schools, and that the sorts of participation in extracurricular activities recognized as critical today for student success is more possible in smaller schools than in larger schools. We are also finding that equal educational opportunity is more about school and community connections and uniform curricular opportunities that have typically been the forte of rural, not urban, schools.

Leadership for Rural Schools is an excellent contribution to the reemergence of rural school scholarship because is covers almost every critical topic involved in rural education today. For the academic, it deals with rural school philosophy and history; for practitioners, it points to the studies and strategies used throughout America, which are used daily in rural schools; the politics of rural schools in an urban nation are addressed; and the demographics of rural places are seriously considered. I know of no other book on the current market that is as comprehensive and complete as this one. I suspect that its contents will entice and fascinate multiple audiences. Don Chalker and his contributors are to be commended.

ALAN J. DEYOUNG
University of Kentucky

Acknowledgements

M ANY authors have contributed their rural school expertise to this book. Several are on the faculty of Western Carolina University where rural education has become a prime interest: Bill Clauss, Dick Haynes, Mary Jean Herzog, Anna Hicks, Ellie Hilty, Bob Houghton, Casey Hurley, Robbie Pittman, and Penny Smith. Other contributing authors, from a variety of locations in the United States, have contributed to the rural education knowledge base for many years: Ed Chance, University of Las Vegas-Nevada; Alan DeYoung, University of Kentucky; Marilyn Grady, University of Nebraska-Lincoln; Emil Haller, Cornell University; Bernita Krumm, Texas A & M University Commerce; David Monk, Cornell University; Bob Morris, State University of West Georgia; Janie Nusser, Cornell University; Les Potter, State University of West Georgia. Consult the About the Authors section at the end of the book for names and background. Every author responded to my call for participation without hesitation. Pictures by professional photographer Rob Amberg enhance the book, and treat the reader to a pictorial version of rural living. The editor thanks each contributor for making this book on rural school leadership possible.

The book features many success stories of rural school administrators, teachers, and students. The book would not have been written without these leaders sharing their experiences. These rural practitioners represent thousands of rural educators who deserve respect for the job they perform each day. Those who research and write about rural education would have little success without them.

The editor thanks office assistants Phyllis Cogdill and Carol Oxendine for their technical help in coordinating the difficult logistics of such a book and making data processing software and tables fit the format of the book. Many times each day, I yell for assistance and receive it gratefully. I always appreciate ideas from my co-author on other books, Dick Haynes, and from my other colleagues in the Department of Educational Leadership and Foundations. Bob

Houghton, a contributor to the book, arranged the web page for the book and will maintain it for readers of the book.

I especially thank my teachers who taught me in rural settings and the students who attended with me. I remember with thanksgiving my parents who gently pushed me ahead and the perfect small town that was home. I thank my family for inspiring me.

The editor also thanks Technomic Publishing Company for recognizing the importance of rural school leadership and for contributing ideas for this book.

THE RURAL SETTING

CHAPTER 1

Introduction: Educational Leadership for Rural Schools

From the moment I picked up your book until I laid it down, I was convulsed with laughter. Some day I intend reading it.—Groucho Marx

This book, *Leadership for Rural Schools,* grew from a belief that rural schools have unique characteristics, and that these unique characteristics require unique leaders. Successful authors who have worked in rural schools and studied rural school characteristics have combined their talents to make this collection useful. Two characteristics of the book are: (1) The book will help educational leaders who work in small schools or rural settings better understand their role, and (2) The book will help all educators learn elements of the rural model that can enhance every school. Chapter 1 introduces the concept of rural school leadership, and introduces the authors and their contribution to rural school research.

RURAL ROOTS: FROM THE EDITOR

THE PERSONAL EXPERIENCE

W HEN I was about to enter a K–12 high school in a small Ohio village, my father came home one evening from the barber shop and handed me a four-year schedule that he declared would properly prepare me for college. While waiting his turn for a haircut at the village barber shop, he conversed with one of my teachers (also the school's only coach). Coach George developed a high school program for me and had his hair trimmed at the same time. So, for the next four years, I took every course outlined, studied enough to earn pre-

Donald M. Chalker, Department of Educational Leadership and Foundations, Western Carolina University.

sentable grades, played all three sports the school offered (coached, of course, by Coach George), delivered the commencement address and then, indeed, matriculated successfully to college. My parents, my teachers, and community members never really offered another choice. I am thankful that I grew up in a small town and attended a small school. Editing a book on rural school leadership is a rewarding way to celebrate my rural roots.

Small schools in rural communities offer a path to excellence that eludes others. Close cooperation between teacher and parent, a basic curriculum easily understood and goal directed, and a small town population that values its local school are but a few examples of the rural advantage. The barber shop and the school the author attended for twelve years are in the small village of Mantua, a town of 1200 people in Northeast Ohio. One building housed all grades and students attended elementary school on the first floor, junior high school on the second floor, and finally moved to high school on the third floor. The word "opportunity" was carved over the door and, indeed, opportunity was there for the asking. I remember a great deal about the "opportunity school." Even today, I can name every teacher I had through the twelve grades and almost every student in the school. Many of the experiences are vivid—some pleasant and some troubling. As this book took shape, the experiences continued to surface in my mind. It is fascinating that small or rural schools like the "opportunity school" survived in spite of conditions that educators would consider intolerable today such as:

(1) Multi-age grouping: The "opportunity school" had two grades grouped together because each grade housed only enough students for half a class.

(2) Grade teachers as specialists: Teachers not only taught two grades but also taught art, music, and physical education. The integrated curriculum existed long before the experts claim to have invented it. Special education students or gifted students did not exist in the "opportunity school." Well, they were probably there but nobody told the students or the teachers that they should be treated differently.

(3) Basic education: Since there were only enough students for one class, high school teachers taught the basics. There were four English classes, four social studies classes, four science classes, etc. Needless to say there was no tracking. There was one vocational class—agriculture—and the Future Farmers of America was *the* club.

(4) Few student services: There was no lunch program and no school buses; band met after school; and the superintendent was also the principal and a civics teacher.

(5) Community ownership: The citizens in town owned the school, used its facilities extensively, and attended school functions in the absence of a movie theater, bowling alley, and shopping mall.

The rural experience became more realistic when the "opportunity school" consolidated, and two adjoining small, rural schools joined the still rural system. Suddenly there were enough boys to play eleven-man football. The graduating class grew to thirty-six. And the school went into the cafeteria business and developed a transportation department. The "bigger is better" syndrome reached rural Ohio.

THE PROFESSIONAL EXPERIENCE

I graduated from the "opportunity school," earned my teaching certificate at the nearest university, and headed for the big city (another rural characteristic: Success means heading for the big city). I taught and served as an assistant principal, principal, and assistant superintendent in several suburban school districts in Ohio and Michigan. The schools were large, the buildings new, the resources plentiful and, of course, the salaries attractive. I had shed my small town image.

When the time came to seek the superintendency, however, I began to evaluate the quality of my personal and professional life in the big city. I had dealt with the "new rich" (those who suddenly move up in life and feel that the school is responsible for their children's drug habits, poor behavior, and lousy work ethic). I had dealt with the politics that school boards, pressure groups, and teacher unions practiced to influence decision-making. I had been responsible for schools of over 2000 students and struggled with the varied problems that come with large schools. But, when I was ready for the superintendency, my rural values surfaced, and I sought a smaller, rural-oriented system. I was successful and became the superintendent of the Lincoln Consolidated Schools, close to but still enough outside metropolitan Detroit to qualify as rural.

The Lincoln Schools claim to be the second consolidated in the United States of America. In 1924, thirteen one-room schools consolidated to form the Lincoln District and a brand new unit school opened. The new school burned in 1925, no doubt set on fire by persons known to oppose the consolidation. The community rebuilt the school, however, and the seventy-two-year-old building still serves Lincoln students. The Lincoln district is about 70 square miles of flat land mostly devoted to farming. A majority of the roads in the Lincoln District are dirt roads, and the district usually closes each spring because of impassable roads. We called these days "mud days," a term suburban neighbors found amusing. The farm calendar dictated the school calendar, and when the teacher union wanted to move the starting date earlier than the traditional post-Labor Day start, some farmers protested and said they would employ no more Lincoln students because they could not work the entire summer. Communications in the district flowed through three small post offices serving the three townships in the area. If anyone wanted to know how the district was faring, he or she took the mail to the post office. The teachers knew the parents and the parents liked their schools. Problems seemed livable in an atmosphere where values such as community, civility, and respect for education prevailed.

Today builders are developing some of the farm land. The federal government combined the three rural post offices into one large post office. The school district is under transition—rural to suburban. Lincoln is losing much of the rural advantage and, although it might be coincidence, is experiencing growing pains and a loss of stability.

IMPLICATIONS FOR RURAL SCHOOL LEADERSHIP

The editor and several of the contributors to this book now teach, write, and serve the public schools at Western Carolina University. Western is located in rural Appalachia in Cullowhee, North Carolina. The College of Education and Allied Professions and more specifically the Department of Administration, Curriculum and Instruction maintains a mission to train rural school leaders. In fact, the first doctoral program at Western is a unique program designed to prepare *rural* school administrators. The idea for this book developed from conversations about this rural leadership mission. The need for rural research is vast, and the educational system needs to understand the value of rural educational settings and the appropriateness of small schools. *Bigger is no longer better.*

The content of the book comes from beyond the Western Carolina contingent, however, and contributions for the book come from experts around the country who study and write about rural education. Collectively, the authors answer important questions about rural education:

(1) Can ruralness and smallness be defined?

(2) Are rural and/or small schools unique?

(3) Is the uniqueness of rural schools a positive condition?

(4) Do rural schools require leaders who understand rural uniqueness?

(5) Can research and a study of best practice in rural school leadership lead to knowledge that educational leaders can use to improve rural schools?

ORGANIZATION OF THE BOOK

Alan DeYoung, a scholar specializing in rural school research, wrote the Foreword for this book. In Section I, three authors establish the parameters of rural education. Mary Jean Herzog and Robert Pittman, Chapter 2, look for the elusive definition of rural schools and find it through the experiences of students recently graduated from public school. In Chapter 3, Penny Smith explores the history of rural education, and in the process proposes that the positive characteristics of rural education are currently positive characteristics that should exist in all schools.

> Ironically, we now find that our "one best system" no longer functions well and are discovering reforms that were at one time embedded in the ways effective rural schools operated.—Smith, Chapter 3 of this book

Section II, The View from the Top, examines rural school leadership at the district level. Typically, the rural school central office must process the same paper work as the larger urban district and accomplish the task with a smaller staff. Administrators must often assume dual roles and perform those roles within the expectations of the rural population. In Chapter 4, Marilyn Grady and Bernita Krumm look at the behavior of school boards in the United States and filter out characteristics that are uniquely rural. Ed Chance has studied the rural superintendent extensively, and in Chapter 5, he brings fresh insights into the successes and failures of the chief executive officers of rural schools. Robert Morris and Les Potter, in Chapter 6, study the function of personnel and human resource development in rural schools. Richard Haynes (Chapter 7) explores teaching and learning and the improvement of these most important school characteristics.

Section III features the rediscovery of site-based leadership in America's schools. The authors paint a picture of rural site-based leadership with a broad stroke. In Chapter 8, Casey Hurley looks at the role of site-based leadership through the eyes of several rural or small-school principals. Eleanor Hilty (Chapter 9) presents the argument that teachers need to assume a stronger leadership in their school, and Anna Hicks, in Chapter 10, argues that "students are leaders too" particularly in the rural environment. Each of the three authors uses interviews and case studies extensively in their reporting.

Educational leadership in all schools exists in a climate where knowledge about social, economic, political, and technical forces is essential for success. Educational leaders, particularly in rural settings, must understand the community they serve and the people that influence educational decisions. Educational leaders can no longer ignore technology. Section IV features leadership and organizational skills that all educators should understand and internalize. In Chapter 11, Robert Houghton tells school leaders about the most current uses of technology in schools.

> Long after city dwellers gave up hand wringers for washing machines, rural inhabitant did their work manually. It took special legislative pressure and funding in the 1950s to complete the effort of extending the electrical grid into the farthest reaches of rural communities. The similarities of providing rural electrification and providing rural communities with technology are sufficient to disguise important differences.—Houghton, Chapter 11 of this book

William Clauss (Chapter 12) talks about cooperation and collaboration between universities, communities, government agencies, and public schools in rural America. Edward Chance returns in Chapter 13 with a study of two rural school districts that collaboratively developed a school-community vision. The politics of educational decision-making surface in Chapter 14, as the editor, Donald Chalker, explores the overwhelming presence of politics in the educational scene and offers suggestions for combating the negative effects of political turmoil. Chapter 15 features a study by Emil Haller, Janie Nusser, and David Monk that compares the similarities and differences of school district quality as reported by local school citizens to those developed by the State of New York Department of Education. Chapter 16, by Doris Hipps, looks at the unique educational needs of Native Americans in rural America. Native Americans are, perhaps, the first rural inhabitants of this country.

Information about each author appears in the About the Authors section at the end of the book.

Rob Amberg, a professional who specializes in rural photography, provided the pictures scattered throughout the book. Behind every picture is a story that defines rural America.

HOW TO USE THIS BOOK

The content of the book, *Leadership for Rural Schools,* touches nearly every aspect of rural school leadership. Educators who read the entire book will find fresh ideas and yet be able to reinforce present knowledge. Each chapter is an independent study of a leadership position or issue, thus allowing the reader to pick and choose. Each chapter starts with an abstract to make choices easier. Each chapter features at least one quote. The quotes also identify the content of the chapter. Readers who seek additional information about rural leadership will find a list of resources at the end of each chapter.

The editor has created a web page on the Internet accessible at http://www. wcu.edu/Houghton/RuralCyberspace/ruraledcontents.html. The authors encourage your reaction to the book and, in many cases, have provided an E-mail address. Most of the authors provide services to the public schools in their specialty area and are available for consulting activities. The authors also encourage readers to respond to the book using the "talk" feature of the web page. The editor will attempt to respond to readers' comments and questions.

The Nature of Rural Schools: Trends, Perceptions and Values

Common people, good people, love of land, men without shirts, kids without shoes, women without makeup, people without a care in the world, small churches, not much traffic on dusty, back roads.—A student's response to the survey question: "What do you think of when you hear the word rural?"

Chapter 2 explores the constructs of rural communities and schools through an examination of demographic, economic, and educational trends and through a study of perceptions of rural college students preparing to enter the teaching profession. The results of the analysis and the study indicate that rural schools and communities have strengths that should be part of the prescription for remedying problems and directing changes in rural education. In order to develop an image of the shape of reform in rural education, it is necessary to understand the problems as well as the strengths of rural social and educational communities. For rural schools to be successful in combating their problems, they will have to capitalize on the community and family ties that rural students rated as so important. Educational leaders need to capitalize on the strengths of rural life and build the preparation of rural educators around them.

WHEN *Savage Inequalities* was being passionately debated around the country, Jonathan Kozol (1991) often inspired idealistic college students, raising their level of awareness about school funding equity issues. One such student, after hearing Kozol speak on a college campus, remarked with some relief, "I'm glad *our* schools aren't that bad. We don't have any of those prob-

A version of this chapter appeared originally in *Phi Delta Kappan*, volume 1, number 2, in October 1995. The authors thank *Phi Delta Kappan* for permission to use the contents.

Mary Jean Ronan Herzog and Robert Pittman, Department of Educational Leadership and Foundations, Western Carolina University.

School bus in rural Duplin County, NC. © Photo by Rob Amberg.

lems." Her comment reflected a commonly held belief that rural schools are in good condition, especially in contrast to schools in urban areas where racism, violence, financial problems, and general decay are prevalent images. But is she correct? Are rural schools really in good condition? Do rural school leaders agree with the statement made by this student?

Like their urban counterparts, schools in rural areas face financial inequalities, but they also have problems that are uniquely rural. A comprehensive report on rural schools (Stern, 1994) found high rates of poverty and low levels of educational attainment. It found that rural schools were staffed by younger, less well-educated faculty members and administrators who earn lower salaries and benefits than their metropolitan counterparts. The report documents persistent problems related to rural school finance, teacher compensation and quality, facilities, curriculum, and student achievement (Stern, 1994). Rural communities are said to be suffering from a "bitter harvest," with the well-educated emigrating to metropolitan areas for better jobs (Harp, 1994; Stern, 1994). Rural schools have image problems that stem from long-standing negative attitudes toward "country people."

These problems stand in stark contrast to the student's naive reaction to Kozol. However, she was correct in some respects. Rural schools and communities have strengths that should be part of the prescription for remedying problems and directing changes in rural education. An examination of the strengths and problems of rural social and educational communities must be undertaken in order to develop a picture of the direction reforms in rural education must take.

RURAL IMAGES

WHAT IS RURAL?

One problem facing rural education is the lack of a definitive understanding of the meaning of "rural" (Haas, 1991; Stern, 1994). The word is often defined from an outsider's and urban perspective, in much the same way that the dominant culture has traditionally spoken for minority groups. The U.S. government's term for a rural area is "nonmetropolitan." What does "nonmetropolitan" mean? An area without skyscrapers and interstate junctions? The Census Bureau defines rural areas as communities with *fewer than* 2,500 inhabitants or *fewer than* 1,000 inhabitants per square mile. Imagine the absurdity of placing New York City or Chicago in a category defined as "nonrural areas with more than 2,500 people" or as "areas without barns." The pervasiveness of the urban perspective seems to have contributed to a weak identity among our students: they often appear apologetic for being from the country.

ATTITUDES TOWARD RURALNESS

Another basic problem that students of rural education must face is the preponderance of negative attitudes toward rural people and places. As Toni Haas (1991) argues, modern American society does not value ruralness; prejudices against rural people and places are strong. Rural students seem to have internalized those prejudices, and they often seem to have an inferiority complex about their origins. Although the term "rural" conjures rich images, many of those images are based on negative stereotypes.

Consider one rural image with roots in antiquity—this is the "country bumpkin"—the healthy, naive, slow-witted, unsophisticated, ignorant, ultraconservative, penniless soul from beyond the outer fringes of the interstate. The *Oxford English Dictionary* provides references from the sixteenth and seventeenth centuries for the unflattering characterization of a rural person as a bumpkin. While the side of the interstate on which one lived was not a defining feature of Western Europe at that time, rural people were an easy target for the sixteenth-century equivalent of present-day prejudices and slurs. One can imagine the bumpkin persona arising from particular demographic, economic, and educational conditions in rural areas of sixteenth-century Europe, and the same relative conditions exist today to sustain the image. Even though our times are characterized by a heightened awareness of sensitivity to cultural differences, it is still considered socially and politically acceptable to poke fun at "rednecks," "hillbillies," and "hicks."

A key to success in educational reform is the school staff, and yet university education programs have done little to provide educators with specialized training for work in rural areas (Stern, 1995). Training for rural educators must go beyond superficial sensitivity training to an examination of the ways in which prejudices are developed against rural people and places. For example, elementary school social studies texts frequently portray rural areas in unflattering terms; children are taught that "urban" means, as a third-grade child recalled, "skyscrapers and people prancing around in fur coats," while rural means "barns and girls with pigtails." One North Carolina social studies text labeled the rural, mountainous western part of the state as an "unproductive region." Click on thesaurus when the cursor is on the word "rural" and see what appears. Our computers listed "provincial," "uncultured," "unrefined," "hinterland," "backwoods" and "forsaken" as synonyms for rural. For "urban," the thesaurus listed "civic," "civil" and "cultured." Over time, such negative connotations have a way of becoming the norm.

TRENDS AFFECTING RURAL SCHOOLS

While image is certainly one of the obstacles facing rural school leaders, it is not the only one. Educational, demographic, and economic trends also pose challenges for rural education.

Demographic Trends

Clearly, the standard definitions of rural areas and people paint a bleak picture. Are these images an accurate portrayal of conditions? Three population trends reflect much of what is happening in rural America. First, the U.S. population that is rural is decreasing. Second, the proportion of the population that is of working age (i.e., 18 to 64) continues to be higher in metropolitan areas than in rural areas. Finally, the older segment of the population has increased more in rural areas. The figures in Table 2.1 illustrate these demographic trends.

A larger percentage of the U.S. population lives in metropolitan areas than ever before. When the figures for the past thirty years are projected forward, this trend is expected to continue. Accompanying the relative decrease in the rural population, the proportion of the different age groups has changed. The working-aged segment of the rural population (those between the ages of eighteen and sixty-four) has increased in size. Metropolitan areas follow a similar pattern, but on careful inspection some differences appear. Discrepancies in the proportions decreased from 1960 to 1970, but have been increasing since 1970. While the segment of the population aged sixty-five and older has steadily increased in both rural and metropolitan areas, the increase has been greater in rural areas. Obviously, the operative population dynamics for rural and metropolitan areas are quite different.

John Cromartie (1993) sheds light on these differences by noting that migration between rural and metropolitan areas is a major factor in population growth and decline. The current rural-to-metropolitan migration is primarily due to working-age adults moving for better employment opportunities. On the other hand, rural areas attractive to individuals of retirement age are the recipients of a metropolitan-to-rural migration (Hobbs, 1994). Thus there are two contrasting migratory forces at work in the rural population. The challenge facing education in rural areas will be partly defined by these shifts. The different age groups are likely to have different views on the relative importance of education.

Economic Trends

Economic factors will likewise play a major role in defining the challenges for rural education. Table 2.1 shows that the median family income in rural areas in 1990 was about three-fourths that in metropolitan areas. The fact that participation in the labor force was approximately 6 percent less for rural areas than for metropolitan ones in both 1980 and 1990 (Parker, 1993b) does not completely explain the income differentials. As indicated in Table 2.1, metropolitan areas have a proportionately greater share of professional and upper-level managerial positions. These jobs pay more than others, thereby heightening the income differentials between rural and metropolitan areas. In contrast,

TABLE 2.1. Selected Demographic, Economic and Educational Factors, 1960–1990, by Rural/Metropolitan Residence.

	Year							
	1960		1970		1980		1990	
Factor	Rural	Metro	Rural	Metro	Rural	Metro	Rural	Metro
Demographic Factors								
Percentage of the population classified as living nonmetro/metro areas	30.1	69.9	26.4	73.6	23.8	76.2	22.5	77.5
Percentage of the population aged 18–64	52.2	56.3	53.3	56.4	57.5	61.5	58.6	62.8
Percentage of the population aged 65 or older	10.1	8.6	11.7	9.3	13.0	10.7	14.7	11.9
Education Factors								
Percentage of the population completing high school or more	34.0	43.3	44.3	54.8	58.7	69.0	69.2	77.0
Percentage of the population completing bachelor's degree or more	5.1	8.5	7.0	11.8	11.0	17.9	13.0	22.5
Economic Factors								
Median family income	$4,278	$6,211	$7,458	$9,962	$16,451	$21,104	$27,620	$37,933
Percentage of the population classified as living in poverty	34.2	17.0	20.9	11.5	15.7	11.4	16.8	12.0
Percentage of children under 18 classified as living in poverty	37.0	17.3	22.4	12.8	18.9	15.0	21.9	17.1
Percentage of the employed classified as working in professional/managerial positions	14.3	21.4			19.9	27.4	22.6	32.0

Note: The information in the table was derived from data in *Rural Conditions and Trends,* Vol. 4, No. 3, Fall, 1993: *Social and Economic Characteristics of the Population in Metro and Nonmetro Counties,* 1970 by Fred K. Hines, David L. Brown, and John M. Zimmer; *Statistical Abstracts of the United States, 1972;* and *Rural People in the American Economy,* by the U.S. Department of Agriculture, Economic Research Service, 1966.

rural areas have a higher proportion of the working poor who are stuck in low-wage, low-benefit jobs.

The incidence of poverty provides another perspective on the impact of the economy on rural education. Poverty is more prevalent in both the general and the school-aged segments of the rural population than in the metropolitan population. The data in Table 2.1 indicate that there has been neither a steady decrease nor a steady increase in rural poverty rates during the past thirty years. Rather, two mini-trends are evident. First, the incidence of poverty and the difference in the poverty rates for rural and metropolitan areas decreased in the period from 1960 to 1980. Second, overall poverty and the rural-metropolitan discrepancy increased from 1980 to 1990—but not back to 1960 levels. Of special significance to education is the fact that the percentage of school-aged children in poverty remains essentially the same as it was twenty years ago. The reduction in the poverty rate for the total population has not extended to children. Darryl Hobbs (1994) documents the increase in poverty for this population, and Michael Lahr (1993) reinforces the point by noting that more than one third of the rural Americans who are in poverty are children.

What are the implications of these economic conditions? In the future, rural schools will exist in communities with higher unemployment, lower median family income, and higher rates of poverty than metropolitan areas. In other words, more rural students will come from economically impoverished backgrounds, and fewer will come from homes in which the parents have professional or managerial positions.

Educational Trends

Two related educational factors—high school and college completion rates—are notable in defining the challenges facing rural education. The figures in Table 2.1 indicate that the average American now attends school longer than in the past. This tendency for more schooling is equally evident in both rural and urban populations, but that is where the similarity ends. From 1960 through 1980, high school completion was approximately 10 percent lower for the rural population than for the metropolitan population. From 1980 to 1990, the difference dropped to 7.8 percent. This suggests that the gap in the level of basic education between the rural and metropolitan populations has been reduced. However, the gap in college completion rates between the two populations has increased in each decade. In 1960, only 3.4 percent more of the metropolitan population than of the rural population had completed college. By 1990, this discrepancy was 9.5 percent. A portion of the difference can be explained by the outmigration of the more highly educated to obtain jobs in metropolitan areas (McGranahan, 1994; Parker, 1993a).

A third factor, school consolidation—a means of both cutting costs and improving quality—has been the single most frequently implemented educational trend in the twentieth century (Stephens, 1988, in Stern, 1994, p. 43). Emil Haller (1992) noted that consolidation has resulted in a marked decrease in the number of rural schools and school districts, yet more than 45 percent of the school districts in the U.S. are rural. Only 4.8 million students attend those numerous rural schools compared to more than 36.5 million students in urban districts (Stern, 1994).

Although consolidation has resulted in bigger districts and bigger schools, rural schools are still smaller and poorer than nonrural schools (Stern, 1994). Historically, student population has determined funding allocations, and smaller numbers mean fewer dollars. Fewer dollars mean fewer teachers and fewer advanced or specialized courses, thus putting students in rural schools at a disadvantage, a situation not unlike the urban inequalities Kozol describes.

A recent study of educational inequity in North Carolina schools conducted by the North Carolina Civil Liberties Union and the American Civil Liberties Union (1991) illustrates a form of geographical predestination. Blue Ridge School is a consolidated school that has 390 students in kindergarten through grade 12, with about 120 students in grades 9 through 12. By cmparison, Northern High School has 1,640 students in grades 9 through 12. According to the Civil Liberties Union report:

> Students at Blue Ridge High School in rural Jackson County . . . have 116 fewer courses to choose from than students at Northern High School in Durham County. Poorer schools are unable to provide students with a range of courses, especially in critical areas such as math and science. In 26 poor school districts, not one student sat for an AP exam. (p. 26)

Such curriculum differences between very large and very small schools are commonplace (Smithmier, 1994). School consolidation does not seem to have met the promise to erase inequities. Other than the fact that they are in the same state, Blue Ridge School and Northern High School might as well be on different planets for all they have in common. Students from poor, rural schools experience disadvantages in college attendance and graduation. The Rural Initiative, a study of educational opportunity in North Carolina (Public School Forum, 1990), compared the five wealthiest counties with the five poorest counties and revealed a 120-point SAT score deficit for the poor counties. The Civil Liberties Union found that "over 25 percent of the students attending the University of North Carolina (UNC) system campuses from 37 separate, predominantly poor counties required remediation upon their arrival at college" (NCACLU, 1991, p. 13). The poor counties in both studies were predominantly rural.

A number of conclusions can be drawn from an analysis of the demographic, economic, and educational trends displayed in Table 2.1. In rural areas in general, working populations are shrinking, economies are declining, and students are not competing well in college attendance and completion. Although there are mixed findings about the successes of rural students beyond high school (Smithmier, 1994), and although some states fare better than North Carolina, for more than 85 percent of rural students nationwide, the goal of a college education that leads to a professional career remains out of reach (see Table 2.1).

In the past when rural economies were self-sufficient, perhaps education did not matter as much, but today that is not the case. Additional resources could alleviate many shortages and buttress the system against problems that cannot be directly addressed such as the outmigration of many well-educated, adults of working age. If rural communities are to survive, they must develop new economies, attract working-aged people, and redesign schools so the students are not at a disadvantage simply because of geography.

STRENGTHS OF RURAL COMMUNITIES

The problems of rural communities are formidable, but developing solutions is the real question. What strengths does rural America possess upon which to create a foundation for addressing its problems?

THE RURAL ATTITUDE SURVEY

As a beginning point in this endeavor, the authors gave a questionnaire designed to investigate students' experiences with rural life to 108 students enrolled in educational foundations courses at Western Carolina University in Cullowhee, North Carolina. A majority of the respondents were sophomores or juniors in teacher education programs. The university has about 6000 students and is in the southern part of western North Carolina, 60 miles from Asheville and 150 miles from Atlanta. Cullowhee is in the Southern Appalachian Mountains about 20 miles southeast of the Cherokee entrance to the Great Smoky Mountains National Park. Raleigh, over 300 miles to the east, is the state capital and technological center and a place many natives will never visit. Raleigh is considered by many mountain people to be the place where rules are made without regard for the people who will be affected.

Regardless of their origins, attending Western Carolina University gave the respondents a rural experience. To illustrate the rural context in which the survey took place, the authors asked the students to "describe WCU and its surroundings as if you are telling an old friend about them." The majority of students described it in rather glowing terms, but a student from Raleigh responded from an urban perspective: "They call it 'Cullowhat' because you don't know where in the world you are, stuck here in these mountains. All of the people here are from the hills, and they intend to stay in these hills."

For the students in our survey, the positive feelings they had about living in rural areas were connected with their families, homes and small communities and with peace, safety and caring.

Some 40 percent of the students attending the University are first-generation college students. The questionnaire contained open-ended questions designed to elicit reflections on personal experiences. The students' responses were a sharp contrast to the images and trends of rural areas described above. One question was: "What do you think of when you hear the word rural?" Contrary to typical definitions, the students' answers did not rely on negative terms or urban contexts. In fact, the students used images that, taken together, told good stories about country life. One student, for example, responded that, when he thinks of "rural," he thinks of "common people, good people, love of land, beautiful scenery, men without shirts, kids without shoes, women without makeup, many people without a care in the world, small churches, not much traffic on dusty, back roads."

The great majority of the responses to this question conveyed images evocative of a healthy society. The students indicated that when they thought of rural, they thought of people, nature, and community. When they mentioned people, they emphasized the importance of relationships and relatedness as in "close-knit people; family gatherings; good country folks talking; old people sitting on the porch in a swing; and people who care about each other instead of the amount of money they make." They described a sense of community with phrases such as: "small; involvement; peaceful community; people actively involved in community activities; a community that couldn't survive very long without help from other places." Several students drew a connection between "small businesses" and a sense of community: "one gas station; one post office; convenience stores; no factories or shopping areas; small stores where the owners know each of the customers and each person feels welcome."

References to nature were intertwined with the descriptions of people and communities: "I can see horses, mountains, waterfalls, and I can hear good country folks talking. It makes me think of Highlands, my hometown." One student wrote, " 'Rural' is country; farms and children in the fields playing baseball or cow pasture football. I can visualize gardens, tomatoes and tobacco fields, and cattle grazing in the pastures."

The next question on the survey was, "What feelings does the word 'rural' bring out in you?" Students' responses to this question were, like their answers to the previous question, overwhelmingly positive and idealistic. One woman's response illustrated common themes: "The feelings I get when I hear the word rural are security and a sense of togetherness because a lot of rural communities are tightly knit. Contentment is another feeling I get when I think of rural. People living in the rural community seem to have a sense of fulfillment, being happy with what they have."

Another woman wrote, "I love the word rural. This, to me, is the best place to bring up children and to live a happy, relaxed life. Nice people and friendly atmosphere—relatively crime-free. Maybe even some backwoods type of people. Rural brings out happiness in my mind."

From all the responses students gave to this question, the authors extracted a total of eighty-eight different positive words, several of which occurred frequently. The most commonly used words in the responses were "peaceful," "safe," and "warmth." "Closeness," "comfortable," "friendly," "home," "quiet," and "relaxing" were also used frequently. Only fourteen of the students had negative responses and we compiled a list of seventeen different words and phrases including "negative," "no culture," "none," "nothing" and "isolated."

HIGH SCHOOL EXPERIENCES OF RURAL STUDENTS

Schools reflect their time and place, and students described their high schools, like their communities, as having positive qualities. One of the questions asked them to "Describe your high school as if you are telling a new friend at WCU about it." To analyze students' responses to this question, we separated those who were originally from rural areas from those who were from urban or suburban areas. A few examples of the responses from the rural students illustrate school-community themes: "My school is a school everybody is proud of." "My high school was very small, and I knew almost everyone by name. It is a close-knit family." "It was very comfortable in the school because the teachers and students were like family." "The teacher knew his/her students, and all the students knew each other. I knew the name of every student that I graduated with." Athletics were often mentioned as positive aspects of the high schools.

But rural students were also critical of their high schools. Their criticisms reflected the negative stereotypes of rural areas and were related to the demographic and economic issues discussed above. Some students described poor school facilities. For example, one respondent said, "I went to this high school that was so old we were lucky to walk out alive." Students reported negative experiences regarding their socioeconomic status. Two students wrote similar comments: "It was hard to get into college prep classes if you were poor because there was only one counselor, and she figured if you were poor, you were automatically a loser." Several students described their high schools as "hick schools." Another student said that her high school was ". . . a kind of rundown rural school compared to the city school in the area. Our SAT scores were not as high as the city school's."

THE BRAIN DRAIN

Another question asked, "Do you plan to go back to your community to work after college? If so, what kind of job do you hope to get?" Almost half (43 percent) plan to go back home, and about 15 percent are ambivalent. Of those who want to go back home, 85 percent plan to work in an education career, most as teachers. (Given our sample, this career choice is not surprising.) Our students' responses are consistent with the portrayal of rural areas as losing a large portion of their educated young adults because of the lack of professional and managerial jobs. Teaching continues to be one of the few professional opportunities available in many rural areas.

HOME, FAMILY, COMMUNITY, CARING

In the context of the violent and materialistic world of the waning twentieth century, the students at Western Carolina University may sound unduly optimistic. But their voices should be heard. They are saying that there is true value in relationships, that community is an anchor, and that peace and safety lie within their rural communities. They are also telling us that their schools had good qualities but could have been better—that they could have provided more opportunities for disadvantaged students and better preparation for college and the workplace.

As noted earlier, rural education did not get much attention in the national Reform Movement that began in the 1980s. The Reform Movement missed the importance of the home, family, and community in reshaping schools (Bell, 1993). Evans Clinchy (1993) argued that all schools should be "small, safe, intimate, family-like institutions" (p. 610). Paul Theobold and Ed Mills (1995) hold that schools have to rediscover community and caring. Finally, Joyce Stern's (1994) discussion of rural school-community relationships reaffirms our students' impressions of the sense of community and smallness of scale that represent the best qualities of rural life.

For the students in our survey, the positive feelings they had about living in rural areas were connected with their families, homes, and small communities and with peace, safety, and caring. Many of them have chosen a career in education so they will be able to return to their homes after college. For rural school leaders to be successful in combating their problems, they will have to capitalize on the community and family ties that our rural students rated as so important. It is curious that rural communities, which for so long have been marginalized by the dominant culture, present precisely the qualities for which the critics of American schools are now looking. As educators, we need to recognize these strengths, take advantage of them, and build the preparation of rural school leaders around them. We have neglected this task for too long.

REFERENCES

Bell, T. H. 1993. "Reflections One Decade After a Nation at Risk," *Phi Delta Kappan*, 74 (8), 592–597.

Clinchy, E. 1993. "Needed: A Clinton Crusade for Quality and Equality." *Phi Delta Kappan, 74* (8), 605–612.

Cromartie, J. 1993. "Nonmetro Outmigration Exceeded Inmigration During the 1980's," *Rural Conditions and Trends, 4* (3), 24–25.

Haas, T. 1991. "Why Reform Doesn't Apply," in A. J. DeYoung, *Rural Education, Issues and Practice.* NY: Garland, 412–446.

Haller, E. 1992. "High School Size and Student Indiscipline: Another Aspect of the School Consolidation Issue?" *Educational Evaluation and Policy Analysis, 14* (2), 145–156.

Harp, L. 1994. "The Bitter Harvest," *Education Week,* XIV (8), 24–29.

Hines, F., D. Brown, & J. Zimmer. 1975. "Social and Economic Characteristics of the Population in Metro and Nonmetro Counties, 1970," *Agricultural Economic Report No. 272.* Washington, DC: U.S. Department of Agriculture, Economic Research Service.

Hobbs, D. 1994. "Demographic Trends in Nonmetropolitan America." Paper presented at the Annual Meeting of the American Educational Research Association, New Orleans.

Kozol, J. 1991. *Savage Inequalities.* New York: Crown Publishers.

Lahr, M. 1993. "Families with Children and Headed by Women Fare Worst," *Rural Conditions and Trends, 4* (3), 50–53.

McGranahan, D. 1994. "Rural America in the Global Economy: Recent Socioeconomic Trends." Paper presented at the Annual Meeting of the American Educational Research Association, New Orleans.

North Carolina Civil Liberties Union/American Civil Liberties Union. 1991. "A Right Denied: Educational Inequity in North Carolina's Schools." (A Report to the North Carolina General Assembly.) Raleigh, NC: Author.

Oxford English Dictionary, Volume II, 2nd ed. 1989. Oxford: Clarendon Press.

Parker, T. 1993a. "Nonmetro College Completion Rates Fall Further Behind Metro," *Rural Conditions and Trends, 4* (3), 32–33.

Parker, T. 1993b. "Nonmetro Labor Force Size and Participation Rate Up Moderately," *Rural Conditions and Trends, 4* (3), 34–37.

Public School Forum. 1990. *All That's Within Them: Building a Foundation for Educational & Economic Growth.* Raleigh, NC: Public School Forum.

Smithmier, A. 1994. "Constructing a Culture of Community," *Journal of Research in Rural Education, 10* (2), 89–96.

Stern, J. D. Spring, 1995. "Reflections of a Recently Retired Federal Analyst in Rural Education," *The Rural Education Newsletter.* Charleston, WV: Appalachian Educational Laboratory. (Supplement), pp. 1–2.

Stern, J. D. (Ed.). 1994. *The Condition of Education in Rural Schools.* Washington, DC: U.S. Department of Education.

Theobald, P., & E. Mills. 1995. "Accountability and the Struggle over What Counts," *Phi Delta Kappan, 76* (6), 462–466.

Theobald, P. January, 1992. "Rural Philosophy for Education: Wendell Berry's Tradition," *ERIC Digest. Clearinghouse on Rural Education and Small Schools* (Digest EDO-RC-91-12).

U.S. Bureau of the Census. 1972. *Statistical Abstracts of the United States: 1972* (93rd edition). Washington, DC: Author.

U.S. Department of Agriculture, Economic Research Service. 1966. *Rural People in the American Economy. Agricultural Economic Report No. 101.* Washington, DC: Author.

CHAPTER 3

"It's Deja Vu All Over Again":
The Rural School Problem Revisited

Most of the change we think we see in life is due to truths being in and out of favor.—Robert Frost, "The Black Cottage"

This chapter will review the general form of criticisms made of rural schools from the nineteenth century onward. It will suggest several reasons for the persistence of charges made against those schools. Finally, it will offer current educational leaders a few policy and pedagogical implications of that history.

THE historian Richard Hofstadter (1966) once observed that "the educational jeremiad is as much a feature of our literature as the jeremiad in the Puritan sense" (p. 301). Early American authors, primarily colonial ministers, designed jeremiads to remind their congregations that they were all sinners. If their sermons were effective, the resultant guilt was palpable. Transgressors sought, immediately and with an anxious sense of urgency, redemption. A recitation of sins, these ministerial admonitions were simultaneously calls to action.

Those of us who work in our nation's public schools are all too familiar with contemporary secular variations of the jeremiad. Presaged by Jimmy Carter's National Agenda for the Eighties, the year 1983 marked the beginning of a barrage of criticism, of subsequent demands for reform, and, ultimately, of a plethora of proposals for improvement. "The current crisis in confidence in public schooling is more widespread, persistent, and intense than at any previous point in history" (Reisler, 1981, p. 413). "Each generation of Americans has outstripped its parents in education, in literacy, and in economic attainment. For the first time in the history of our country, the educational skills of one genera-

Penny Smith, Department of Educational Leadership and Foundations, Western Carolina University.

Children waiting for the school bus, Iredell County, NC. © Photo by Rob Amberg.

tion will not surpass, will not equal, will not even approach, those of their parents" (National Commission on Excellence in Education, 1983, p. 11). "We have expected too little of our schools over the past two decades . . . if we are serious about economic growth in America . . . then we must get serious about education. And we must begin now" (Task Force on Education for Economic Growth, 1983, p. 32).

The language of our current season of discontent has continued shrill and insistent since that initial round of task force and special commission reports. For example, in his 1997 State of the Union address, President Clinton called for "a national crusade for educational standards." In their allusions to educational disaster and imminent academic decline, in their use of rhetorical devices associated with sacred enterprises (crusades) or national emergencies (wars), and in their call to act *now*, these catalogues of complaints embody the basic elements of Hofstadter's educational jeremiad. Politicians extol from bully pulpits; their messages are no less guilt-inducing than those Jonathan Edwards penned in eighteenth-century Massachusetts.

Although all schools are by implication subject to the current critique, one set of those institutions has been the focus of condemnation since the colonial period—our rural schools. They were, initially, because they were the only schools we had. As the United States entered the nineteenth century, increasingly they became the "other schools," educational facilities whose remediation was promised when they assumed the look and practice of improved schools, those found in cities—the legacy of the reform initiatives that David Tyack (1974) described in his book *The One Best System*. The list of ways in which rural schools failed their students has remained remarkably unchanged over most of the last two centuries, as have the ways by which critics recommend that they be made better. Now, as then, the route to educational salvation is in getting bigger, in consolidation along the lines of modern, a signifier for urban or suburban, schools. As Stern (1994) reminds us, the single most often used reform effort to improve rural schools in the twentieth century has been the merging of smaller buildings into a single, centralized, large facility.

FINDING THE ONE BEST SYSTEM

If, in many history of education books, the dominant theme of the antebellum period in the United States is the introduction and rise of the common school, then the theme in many of those same books of the period after the Civil War is the development of the consolidated, graded school. It is the managed evolution of "one best system." The nineteenth century began with the little red schoolhouse and ended with an educational factory. We moved from small community to bureaucracy in the span of a century, establishing first a system of city schools and then turning to the merger of county schools to ensure that they, too, provided the economic skills requisite for individual and national success in a changing economy.

As the authors of *The Theory of American Education as Approved by Influential Educators* (1874, reprinted in Cohen, 1974) asserted, "the modern industrial community cannot exist without free popular education carried out in a system of schools ascending from the primary grade to the university" (Vol. 3, p. 1903). "The commercial tone prevalent in the city tends to develop, in its schools, quick, alert habits and readiness to combine with others in their tasks." Students in such schools learned "(1) punctuality, (2) regularity, (3) attention, and (4) silence, as habits necessary through life for successful combination with one's fellow-men in an industrial and commercial civilization" (Vol. 3, p. 1905). Civilization meant technological progress. Bigger came to mean better, because size ensured that the course of study could be graded, the curriculum could be standardized, the faculty closely supervised, the staff professionally trained and licensed, the students regularly assessed, and the management of the enterprise entrusted to educational experts exempt from the petty politics of an illiterate public. The words one began to associate with the modern factory—"routine," "standards," "scientific management," "regulation," "orderliness," "control," "efficiency"—became the vocabulary of that new school.

Robert Wiebe (1967) entitled his book about the United States at the turn of the century *The Search for Order, 1877–1920*. It was order we sought in our economic, social, and cultural lives; to achieve it we often looked, as David Nasaw (1979) and Raymond Callahan (1962) remind us, to our schools. Urban schoolmen eagerly complied with demands for docile, skilled, technically proficient workers. Reformers "saw the school as a critical means of transforming the pre-industrial culture—values and attitudes, work habits, time orientation, even recreations—of citizens in a modernizing society" (Tyack, 1974, p. 29). Andrew Carnegie argued that schools should become "a ladder on which the aspiring could rise" (Quoted in Perkison, 1968, p. 156). They should be the formal instrument of economic mobility. The resultant industrial paradigm of schooling ensured that public institutions were bureaucratic in the Weberian (1958) sense: They were authoritarian, hierarchical, and impersonal. The majority of workers were certified teachers, overseen by certified managers, who perceived students as passive participants on an educational assembly line whose end products were designed to meet the needs of business and industry nationwide.

There were few more prolific and influential authors about school matters in the early twentieth century than Ellwood Cubberley, the man who put the educational department at Stanford University on the scientific reform map. Convinced that schools could serve as buffers between the body politic and perdition, helping to prevent crime and poverty, enabling the nation to assimilate millions of new immigrants, and preserving our western Euro-centric culture, Cubberley embraced the educational changes of urban school leaders. He effectively perpetuated those changes from his position at Stanford, becoming a teacher of the next generation of educational leaders and a consultant to systems wanting to modernize. He wrote in 1916:

> Our schools are factories in which the raw materials are to be shaped and fashioned into products to meet the various demands of life. The specifications for manufacturing come from the demands of the twentieth century civilization, and it is the business of the school to build its pupils to the specifications laid down. This demands good tools, specialized machinery, continuous measurement of production to see if it is according to specifications, the elimination of waste in manufacture and a large variety of outputs. (p. 338)

In spite of critics who saw flaws in that new system and who anticipated many of the complaints that contemporary reformers make about urban schools today, that factory model prevailed in our cities. It became the standard for up-to-date, effective schooling.

In 1886 Charles Ham described "the distinguishing characteristic of the ideal school building" as its "chimney, which rises far above the roof, from whose tall stack a column of smoke issues, and the turn and whir of machinery is heard." In that building "which resembles a factory or machine-shop an educational revolution is to be wrought." Americans were, he argued, in the process of replacing "the enervating influence of Grecian aestheticism" with "the scientific direction of the followers of Bacon, whose philosophy is common sense and its law, progress" (Quoted in Cohen, Vol. 3, p. 1857). Once the city common school became a pristine factory, reformers shifted their attention to the country and to rural schools.

DISCOVERING THE RURAL SCHOOL PROBLEM

Criticism of rural schools is as old as schooling in the United States. However, initial criticism was of schooling itself, not of place. It was of the institution and practices therein and considered germane to educational institutions globally, be they in the country, in villages, or in port towns. The ante-bellum common school movement was not so much an effort to improve what happened in a certain place as to institute a set of general standards about what should happen in all places. As part of a campaign for improved schooling, common school leaders criticized the status quo. Teaching, they complained, was merely a series of recitations; learning was rote. Teachers were sometimes transients, all too often political appointments, and occasionally unprepared to teach. Rarely had they received formal training. Most practitioners did not see themselves as members of a profession engaged in a life-long career. For men, teaching was something one did in the winter months when one could not farm, or what one did before going away to college or preparing for a *true* profession. For women, teaching was a temporary stop on the journey from daughter to spouse. School buildings were cold, dirty, and sometimes unsafe. At times the most vociferous discussions about local education involved the placement of the building itself, rather than what went on therein. Students came sporadically and, particularly if older, behaved badly. Parents who could afford private academies continued to send their students to them, thereby diminishing popular support for publicly funded educational opportunities for all citizens. Corporal punishment was the norm. Communities supported formal education less than enthusiastically and were renown for their unwillingness to provide adequate resources. Comparisons with other countries, particularly with Prussia, highlighted for early reformers like Calvin Stowe, Horace Mann, and Henry Barnard the inadequacies of American schools.

To make their cases for common schools, these reformers linked the educational well-being of individuals to the economic and social well-being of the state. Mann, writing in 1848, noted that "education . . . beyond all other devices of human origin, is the great equalizer of the conditions of men—the balance-wheel of the social machinery" (Quoted in Knight & Hall, 1951, p. 166). In 1867 an editor of the *New York Sun*, arguing in favor of the passage of a compulsory school law, wrote that "the stability and credit of our nation depends in no small degree on the efficiency of our system of popular education, and every state should take measures to render compulsory such a share of education as is indispensable to intelligent citizens" (Quoted in Knight & Hall, 1951, p. 368).

The solution to a lack of uniform educational opportunity was to create an organization, to establish a cohesive, interactive whole from disparate parts. As Mann (1955) observed in a 1837 lecture:

> In this Commonwealth there are about three thousand public schools, in all of which the rudiments of knowledge are taught. These schools, at the present time, are so many distinct, independent communities; each being governed by its own habits, traditions, and local customs. There is no common, superintending power over them; there is no bond of brotherhood or family between them. They are strangers and aliens to each other. The teachers are, as it were, imbedded, each in his own school district . . . As the system is now administered, if any improvements in principles or modes of teaching is discovered by talent or accident, in one school, instead of being published to the world, it dies with the discoverer. (p. 19)

Mann anticipated the efforts of the city schoolmen, who intensified the pressure to establish an orderly process of educating America's children. A school system was, to those individuals, a machine, whose parts should be designed to work efficiently and effectively in concert. It was easiest to put those parts together in large towns, because there was, in such places, a concentration of resources, potential teachers, educated reformers, and vacant job for graduates.

Yet, by the 1890s reformers were viewing the rural components of their state school systems as defective and were arguing that one reason for those defects was the rural environment in which they operated. The increasing need for compliant workers in urban factories, the rise of populist protests primarily in rural communities, the growing disparity of wealth between the countryside and the city, the fear that such disparity would compromise the agricultural base upon which turn-of-the-century reformers believed industrialization rested, a vestigial romanticism about nature and agriculture, the flight of farmers from the countryside to towns and cities, and the influx of immigrants whose cultures were distinctly different from the distinctly English one that had theretofore dominated American cultural life contributed to a growing urgency to transform rural life and, by extension, rural schooling. In the late 1890s, the National Education Association (NEA) established the Committee of Twelve on Rural Schools to determine the nature and causes of the public's concerns and to suggest remedies. The committee recommended centralizing services by consolidating schools, a move designed to lead, they believed, to better supervision, more professional administration, a diminution of local politics, competent teachers, and additional resources. Professionalization of education, then being perfected in city schools, would relieve the countryside of its current difficulties. School problems were connected to rural problems, both as cause and cure. The Country Life Movement was born from and motivated by those connections.

THE COUNTRY LIFE MOVEMENT AND EDUCATIONAL REFORM

Coming partially in response to increasing calls for rural school reform and partially in response to growing anxieties about the deteriorating condition of rural America in general, the Commission on Country Life was appointed by Theodore Roosevelt and asked to investigate and report on problems unique to the rural experience. Although it was always dominated by men who lived or worked primarily in urban areas, the commission included many individuals who had earned national reputations for being concerned with the growing plight of farmers in negotiating the socioeconomic changes of an increasingly urban, industrial, cosmopolitan United States (for example, Gifford Pinchot of the United States Forest Services, Charles Barrett of the Farmer's Union, and William Beard, editor of *Great West Magazine*). After studying the results of an extensive survey, mailed initially to more than 500,000 farmers, they concluded that education was the single most important vehicle for changing rural conditions. The report of the National Commission on a New Country Life Education, published in 1911, concluded that:

> The schools are held to be largely responsible for ineffective farming, lack of ideals, and the drift to town. This is not because the rural schools, as a whole, are declining, but because they are in a state of arrested development and have not yet put themselves in consonance with all the recently changed conditions of life. The very forces that have built up the city and town school have caused the neglect of

the country school . . . The school must express the best cooperation of all social and economic forces that make for the welfare of the community. Merely to add new studies will not meet the need . . . The school must be fundamentally redirected, until it becomes a new kind of institution. (quoted in Cohen, Vol. 4, p. 2352)

Convinced that something was seriously amiss in rural America, a fact evident in the widespread economic depression found in most rural communities, the Country Lifers blamed the problem on the inability of local schools to respond to changing national and international conditions. A social problem caused by a school problem could be fixed, they reasoned, by eliminating the school problem.

What is taught in a country school must be, they argued, linked to the unique conditions of place. It must be relevant. "As home is the center of our civilization, so the home subjects should be the center of every school" (Quoted in Cohen, Vol. 4, p. 2352). "The school[s] must represent and express the community in which they stand" (Quoted in Cohen, Vol. 4, p. 2353). Simultaneously, schools should serve as centers for the improvement of country life in general; they should uplift the entire community. As a result, educational opportunities were to be supplemented by extension services, reading circles, club activities for young people, and an aggressive program of publications designed for farmers and their families.

Although direct federal actions as a result of the *Report of the Country Life Commission* were limited, the publication stimulated a flurry of formal pedagogical advice, often influenced by a persistent strain of agrarian romanticism, that specifically addressed the school needs of the American countryside. One of the first such books was Mabel Carney's (1912) *Country Life and the Country School.* She began her comments to rural teachers by noting that "there is an American farm problem. The whole nation is astir with it; its significance is commonly acknowledged; and remedies for its solution are proposed on every hand" (p. 1). "The fundamental problem of country life" was not agriculture per se, but "keeping a standard people upon our farms." The farm problem was a community building problem and, as such, was "a matter of education." Consequently, Carney reasoned, because "the school . . . makes the best and most generally available center for the upbuilding" of the surrounding countryside and its people," the school "is best fitted for immediate institutional leadership." To prepare the schools for that leadership, they must be reorganized "upon the principle of consolidation" and their teachers must be "specially trained" (p. 17).

More specifically, Carney suggested that rural schools needed at least nine things to address effectively the rural life problem. They were: (1) Educational redirection so that what happened in classrooms centered on the rural experiences of students; (2) improvement of physical facilities; (3) expansion of the school to include serving the community as a social center; (4) trained teachers; (5) better supervision; (6) legislation sensitive to the needs and conditions of the countryside; (7) consolidation; (8) establishment of teacher-community partnerships; and (9) sufficient resources to meet the challenges of improvement (p. 139). Schools must adopt, Carney reasoned, "a system typical of our present complex social life" and "it must be a several-teacher or graded system, which will make possible a division of labor among teachers" (p. 145). Educators were to assume positions of leadership in the communities they served and, by implication, were to be residents therein.

Carney, to her credit, did not advocate that rural schools become copies of city schools. Reflective of one group of rural education reformers, romantics in the tradition of Ralph Waldo Emerson and the Transcendentalists, she characterized the city school as "a rigid, over-organized machine" (p. 146) and rejected that model. "What we need . . . is not an urban school whose influences lead young people . . . away from the land, but a country school—a country school, improved, modernized, and adapted to the needs of present country life" (p. 177). Carney wanted to keep young people down on the farm, away from growing metropolitan areas. However, she did want country life and country schools changed, (re)formed in a certain direction.

For that reason, she argued for special preparation programs for prospective country educators, noting that most normal schools had in place programs that failed to distinguish between the characteristics and needs of urban and rural schools. "The general normal school training . . . is usually planned with reference to the needs and conditions of city teachers and city schools." As a consequence, Carney argued, "it neglects not only the peculiar problems of country school organization, management, and teaching, but especially those of rural community welfare and social relationship." The rural teacher "needs a deep appreciative insight into the problems of country life, and an exalted faith in its innate beauty and final triumph" (p. 253).

Whereas Carney reflected the philosophical temperament of many of the rural sentimentalists in the Country Life Movement, Ellwood Cubberley represented a position consistent with the rising influence of scientific management. Although he believed that rural schools were important contributors to local culture and renewal, he also saw them as part of a larger whole, as part of a national enterprise. So, even though he cited some of the same complaints and remedies found in Carney's account, Cubberley called for the end of rural schooling as a distinct enterprise, as a set of small, local schools, locally controlled and supervised, responsive primarily to local agendas. In *Rural Life and Education: A Study of the Rural-School Problem as a Phase of the Rural-Life Problem*, Cubberley (1914) demonstrated that the conditions of farm life had, as the nineteenth century advanced, altered dramatically. Americans were witnessing the "urbanization of rural life," a change that brought with it substantive improvements in the quality of that life. Such improvements were marked by better homes; ready access to supplies and markets; timely effective communication; and an end to isolation.

As farmers gained in prosperity, they moved their families to town and operated their farms through systems of tenancy. Agriculture was becoming mechanized, efficient, and businesslike. No longer an enterprise for subsistence or geared to meet the needs of small numbers of people, farming was increasingly commercial and directed toward satisfying the appetites of large, often distant, impersonal markets. When successful farm families left the land, they were often replaced by immigrants. New immigrant cultures and values differed, sometimes significantly, from those of their predecessors. For example, these new arrivals tended to be more insular and less community-oriented; they were more suspicious of the political and economic agendas of policymakers in large population centers. They were definitely less politically astute. Such changes had important consequences for all rural institutions, most publicly perhaps for the country school.

The story, according to Cubberley, became that of the spreading influence of the city to the countryside as older residents tried to assimilate the newly arrived.

> City-school ideals soon began to dominate all educational aims and practices. Textbooks were written more for them, and their commercial and cultural aims became of first importance. Education began to lean markedly toward preparation for clerical and professional employments and rural education began to lead away from rural life. (pp. 92–93)

Teachers made pedagogically and then physically the same moves. Prepared to teach in programs that considered city teaching normative, they came to view country teaching as undesirable or as a stepping stone to town or city employment. Both salary and prestige lured them toward urban settings, thereby impoverishing the pool of potential educators available to work in smaller communities. Cubberley argued that rural schools, staffed by the poorest trained or the youngest practitioners, were further hurt by diminishing student numbers, rendering them more costly per pupil. Because what was taught in such schools followed a city model and served more as an inducement to leave than to stay, communities, particularly those with large numbers of foreigners, were increasingly reluctant to support them. According to Cubberley

> [t]he result of these many changes in rural-life conditions, brought about by the changing economic and social conditions . . . , is that the rural school has lost its importance and finds itself to-day in a somewhat sorry plight. It is no longer, generally speaking, the important community institution which it was . . . It has largely ceased to minister, as it once did to community needs; its teacher no longer plays the important part in neighborhood affairs that he used to play; it has lost much of its earlier importance as a community center; its attendance has frequently shrunk to a small fraction of what it once was; it finds itself in a serious fi-

nancial condition; and it has been left far behind, educationally, by the progress which the schools of the neighboring towns and cities have made. Managed as it has been by rural people, themselves largely lacking in educational insight, penurious, and with no comprehensive grasp of their own problems, the rural school, except in a few places, has practically stood still. (p. 102)

What Cubberley proposed was the remaking of rural schools through legislated changes in their organization, governance, funding, and operation. Alterations in curriculum so that it addressed rural needs and helped accommodate students to the changing realities of the countryside would follow from the introduction of better prepared teachers, better supervision, and less local political interference.

Specifically, Cubberley advocated the elimination of the district plan insofar as possible and its replacement by a county plan. He argued for the benefits of consolidation, claiming that it would increase attendance, eliminate tardiness, and reduce the problems of foot travel in inclement weather (students would be delivered to schools in some form of bus or wagon, driven by an individual who could also serve as a truant officer). Mass transit would ensure supervision by an adult to and from school, thereby providing fewer opportunities to commit mischief. "In some localities the protection thus afforded girls is very desirable" (p. 237). Additionally, the school could then, because of the larger enrollment, be graded, stimulating the educational efforts of the student and reducing the recitation periods of the teacher. Professional instruction in aspects of the curriculum designed to alleviate the isolation and consequent unpleasantness of country life (drawing, music, the study of nature, manual training, agriculture, and domestic science) would be possible. Buildings would be more attractive, better lighted, and with improved ventilation. The school year would be longer, the community more interested in and proud of what happened at the school, and the students more able to interact and engage in healthy social activities. Fewer teachers would be necessary and, consequently, a system could pick the best candidates. Perhaps most compelling, consolidation would save money. Acknowledging that there were arguments against consolidation, Cubberley addressed and dismissed them in favor of centralized teaching.

Country school districts allowed for a more rational way of governing and supervising schools. No longer should educational institutions be forced to rely on a multitude of local trustees; consolidation along county lines meant that systems were governed by single, elected boards of education "who are analogous to a city board of education" (p. 191). That board appointed a superintendent, who, in turn, employed whatever supervisors he deemed necessary for the efficient management of the system. He would, according to Cubberley, oversee "the scattered schools of the county as though they were a compact city school system" (p. 192).

The daily operation of the school depended upon the quality of the persons who worked in them. Cubberley believed that "how to secure an efficient corps of teachers for our rural schools is one of the most important problems now before us" (p. 283).

> [I]t must . . . be acknowledged that the average rural teacher of today is a mere slip of a girl, often almost too young to have formed as yet any conception of the problem of rural life and needs; that she knows little as to the nature of children or the technique of instruction; that her education is very limited and confined largely to the old traditional school-subjects, while of the great and important fields of science she is almost entirely ignorant; and that she not infrequently lacks in those qualities of leadership that are so essential for rural progress. (p. 283)

Because consolidation would reduce the numbers of teachers, improve the social rewards that one could offer those employed by providing them with professional companionship and fewer preparations, and make more likely the provision of a competitive salary, improvement of the organization and governance of country schools would necessarily improve the quality of instruction. Additionally, Cubberley proposed a course of study to prepare these individuals for such employment, noting that "real rural service can never be rendered by the city teacher who goes to the country 'to get experience' " (p. 299). Included with the more traditional school subjects, Cubberley wanted rural teachers trained in physiology and hygiene, agriculture and nature study, library work, rural problems, the arts, and manual training. Those subjects, he argued, provided an element of place consciousness in the rural school curriculum, one that helped students assist their families to improve the quality of life in their communities and that rendered thereby the conditions of rural life sufficiently satisfactory that children remained in the country. In addition, scientific agriculture would flourish, immigrants assimilate, economic disparity cease, and tranquillity, rather than political discontent, would prevail throughout the land.

Books like Evelyn Dewey's (1919) *New Schools for Old: The Regeneration of the Porter School* provided case studies for the changes that Carney and Cubberley advocated. Accepting the basic elements of the Country Life critique of rural America, agreeing that "what is needed is a remaking of the structure of country life, an improvement in the social habits and the work habits of the whole farm family" (p. 19), and affirming that the school was the most important institution in such a transformation, Dewey laid out in detail the ways in which Mrs. Harvey took the Porter School and its surrounding community in hand. When Harvey was finished, the school had been beautified, the teacherage made clean and attractive, the privies rendered sanitary, and the school and community organized into myriad social and educational groups.

In many ways rural school reformers like Carney and Harvey, influenced by the progressive movement in general and John Dewey in particular, sought to make country schools like city settlement houses; conversely, reformers, like Cubberley, believed that the way to accomplish their purposes was to remake them administratively like city schools. Whatever the method, their joint goal was the transformation of America's countryside, because that transformation would help nurture the industrial development of the nation as a whole. Although some reformers sought changes that resonated with local needs and values, they set their work within the context of rural inadequacy. Not as condescending, perhaps, as Cubberley and his followers, romantics like Carney still sought changes consistent with what was happening nationally. Rural schooling was not an alternative paradigm to urban schooling; it was a variation on an accepted dominant theme. Tyack's "one best system" persisted, albeit with acceptable minor shifts in emphasis.

THE RURAL EDUCATION PROBLEM REDUX

Evidence of the limited effectiveness that the Country Life Movement had in altering the conditions of country schools can be found in the introduction to Anderson and Simpson's (1932) book on supervision. "Rural education, with its limited curriculum, inadequately trained personnel, and meager equipment, with its background of rural political, social, and economic life, and with its traditions, whims, and idiosyncrasies, presents an urgent situation in American education" (p. vii). A generation after Cubberley's book, and more than a decade after Dewey's advice to rural educators, not much appeared to have changed educationally or politically. However, several things had changed economically. The United States was more industrialized and more urbanized, farmwork was more mechanized and commercial. Farmers were increasingly able to meet the agricultural demands of the nation using fewer and fewer people. Consequently, many subsistence and tenant farms failed during the Depression, often victims of another type of consolidation—the shift from family farming to agribusiness. Impoverished, now homeless workers, moved to towns or westward in search of jobs.

For educational reformers what changed in the thirties was a shift in emphasis from rural to community schools. The change was a tacit acknowledgement not only that one-room schools were being replaced by consolidated town schools, but also that small towns and their schools, particularly in educationally depressed areas like the rural south, now suffered from many of the problems once identified with the country. In a 1937 publication, *The Rural Community and Its Schools*, Charles Lewis linked both community and school together in ways that became commonplace in school reform literature. He argued that "at no time in the history of our country has there been so great a need as there is today in rural schools for leaders who have a clear and comprehensive understanding of the major problems which they must face and ultimately solve" (p. xi). Further, lamenting the departure of "the higher levels of intelligence" from rural communities, Lewis argued that such places were left intellectually impoverished.

Schools became the institutions to redress that dangerous imbalance of mental resources. To accomplish that task schools must be able "to provide a maximum quality of business and professional efficiency at the lowest possible unit cost" (p. 88). Lewis saw as solutions consolidation, equitable funding formulas, a curriculum that took into account the economic and recreational needs of rural communities, rural-sensitive training for teachers, and better supervision.

Does Lewis's analysis sound familiar? It should, as should the sudden discovery that things had never before been so bad. His assessment was a replay of the rural educational jeremiad. To ameliorate conditions, Lewis attempted to claim a moderate middle ground between Carney and Cubberley; scientific change and place sensitivity must be addressed simultaneously. Although the "methods of teaching are essentially the same in rural and urban schools" (p. 277), accommodations should be made, Lewis asserted, to take into account the need for appealing to different interests and using different examples. Small schools have an obligation to become central cohesive forces for social and economic improvement within small communities.

Whereas the comments of Lewis reflected more of the Cubberley critique of rural schooling, identifying problems and solutions in terms of the modern factory model of education, the 1938 report of the Committee on the Community School, a product of the Society for Curriculum Study, resembled the softer, romantic tones of Carney's criticism. The authors of *The Community School* (Everett, 1938) held that everything we do is educational. We learn through participation in, rather than simply studying about, life. Life includes work and play for both adults and children. Consequently, public educational institutions should serve both adults and children. Schools must be primarily focused on local community improvement, rather than on the transmission of a national culture. Community members were vital participants in the affairs of a school, which should operate as a democratic institution. Adequate teacher preparation included training in active community service, rather than only in narrowly defined, traditional disciplines. Teachers must integrate into the curriculum areas of study that were consistent with rural life—farming, home-making, crafts, cooperative economics, recreation, and health.

While both the romantics and the Cubberley scientific managers identified as problems many of the same things, and while both groups sometimes advocated similar solutions, the results they sought differed as did the fundamental means for attaining them. That is, Carney and the Society for Curriculum Study wanted to perpetuate local schools, maintain local control, and focus on local needs that were locally identified. Cubberley and other scientific reformers, on the other hand, wanted to infuse rural schools with the language, methods, and expertise of urban educators, men who advocated efficiency, diminished differences in favor of more general principles, and were suspicious of the motives and abilities of small community leaders. One group felt that improvement came from within and from the bottom up; the other sought expert guidance, often from outside the community, and advocated change managed top-down. One group advocated curricular reforms; the other focused on structural and governance alterations. One group sought to preserve rural communities in their distinctiveness and agrarian orientation; the other hoped to elevate them, to make those communities as much like cities in ideology and aspiration as possible.

An indication of the tendency for later reports to mix the contradictory directions of those two positions can be found in the American Association of School Administrators' (AASA) yearbook for 1939, *Schools in Small Communities*, the result of a resolution at the organization's 1936 national convention. The Commission on Schools in Small Communities, charged to investigate and make recommendations about such schools, responded with political delicacy. It noted that these schools were unique and faced special challenges, but that they also must become more efficient, better organized, and more professionally supervised. It tried to fuse the advice of Carney and Cubberley by arguing that the school program must be designed to serve simultaneously the child who will remain in that community and the one who will eventually live in an urban setting. The commissioners found that "the school is the central institution of rural life" (p. 9) and that the "consolidated school is the central institution of the new rural community" (p. 21). Some of the problems AASA member superintendents identified included traditional complaints, such as the difficulty of attracting and retaining quality teachers and securing sufficient financial resources. Others included offering an appropriate curriculum to meet the needs of the college-bound as well as those who intended to conclude their formal education with high school graduation, providing adequate guidance to students, and getting effective leaders to serve on local boards of education.

Over the course of the next two decades attempts to join the two positions appeared in various books and reports, many of which contained a general condemnation of school organization and management. For example, E. D. Sanderson (1939) noted that small districts were handicapped by a "lack of competent administration" (p. 372). Poor administration led to the hiring of unqualified teachers, ineffective supervision, and short-sighted leadership. A lack of vision perpetuated a system that was inefficient and, consequently, unable to obtain adequate resources to provide a good education for its students. Visionaries, good administrators in Sanderson's eyes, centralize. Works and Lesser (1942) introduced their book as "an attempt to describe . . . the nation's number-one educational problem—rural education" (p. v). Those schools have been "limited in both means and personnel" (p. 63). Remedies to their problems included reorganization (consolidation), better administration and supervision, a retooled curriculum, and more adequately prepared teachers. Vernon Culp (1950), in a text for teachers first used in 1942, declared that "the crux of the rural school problem is a question of organization" (p. 7). Among specific problems cited were grossly inadequate financial support, teachers poorly prepared and rarely retained for more than a few years, lack of supervision, parochialism, and an absence of effective, efficient high schools (p. 8). Genevieve Bowen's folksy *Living and Learning in a Rural School,* published as a text for teachers in 1944, cited "improved organization" (p. 209) as one way her state was addressing the challenges inherent in rural education.

In 1943 the University of Chicago established the Rural Education Project (Reeves, 1945), which held a conference the following year to discuss the "emerging problems in rural education" (p. 9). Quality, participants concluded, had become, by the 1930s, dismal and should be "a matter of national interest," if only because many of those students eventually found work in cities. Diminished quality existed because "most rural schools were poorly financed, poorly organized, poorly administered, poorly supervised, and poorly taught" (p. 13). Buildings were deteriorating, teachers untrained, school transportation inadequate, and complementary educational services, like libraries, often nonexistent. Although they believed that some strides were made in the early days of the New Deal, the economic necessities of the second world war exacerbated the hardships of rural communities and their schools, particularly in terms of the available pool of teachers. As the nation prepared to end the emergency conditions of war, it must once again, according to conference participants, turn its attention to those communities. Now, however, there needed to be a closer, more explicit connection made between the interests of the city and the country. Conferees noted that "it is urgent that rural young people be provided with an opportunity for education that will prepare them for either rural or urban living" (p. 18). To do that efficiently, economically, and equitably, small schools should be consolidated, rural systems reorganized, and funding formulas revised. Rural schools were, as Carnegie had once argued urban schools were, instruments of social mobility. By the 1940s there was a shift in the acceptability of preparing young people to leave farms and villages. Whereas previously, there had been, the conference speakers found, a tendency "to overemphasize the importance of keeping the young people on the land," it was now increasingly necessary to advocate schooling that would assist their transition from the countryside to the city (p. 93).

The tension between local control advocates and defenders of a rural variation of the one best system did not end with the war. Butterworth and Dawson (1951), for instance, dismissed as extreme the views that rural schools are totally distinct from those in cities; they are, the authors argued, essentially the same. Yet they urged a moderate position that addressed what was unique in small communities, but that also ensured that rural youth could move to urban areas and prosper. The romantic localist tradition, too, continued in the 1950s. In 1956 (Fox et al.) and 1960 (National Education Association Department of Rural Education) publications, rural educators pointed to the advantages of preserving, while making more attractive, small community schools. Now also advocates for a middle or moderate position, they wanted a blended curriculum attuned to marketplace needs endorsed by the reform initiatives that appeared in the wake of Sputnik. They believed that many of those measures were place neutral. However, the reforms focused on a national education agenda designed to meet the country's need for scientists, mathematicians, and second-language experts and, as such, they were decidedly not without geographic prejudice. By the late 1950s public policy was firmly in the hands of moderates whose inclination was toward the structural changes advanced by Cubberley-like policymakers, even if their rhetoric for changes in rural settings sounded a little like the themes advanced by agrarian sentimentalists.

THE IRONY OF MODERN SCHOOL REFORM

Recent writing on rural education tends to align with the previous debate between localists or romantics and traditionalists or advocates of business-oriented, centralized efficiency. It reflects roughly the ideological perspectives of three groups, labeled for convenience neo-romantics, romantic traditionalists, and political traditionalists. None of those categories is exclusive; the borders among them are permeable and positions are sometimes in flux, depending upon the specific issue under discussion. Individuals move among the labels, reflecting the political and ideological tension one found between Carney's localists and Cubberley's schoolmen. Like the AASA in the 1930s, sometimes individuals try to maintain a foot in both camps, fusing arguments for the one best system with sensitivity to the context of a particular group of young people.

Neo-romanticism is a more sophisticated variation of Carney's arguments; its advocates acknowledge the negative as well as the positive aspects of country living, are critical of the bureaucratic organization of urban schools, occasionally sound like John Dewey progressives or George Counts social reconstructionists, believe that geography matters in considering school reform issues, and are sanguine about the potential educational effectiveness of small communities and their schools. Many of the essays in Jonathan Sher's (1977) and Alan DeYoung's (1991) books fall into this category. After noting that "rural" is far too general a term to be applied uniformly to the multitude of different, sparsely populated communities one finds in the United States, Sher observed that, although "rural initiatives must always be based upon the primacy of local circumstances," the use of rural as an important variable to consider "has little political currency" (p. 2). Pointing out that rural schools are, and are likely to be, with us for the foreseeable future, even if consolidation efforts continue, Sher laments the misconceptions that influence policy decisions, acknowledges the reality of small school problems, and calls for reopening "rural education issues as legitimate topics of discussion and debate" (p. 8). The first two essays, in a section entitled "Panaceas as Policy," directly take issue with the urbanization of the rural experience and with the arguments that have promoted consolidation as a cost-effective way to attain equality and efficiency.

DeYoung's introduction to *Rural Education: Issues and Practices* speaks to

the rediscovery of ruralness, which has led to a renewed hope for the revitalization of small community schools. Yet that rekindled interest in things rural, particularly education, has not stimulated a similar discovery of "a burning interest" in the topic on the part of "most educational scholars" (p. xi). Several of the
articles published in the *Kappan*'s special issue on rural education in 1995 are
also Carney-oriented pieces. With an emphasis on culture, a belief in a social
purpose of schooling that transcends preparation for the marketplace, an inclination to cite environmentalists like Wendell Berry and David Orr, and a sense
that rural schools offer us a promise for a brighter future, authors such as Paul
Theobald, Paul Nachtigal, Craig Howley, and Aimee Howley argue for the importance of place in making educational decisions.

Romantic traditionalists hold a nuanced variation of the fusion of localists
and universalists. Often policymakers and scholars whose academic interests
are in practical, rather than theoretical, matters, these individuals recognize the
uniqueness of rural American life, while adhering to the belief that there are
common ways to improve education in both city and country schools. *Rural
Education: A Changing Landscape* (Manno, 1989), published by the United
States Department of Education in 1989, is a collection of symposium papers
that were presented as part of the rural education initiative Congress under-
wrote in 1986. Most of the papers have a romantic cast, but pair that with a tendency to look at ways to make schools work within the current set of assumptions driving educational reform. For example, Herman Meyers closes his essay
with a quotation from Ron Edmonds, whose work on effective schools focused
more on the challenges of race and class, than of place (Manno, p. 67). The language is sometimes that of productivity, efficiency, and standards—the vocabulary of the factory and of business. Joyce Stern, writing on behalf of the Office of Educational Research and Improvement (OERI), oversaw the OERI
project on rural education that culminated in the publication of *The Condition
of Education in Rural Schools* in 1994. The introduction emphasizes the importance of our rural areas, cites romantic icons like Muir, Thoreau, and Berry and
neo-romantic scholars like Theobald and Sher, then focuses on a series of questions and a presentation of "selected findings" that address issues of definition
(what constitutes "rural" and where is it located?), sociodemographic changes,
economics, finance, and governance. Rather than asking should rural youth reform "at levels comparable to their nonrural peers," the report asks if they are.
Rather than questioning whether the "post-high school experiences of those
educated in rural settings" should "compare to those educated in nonrural settings," the report asks how they do. Rather than address how teachers teach differently in rural settings, the report asks how rural and non-rural teachers compare in terms of education, experience, salaries, benefits, and work conditions
(p. 2).

The third perspective is held by political policymakers or public policy administrators who are inclined to want rapid resolutions to clearly described, un-

complicated problems. Nowhere have they been more visible in educational debates than in the South—a region long considered rural and a region whose introduction to modern industrial and city life is comparatively recent. James Hunt of North Carolina, for example, chaired the commission that drafted *Action for Excellence* on behalf of the Educational Commission of the States, continues to chair the National Board for Professional Teaching Standards, and chaired the National Commission on Teaching and America's Future, which issued its report about the preparation of classroom educators in late 1996. Jimmy Carter of Georgia established, when president, the Department of Education. Lamar Alexander of Tennessee has served as secretary of education in a Republican administration; Richard Riley of South Carolina currently serves in that capacity in a Democratic administration. And when President Bush held his education summit, the man who helped chair that meeting was then governor of Arkansas and, as President, Bill Clinton made education the centerpiece of his 1997 State of the Union address. These men are children of rural America; some of them were acquainted directly with poverty, inequities, a lack of privilege—the limitations of life in one of our nation's poorer sections, in the South with its history of uneven public education; they represent constituencies that finished low on William Bennett's national educational report card, a wall chart comparing the fifty states on such student performance indicators as average SAT scores.

They are also men of the New South, of economic revitalization and regional development, of globalization and technology, of Charlotte and Atlanta. "Hillbilly," "bumpkin," "linthead," redneck," "hick," "cracker"—they know the words that denigrate a person because he lives in a particular place, a place long associated with educational inadequacy. Yet these men also know personally the potential education holds; they are its products. That knowledge contributed to their desire to be educational leaders, to create new schools that responded to the socioeconomic conditions of a New South. They adopted the language of Cubberley, respecting the potential and power of centralizing key services and promulgating general regulations, because it reflected their experiences with changing the economies and values of their region. Desegregation, for example, required federal and state action to effect; dependent on local change, it would have continued with even less deliberate speed. These men, and they were uniformly men, proposed basic education plans; standard courses of study; ways to finance education more generously, if not more equitably; statewide, comprehensive, high-stakes testing systems; new teacher recruitment and training initiatives; student accountability plans; school to work transition programs; and more rigorous licensure requirements for teachers and administrators. They did these things without regard to geography, viewing their entire state as at risk. The South's tardiness in taking advantage of the information age, they reasoned, was in part due to its sluggish education systems; its way out of that dilemma was likewise to be found at the schoolhouse door. These governors were economy-oriented, developing coalitions with business leaders to help in their educational reform efforts. They believed in efficiency, quality control, and cost-effectiveness. If cities had answers that would help, they would apply them; if country schools had answers, then it would be to those institutions that they would turn. The bottom line (these men approved of "bottom lines") was what worked, what provided their fellow citizens with the knowledge and skills necessary to be productive. Place was unimportant except insofar as it described their states as a whole.

All three groups would agree that rural schools have limited resources, are not benefiting from economic changes in the same ways that cities are, and are property rich, but cash poor. Rural school teachers have more daily subject area preparations than their urban counterparts, receive lower salaries, are somewhat younger, have fewer advanced degrees, and work in poorer facilities. Rural schools experience shortages in certain instructional areas, such as physics and special education. The curricular opportunities in rural secondary schools are fewer than in urban ones. Fewer rural children continue their education beyond high school, yet rural youth remain the primary export that their home counties have to offer the rest of the nation. The identified problems (see, for example, pp. 69–71 in *The Condition of Education in Rural Schools*) have not changed since the NEA Committee of Twelve began their work a century before.

However, there does not appear to be consensus on resolutions. Traditionalists of both political and romantic variety, whether they talk about rural or small community schools, still advocate universal remedies, use the language of industry, and are inclined to think about schooling as a global or national activity. Place is something one might acknowledge, but it is not as significant a variable as other factors in determining what and how to teach. Essentialist in orientation, they advocate a basic national curriculum as well as national accountability measures. They consider problems of recruitment and retention of teachers more urgent than considering whether there are special teacher qualities or different curricular needs required for work in rural settings. Less inclined to applaud some local practices than romantics, they are policymakers, rule-setters, expertise seekers.

Romantics, however, point to the tendency to affirm in recent reform literature many of the practices that have long been associated with rural education—lower class sizes, smaller schools, the establishment of a sense of community, service education, multi-age groupings, cooperative learning, interdisciplinary projects, paired teacher-student advancement, integration of the community into the program of study, and an emphasis on returning the personal to what has become in large schools an impersonal enterprise. Site-based management, participatory governance, and shared decision-making are all avenues for the restoration of local control. If city schools were once seen as the cure for what was the rural school problem, former rural school practices are sometimes now identified, these critics point out, as the potential remedies for our universal (read "normative" or "city") educational crises.

As ironic as the advocacy of rural practices for universal educational problems might be, what is even more ironic is the need to advocate a return to those practices in the very areas that once used them. Rural schools are now part of our industrial school model; they look and generally act like institutions in urban areas. Consolidation and a century of Cubberley ascendancy in reform thinking has done that. We are now in the position of having to reteach rural school educators things they once did well and that we asked them to stop doing. We do so while simultaneously, in the name of fiscal prudence, asking them to centralize, to consolidate, to get bigger, or to adopt the technologies of distance (satellite feeds, the Internet, distance learning) that, by their natures, diminish the spontaneity and place-centeredness of the physical touch of a live teacher.

Neither the ideological questions of what such schools should do for their communities and children nor the practical questions of what to do about personnel, finance, and governance have been resolved. What remains a given is that the rural school problems that Carney, Cubberley, and the Country Lifers encountered persist in forms that they might recognize as do the solutions we generally propose to address them. Like our predecessors, we usually teach future educators in generic preparation programs to practice in generic schools that will feature a generic curriculum, supported by generic tests, and that will be assessed based on student achievement on generic standardized tests. The romantics notwithstanding, generic has come to mean what we do in suburban and, sometimes, in urban schools; it is education with a city face.

Why is that the case? Are the differences of place unimportant? DeYoung and Theobald (1991) suggest that we might have created conditions that ensure that they are no longer significant:

> For the most part, the combination of modern schooling practices, mass media influences, expanded occupational opportunities and proximity to metropolitan areas appears to have rendered moot . . . the contradictions between older traditional, decentralized, religious, and agriculturally based lifestyles of rural America versus contemporary metropolitan America and what various sociologists and anthropologists have outlined as the norms and values it requires. (p. 11)

Even if they are moot, why did the perspectives of Cubberley and the city reformers prevail? Michael Katz's (1968) work on the decisions that led to the triumph of an "incipient bureaucracy" model of schooling in the ante-bellum period, his critics notwithstanding, indicates that few things organizationally about schools are inevitable. There was not some direct social evolution at work in the nineteenth and twentieth centuries. What we have is the product of choices, deliberately made sometimes, by specific groups of people with specific intentions.

There are, for purposes of this chapter, at least three intertwined and overlapping explanations for that city face: the ideological and cultural implications of the Civil War; pervasive, persistent anti-intellectualism, associated more nega- tively with the country than the city; and our paradoxical love-hate relationship with things rural. That these explanations are not the whole story is obvious; this is a chapter and not a book. However, they contain policy implications for tomorrow's rural schools and indicate that the educational Jeremiahs who have spent the past century making the country school anew every ten years or so will probably not retreat quietly to another place.

THE COUNTRY MOUSE AND THE CITY MOUSE

That there has persisted a tension between country and city since the inven- tion of the latter is suggested by the existence of Aesop's fable about mice. The town mouse, unimpressed by the meager culinary offerings of his country cousin, invites him to visit his urban abode. "When you have been in town a week you will wonder how you could ever have stood a country life" (Aesop, quoted in Eliot, 1937, p. 14). Dining on a more resplendent repast, they are in- terrupted by two dogs who chase them off. The country mouse, departing, de- clares that it is better to have simple food than more varied and refined alterna- tives eaten in fear. The dichotomy Aesop drew between the two persists in our national mythology. The country is the site of natural, hardy, albeit humble and honest living and the town, now city, is the site of artificial and perhaps ill-got plenty. Life in the country is tranquil and safe; life in the city is fast and danger- ous.

As a nation we have a long tradition of belief in the virtues inherent in coun- try living. Thomas Jefferson, for example, wrote passionately about the yeo- man farmer and his role in the creation and preservation of our democracy. By the ante-bellum period, politicians were running for president based partially and sometimes inventively on their log cabins origins. Natty Bumppo, James Fenimore Cooper's creation, is arguably our first novel hero, enacting in fiction the adventures claimed in real life by the likes of Daniel Boone and Davy Crockett. Among the bestsellers in the nineteenth century were dime novels that romanticized the lives of western mountain men. Huck Finn, at the conclu- sion of the novel bearing his name, declares that he intends to "light out for the territory" because he is faced with the prospect of being adopted by Aunt Sally who wants to "sivilize" him (p. 283). Horace Greely admonished young men to head West to seek their fortunes. When Frederick Jackson Turner wrote his fa- mous essay about the end of the frontier, pundits worried that American democ- racy was endangered by the conclusion of its struggle to tame its wilderness.

When Americans talk about "getting away from it all," they often mean heading for the country, for our wild and natural places, for mountains or lakes or sea coast. We are unconcerned by the irony of rusticating in luxury. As a na- tion, we are in love with countryside—a place to backpack, fish, hunt, get in tune with our inner selves; a place to get back to nature, if only for the weekend. Thoreau still sells well; Wendell Berry's books are a cottage industry. We garden, even in city pots. Scarlett O'Hara clutching a bunch of vegetables from the family plantation, Tara, looks directly into the camera in the *Gone with the Wind* scene immediately before the original intermission and waxes eloquent about what she will and will not do to keep her land and all it represents of heritage, the good life, her and, by extension, the southern, rural past.

Yet it is the city that defines modern life and it is city ways and city values that dominate our daily cultural landscape. One reason for that domination is the fact that the North won the Civil War, a conflict that some historians view as a struggle for our national consciousness and identity as much as or more than a fight for our collective conscience. William Taylor (1961), for example, saw the nation as divided into two ideal types prior to that war: the Cavalier or southern gentlemen and the Yankee or northern entrepreneur. Acknowledging that these types were as much myth as they were reality, he noted that we act on our mythologies as well as our realities. By the 1830s, Taylor argued, that

> a significant number of Americans had begun to express decided reservations about the direction progress was taking and about the kind of aggressive, mercenary, self-made man who was rapidly making his way in their society. In everyone's eyes this type of parvenu came to express a worrisome facet of the national character, to symbolize, in fact, both the restless mobility and the strident materialism of new world society. In the face of the threat which seemed to be posed by this new man, Americans—genteel and would-be genteel—began to develop pronounced longings for some form of aristocracy. They longed for a class of men immune to acquisitiveness, indifferent to social ambition and hostile to commercial life, cities and secular progress. (p. 334)

The southern gentleman, epitomized by the plantation owner and evident in the lifestyle of Thomas Jefferson when he retired to Monticello to write about his yeoman farmers, was one reaction to the emergence of commercial America—a reaction linked directly to the countryside.

Another version of American agrarian romance emerged at approximately the same time in New England and included many of the most famous literary minds in our young nation. Both George Fredrickson (1965) and Leo Marx (1964) address the importance the pastoral ideal played in the writing of authors like Nathaniel Hawthorne, Ralph Waldo Emerson, and Henry David Thoreau. Although they eschewed the image of the plantation Cavalier, like their southern intellectual counterparts they were disturbed by the emergence of a consumerism that seemed to threaten the agrarian values of their young nation. Using the locomotive as a symbol of the brutish and polluting power of industrialization, Hawthorne, in his short story "The Celestial Railroad," suggested that the economic transition in which the United States was engaged in the ante-bellum period was as morally charged as it was economically motivated (Hawthorne, 1982, pp. 808–824).

In spite of criticisms, in the nineteenth century a *new* America came of age, one defined by mobility and materialism. Its citizens, these *new* Americans, were acquisitive and ambitious. They lived in cities, often originally port towns, and worked in commerce. Their values were secular and relative. If the wilderness of the Puritans became metaphorically an ante-bellum pastoral Eden to the Transcendentalists and their followers, then the Civil War, fueled by the engines and engineers of the North, abruptly introduced Americans to a reality of steam, factories, and competition in which the winners were exalted and lived in Newport palaces whereas the losers huddled in New York tenements and rural tenant farms. For all the complaints of country mice and all the conscious back-to-nature literal and imagined journeys of their urban cousins, it was town mice that came to mean the United States. We admire a Donald Trump, a Ross Porot, or a Bill Gates because each is a venture capitalist, a lone competitor willing to take big-city risks; each is an urban mountain man.

When the progressive education reformers began defining and then fixing the country life problem, their models for what worked were found in urban settings. At the turn of the century the national stage was dominated by tinkerers like Thomas Edison and Henry Ford and business moguls like Andrew Carnegie and John Rockefeller. These were men whose adult successes were influenced by the marketplace, by commerce, by the generation and distribution of mass-produced merchandise, by being responsive to and located near cities. Although Theodore Roosevelt might preach the virtues of the strenuous life and write books about his experiences on western ranches, he lived most of that life in cities and it was there that he found his political destiny. To reformers who continued the American romance with the countryside, the Country Life Movement made sense—in order to preserve what was good and wholesome and pure in rural America, we had to ensure that it adopted the ways of business and modernity. To them there was no internal contradiction, partially because the Civil War had marked the changing of our ideological guard. A "new" American was not a yeoman farmer, a southern Cavalier, or a romantic individualist, except in myth and nostalgic memory; that American was a Yankee merchant making economic hay in a growing global market. Country mice were sentimental icons, fodder for lyrical poetry perhaps, but city mice were where the action was and would stay. Country mice needed to be prepared to move, even if they might not want to do so.

A TALE OF TWO PEDAGOGUES

Two stories about teachers bookend the popular literature of the nineteenth century: Washington Irving's "The Legend of Sleepy Hollow" and Edward Eggleston's *The Hoosier Schoolmaster*. Irving's portrait comes in a short sketch found, appropriately enough, in a collection entitled *Sketch Book* (Reprinted in

Irving, 1983). Written prior to the Civil War, it chronicles the short adventures of one Icabod Crane, employed by a local Hudson River Valley community in New York to instruct the neighborhood children in the ubiquitous one room school house. Crane

> was tall, but exceedingly lean, with narrow shoulders, long arms and legs, hands that dangled a mile out of his sleeves, feet that might have served for shovels, and his whole frame most loosely hung together. His head was small and flat on top, with hugs ears, large green glassy eyes, and a long snipe nose, so that it looked like a weathercock perched upon his spindle neck, to tell which way the wind blew. To see him striding along the profile of a hill on a windy day, with his clothes bagging and fluttering around him, one might have mistaken him for the genius of famine descending upon the earth, or some scarecrow eloped from a cornfield. (p. 1061)

Irving's description was not a picture to inspire scholarly aspirations nor one to encourage young people to become educators. Partial to the hickory stick as his favored mode of motivation, Crane was fond of food, country girls, light farm labor in exchange for congenial boarding arrangements, dancing, and singing. "He was . . . esteemed by the women as a man of great erudition, for he had read several books quite through, and was a perfect master of Cotton Mather's *History of New England Witchcraft*, in which . . . he most firmly and potently believed" (p. 1063). Superstitious, gawky, given to daydreaming, Icabod Crane was used as a foil for the real hero of Irving's sketch, the local rowdy Brom Bones. Bones was "a burly, roaring, roystering blade . . . the hero of the country round, which rung with his feats of strength and manhood" (p. 1069). A man's man, Bones ultimately wins the girl, humiliates Crane, and chases him from the county—a series of events any reader could have foreseen given the two men's contrasting physiques and interests.

Conversely, Eggleston's teacher, Ralph Hartsook, although admittedly slight of frame, is able to address the problems presented to him in his one-room school with a cunning that ultimately triumphs over false accusations, duplicitous villains, and local bullies. He outwits, rather than outboxes, his opponents and, unlike Carne, emerges as someone due our attention; he even gets the girl, a sure sign of qualities worthy of emulation. Eggleston makes clear that nineteenth-century teaching was not for the faint of heart, that it was difficult, challenging task that all too often pitted the teacher against older students hoping to embarrass him and trustees hoping to secure his services for as little money as possible. A countrified Mr. Chips, Hartsook was a hero to Crane's buffoon.

Yet, which is the picture of country schoolmaster that has persisted? If one goes to a local discount store and rummages through the videotape collection, one is likely to find Walt Disney's version of the Sleepy Hollow legend. Narrated by Bing Crosby, the cartoon is a story of muscle triumphing over mind.

Crane, pictured in amusing detail by Disney's animators, is no match for the handsome Brom Bones. A viewer knows without watching past the initial, contrasting images who wins the girl and who is scared out of town. As to the Hoosier schoolmaster, there is no contemporary account on tape. The closest, perhaps, one comes in the popular media are the books about schooling by the Kentuckian Jesse Stuart, particularly *The Thread That Runs So True* (1949), *To Teach, To Love* (1970), and *Mr. Gallion's School* (1957). The first two recount Stuart's personal experiences as a country educator; the last book is a fictional account of his return to school administration after an absence of several years. *The Thread That Runs So True* particularly reads like a twentieth-century version of Ralph Hartsook's trials and triumphs. One finds therein the challenges of getting students to attend to their duties as scholars, the importance of the community in determining the direction of and the prestige accorded to education, the difficulties of boarding out and working with semi-literate trustees, the drama of competitions like spelling bees and countdowns, the need to be entrepreneurial about resources and flexible about teaching strategies, and the discovery of the woman with whom one wants to live one's life—all events in somewhat different guises that appear in *The Hoosier Schoolmaster*. Yet Crane lives on in our popular culture, a vital image that even today's young children recognize and ridicule. Stuart's books are mostly out of print; few young people we prepare for rural schools have ever heard of him.

Richard Hofstadter would not have been surprised. In *Anti-Intellectualism in American Life* (1966), he argued that our nation has always been somewhat uneasy about brain work. Talented men (Hofstadter can be faulted for not considering the ways in which talented women used teaching as a means of social mobility) did not, by implication *do* not, become educators. "In the history of the United States, the schoolteacher has been in no position to serve for an introduction to the intellectual life. Too often he has not only no claims to an intellectual life of his own, but not even an adequate workmanlike competence in the skills he is supposed to impart." Certainly Crane would fit that description. His role is "associated with exploitation and intimidation" (p. 310). "Misfits seem to be so conspicuous that they set an unflattering image of the teaching profession" (p. 314).

The reasons for our unique tendency to diminish observations of the head in favor of conclusions made by the heart or intuition are multiple, according to Hofstadter. Our religious heritage is emotional, not rational. We have a penchant for evangelicalism and revivals, rather than Acquinas-like reasoned discourse. Our politics, once the era of gentleman politicians ended with the election of Andrew Jackson, is dominated by contestants attempting to prove that they are the true defenders of the common man, of the American people, rather than defenders of some set of rationally derived principles. Our culture is the servant of practicality, of what works and gets the job done now. It is the servant, too, of business, self-help, technology, gadgets, and fancy machines. The environment in which a teacher struggles to introduce young people to a life of the mind is inimical, according to Hofstadter, to that task. A clear indication of the position that intellectual pursuits hold in the hierarchy of our popular preferences is the ways in which we honor and reward education workers in our nation's public schools. By and large, we reward them infrequently and inadequately; publicly we are more inclined to mock or denigrate them than to place them on pedestals.   ·

Occasionally we have a Ralph Hartsook who wins his fifteen minutes of fame on some type of educational stage (Jaime Escalante comes to mind), but we are more likely to have a William Bennett or a Diane Ravitch or a Lynn Chaney, themselves not P–12 teachers, assume a starring role in matters educational. So, although we cling to a rhetorical defense of schooling, we simultaneously mock nerds and geeks, the 1990s versions of eggheads. We have always insisted on the importance of book learning and have paid attention to it through the establishment of early, accessible, publicly funded institutions, but we have compromised that position by, at the same time, belittling teachers, paying them poorly, and not supporting reflective, critical, intellectual activities. The old saw about "those who can, do and those who can't, teach" is better known than any refutation of it.

Such anti-intellectualism is common throughout our society. It can be found in cities, suburbs, small towns, and farms. But as Hofstadter (1955) observes in another book, *The Age of Reform*, "populism had been overwhelmingly rural and provincial. The ferment of the Progressive era was urban, middle-class, and nationwide" (p. 131). Both populism and progressivism were reform initiatives at the end of the nineteenth century, but the latter triumphed in part because the former was perceived by city policymakers as emotional, backward, parochial, somewhat fanatical, unscientific, and unfriendly to business. It was the relatively safe, domesticated, Teddy Roosevelt version of progressivism that provided the political frame upon which education critics like Cubberley built their arguments. It was the countryside that they ultimately hoped to reform by bringing it and its stubborn populist inclinations into their definition of nation. When they looked at country schools they saw Icabod Crane, never Ralph Hartsook.

Reinforced by the triumph of city values and an industrial, urban economy, of Yankee entrepreneurship, the anti-intellectualism of the country was characterized as different from that of the city. In the city, it translated into a preference for getting on with things, for making products of substance, for efficiency and speed over reflection. It serviced industrialization and tolerated a modicum of scholarly and high cultural activity. In the country, however, it translated into a pathology, a defect, an attribute of misguided, superstitious people. Hartsook, after all, eventually worked at a town school, leaving the country schools only Crane and his colleagues. Those impressions, of a countryside replete with William Jennings Bryan demagogues with little business sense and suspect personal beliefs, were reinforced by simultaneous attraction for and repulsion of things rural.

DELIVERANCE MEETS DUKES OF HAZARD

We continue to have a love-hate relationship with our notions of ruralness. Consider, for example, the portrait of backwoods America that one finds in the film *Deliverance*. There reside mean-spirited men and cowed women. Unlike the equally impoverished Joads in Steinbeck's *Grapes of Wrath* they are capable of, indeed inclined toward, violence and perversity. Suspicious of strangers, sadistic, and ignorant, they taunt, maim, and demean the main characters of the film based on James Dickey's novel. As J. W. Williamson (1995) wrote, *Deliverance* "imagined the southern mountains as supercharged with an active human-hating evil" (p. 150). Yet these are the same mountains in which we find Li'l Abner and Daisy Mae, the strong-armed and good-hearted Duke boys, Ma and Pa Kettle, and the Clampetts.

On the one hand we are deeply suspicious of things savage, of the lack of civility and control possible in our nation's backwoods. When the Puritans redefined their errand into the wilderness during the first decades of their sojourn in Massachusetts, they did so in a way that incorporated the idea of subduing and taming the land—a metaphor, perhaps, for subduing and taming the natural, but unchristian, passions they feared within themselves. Nationally we have a history of identifying those emotions that seem to us wild or irrational and transferring them to "the other," to the Native American, whom we called savage, and, in the South, to Africans, whose otherness and connection with that foreign continent provided us with a rationalization for their enslavement. In some respects the mountain people of *Deliverance* were but another chapter in that series of displacements. They represented the existence of inhumanity and of monstrosity.

Yet we are also a people who find the wilderness a place of simplicity, truth, beauty—a place in which we can come of age. When Ralph Hartsook goes to work in a country school, he does so partially to become a man. As often as we populate the countryside with fools and monsters, we place upon it upright, good-hearted "real Americans." The Marlboro Man sold cigarettes not because westerners look better smoking, but because he embodied what our citified situation precludes, an independent life amidst vast space in which we ride comfortably and are in command. John Wayne remains the American film archetypal hero. We all recognize the plot of *Shane*. A stranger rides into town, gets rid of the bad guys, sets an example for the good, albeit temporarily cowardly, guys, makes life safe again for the women and children, and rides silently into the sunset. The film *Hoosiers* combines elements of the western and the Hartsook myth. It is, ultimately, a story about David defeating Goliath, the small country school bringing to its knees the large, urban school on a basketball court of honor. Everyone, the misplaced coach, the schoolboy hero, the drunken father, is made better by the experience. *Green Acres* was popular as much for its contrast of city and country, to the advantage of the latter, as for its two popular stars. The theme of simple decency triumphing over greedy, grasping, manipulating city slickers (*The Beverly Hillbillies* comes to mind) is commonplace, a staple in our national literature. When we remember Ronald Reagan it is not so much the man in the expensive suit and perfectly knotted tie that attracts us, but the man who rode horses and chopped wood, who stood tall both literally and figuratively.

PEOPLE OF PARADOX

That these themes are contradictory is obvious. We both hate and love wilderness, rurality, the countryside. We see it as the cauldron in which our democracy is forged; we see it as a repository of ignorance and fanaticism. It embodies virtues we want to claim as distinctly American—rugged individualism, independence, hard work, perseverance, and simplicity; it represents conditions that we find antithetical to progress—parochialism, narrow-mindedness, superstition, and a reluctance to change. It can save us; it can serve to limit our horizons.

These themes are also illusionary. There is no one countryside, no one rural place, no one wilderness. There is also no one set of country people, rural dwellers, settlers on the edges of our civilization. We enlarge our frontiers, making them the sites of national mythologies, and, consequently, we make them illusions. However, as Taylor reminded us, we act on such illusions as often as we act on realities. What "nation" means is contested territory; it means different things to different people at difference times. Who we are and what we represent have been the subjects of our politics, our literature, and our history. Never definitively decided as long as we persist, it is the stuff of disputation—sometimes humorously, sometimes accidentally, often deliberately, and all too often in ways that are divisive and damaging to one or another group.

Michael Kammen (1973) called us "people of paradox." A product of pluralism, we are biformational. We see our world in dualities. We are black or white, American or un-American, city or country. To Kammen, that tendency comes from our inability to resolve the tensions between authority (what the state decrees) and individualism. "Americans have managed to be both puritanical and hedonistic, idealistic and materialistic, peace-loving and war-mongering, isolationist and interventionist, conformist and individualist, consensus-minded and conflict-prone" (p. 290).

Hofstadter (1955), too, recognized the dualistic character of our national consciousness. In writing about populism, he noted that our agrarian heritage wears two aspects. The genteel side is characterized by yeoman farmers not unlike Wendell Berry today, by utopian idealism, and by social radicalism; its practical side emphasized technological improvement, efficiency and the adoption of business methods, and advocacy politics. In our national identity debates, the side that is currently in ascendancy is the one characterized by scientific practicality.

Although we give our occasional affection to the country mouse, the national forests, and *Shane*, we keep our day jobs in the city, recreate in rustic comfort on weekends, and hope to become the next Bill Gates. Consequently, country schools and the alternative model that some romantic country schools reformers offered to the factory model found in the city failed to thrive. Rural and small schools that still exist have become, in most cases, successfully urbanized at precisely the time that we are discovering that both cities and their schools are in crisis. As we refigure the costs of centralization, including this time what consolidation, for example, did to the vitality of small communities and what bus transportation has done to rural school budgets, we find that our initial bottom line figures were in error. Cubberley did not lie; he misadded because he misdefined what constituted quality.

And, because we are people of paradox, we are prone to err in large measure. As Kammen observed:

> Because of our pluralist inheritance of biformities, we are given to forms of inadvertent overcompensation. Take for example our longstanding vacillation between nature and civilization. After generations of abuse and neglect, we are beginning in sizable numbers to appreciate the spiritual value and aesthetic beauty of the American wilderness. Yet this very increase in appreciation may ultimately prove to be its undoing, for we are beginning to love our national forests and wonders right out of existence, so crowded have they become with campers and their litter. (p. 297)

In our rush to eliminate the problems of one-room and small schools, we built large ones and, in so doing, made city schools in the country, resulting in country schools that today have some of the same disadvantages of size, impersonal bureaucracy, and uniformity without context that we find in our cities.

IMPLICATIONS FOR ADMINISTRATORS

Hofstadter is right about educational jeremiads. They have always been with us and are unlikely to vanish in the future. When educational critics turned their attention to our countryside, what they found objectionable was that it was not the city located among trees and cultivated fields. The solution to that rural problem became the rural school and the solution to the problems of the rural school became to make it, either partially or wholly, like its urban counterparts. Partial revisionists maintained a localist perspective, sought bottom-up improvement, and wanted the schools to remain close to the needs of particular communities. However, the reforms they advocated had the unintended consequence, when taken to extremes, of making schools precisely what the total revisionists wanted—consolidated, centralized, scientifically managed, businesslike enterprises. During the twentieth century we closed schools throughout the United States at a remarkable pace, centralizing services and educational ideologies, creating "one best system" throughout the land.

> Rural educators can lay claim to some of the most recent school improvement initiatives, because they are essentially attributes that good country or small schools once, and sometimes still do, possessed—an emphasis on community and community involvement, multi-age groupings, inclusion, close ties between teachers and students, authentic forms of assessment, experiential learning, and an integrated curriculum.

Ironically, we now find that our "one best system" no longer functions well and discover reforms that were at one time embedded in the ways effective rural schools operated. Yet, even in rural and small community schools, the very institutions in which they were once practiced, those better ways of doing things no longer exist. We consolidated them out.

What can a rural school administrator learn from this experience? Certainly, that administrator knows that there will always be criticism of public schools and that there might be unfair, inaccurate, or inappropriate criticism of rural schools. However, administrators in rural settings need to become sensitive readers of such critiques. Is this criticism one of schooling in general or of rural schooling in particular? Does it fit the situation of a specific rural setting? We need to acknowledge that some of what we did in the past we did because we were told (and we believed) it was good for us; we also need to acknowledge that some of those actions were wrong-headed. We need to examine which benefits of rural schooling are worth retaining (some are) and which liabilities should be labeled as such and discarded or altered. We also need to recognize that the results of such a review will vary from place to place. There is not a monolithic place called "Rural," even though both Carney and Cubberley suspected that there was.

In other words, rural administrators should be trained to think within a particular rural context—something few university preparation programs do today. They should also act within such a context—behavior that requires courage, perhaps, in an era of national standard-setting and standardized test accountability systems geared to an urban school model and urban, industrial, and largely impersonal economic aspirations. One of the encouraging aspects of a reacquaintance with rural school history is how much of it is a story of good, effective, and hopeful practice. There exists a healthy and vibrant literature upon which to base a reexamination of rural and small schools. Likewise, there exists an alternative organizational model, one that is student- and community-centered and place-sensitive, one that leavens the three R's with lessons in compassion, concern, and connections (see, for example, the more general work of Nel Noddings, 1984, and Jane Rowland Martin, 1985), one that treats the acquisition of the basics as an act that incorporates personal as well as discipline-grounded knowledge and skills.

Rural administrators must be suspicious of "one best system" thinking and reform efforts. That means that they must be politically active and visible, both at the local and at the state level. Metaphorically, it means being able to declare the emperor naked if he pretends to wear an inappropriate city coat in the country. Rural educators can lay claim to some of the most recent school improvement initiatives, because they are essentially attributes that good country or small schools once, and sometimes still do, possess—an emphasis on community and community involvement, multi-age groupings, inclusion, close ties between teachers and students, authentic forms of assessment, experiential learning, and an integrated curriculum. That rural schools must reclaim what they once had indicates that we did not conserve well our resources in the past and that we would profit from becoming more conscious of our role as educational conservationists in the future.

Today one can be rural unapologetically, naming such urban initiatives as schools-within-schools what they are: attempts to reclaim community by becoming small, attempts to remake the city in a country way. However, rural administrators are obliged not simply to reclaim what they once had, but to demand that attention once again be paid to place and the unique importance of geographic and, consequently, the cultural context in learning. Such an obligation does not necessarily lead to a tribalism or parochialism that denies the need for certain educational universals. We will never again reclaim a time in which economic or geographic mobility was severely limited, nor should we want to do so. However, it does mean that we should expect schools of education to pay attention to place, particularly if they are in locations that are themselves rural and they prepare educational practitioners who will likely work in rural areas. It does mean that we should attend to the presence, or lack thereof, of curricular materials that address rural environments and that we should encourage our faculties to incorporate the literature, history, geography, ecology, and economics of rural places into any standard course of study. We know that rural schools are uniquely teacher-dependent, that they require multiple things from the educators who work in them and that those obligations differ from what might be required in urban settings. Consequently, we should seek ways in which professional development programs likewise address the needs of place, in which they prepare sensitive generalists as well as discipline-oriented specialists.

We know that eco-systems that limit diversity are more fragile, less healthy, and more susceptible to abrupt changes. Yet haven't we made our schools into such systems when we demand that they become the same, when we prepare each educator as we prepare all educators, when we require that each school becomes all schools? Surely, as a nation, we gained when we equalized salaries, advocated a more comprehensive curriculum, and required safe, adequate facilities of all schools. We also gained when we asked all schools to ensure that students are adequately prepared for further educational opportunities. Yet we lost something important when we extended our list of requirements to more specific aspects of what we did in the public schools, when we distanced schooling from the communities and the people it served. Rural educational leaders can regain that educational ground; no longer should the rural school problem be that rural schools are not city ones, nor should the city school problem become that they are not rural ones. School problems should be those that indicate that an educational institution does not meet the dual needs of its unique, place-specific students—the need to introduce them to lessons that will help them understand who they are and how they came to be that way and the need to prepare them to make conscious decisions about how to live their lives well either in that community or elsewhere.

REFERENCES

American Association of School Administrators. 1939. *Schools in Small Communities: Seven-Tenth Annual Yearbook.* Washington, DC: American Association of School Administrators.

Anderson, C.J., & J.I. Simpson. 1932. *The Supervision of Rural Schools.* New York: D. Appleton and Company.

Bowen, G. 1944. *Living and Learning in a Rural School.* New York: The Macmillan Company.

Butterworth, J.E., & H.A. Dawson. 1952. *The Modern Rural School.* New York: McGraw-Hill Book Company.

Callahan, R. 1962. *Education and the Cult of Efficiency: A Study of the Social Forces That Have Shaped the Administration of Public Schools.* Chicago: The University of Chicago Press.

Carney, M. 1912. *Country Life and the Country School.* Chicago: Row, Peterson.

Clinton, W.J. 1997, February 5. "The State of the Union Address," The *Washington Post,* A05.

Cohen, S. (ed.) 1974. *Education in the United States: A Documentary History.* 4 Vols. New York: Random House.

Committee of Twelve on Rural Schools, National Education Association. 1898. In *Report of the Commissioner of Education for the Year 1896–97.* Washington, DC: U.S. Government Printing Office.

Cubberley, E. 1916. *Public School Administration: A Statement of Fundamental Principles Underlying the Organization and Administration of Public Education.* Boston: Houghton Mifflin.

Cubberley, E. 1914. *Rural Life and Education: A Study of the Rural-School Problem as a Phase of the Rural-Life Problem.* Boston: Houghton-Mifflin.

Culp, V.H. 1950. *How to Manage a Rural School.* Minneapolis, MN: Burgen Publishing Co.

Dewey, E. 1919. *New Schools for Old: The Regeneration of the Porter School.* New York: E.P. Dutton and Company.

DeYoung, A.J. (ed.) 1991. *Rural Educational: Issues and Practice.* New York: Garland Publishing, Inc.

DeYoung, A.J., & Theobald, P. 1991, Summer. "Community Schools in the National Context: The Social and Cultural Impact of Educational Reform Movements on American Rural Schools," *Journal of Research in Rural Education, 7*(3); 3–14.

Eggleston, E. 1957. *The Hoosier School-Master.* New York: Sagamore Press, Inc.

Eliot, C.E. (ed.) 1937. *Folk-Lore and Fable: Aesop, Grimm, Andersen,* Vol. 17 of *The Harvard Classics.* New York: P.F. Collier & Sons, Publishers.

Everett, S. 1938. *The Community School.* New York: D. Appleton-Century Company.

Fox, R.S. (ed.) 1956. *Teaching in the Small Community.* Washington, DC: National Education Association.

Fredrickson, G.M. 1965. *The Inner Civil War: Northern Intellectuals and the Crisis of Union.* New York: Harper Torchbooks.

Hawthorne, N. 1982. *Hawthorne: Tales and Sketches.* New York: The Library of America.

Hofstadter, R. 1955. *The Age of Reform.* New York: Random House.

Hofstadter, R. 1966. *Anti-Intellectualism in American Life.* New York: Vintage Books.

Howley, C.N., & A. Howley. 1995, October. "The Power of Babble: Technology and Rural Education," *Phi Delta Kappan, 77*(2); 126–131.

Irving, W. 1983. *History, Tales and Sketches.* New York: The Library of America.

Kammen, M. 1973. *People of Paradox: An Inquiry Concerning the Origins of American Civilization.* New York: Vintage Books.

Katz, M. 1968. *The Irony of Early School Reform: Educational Innovation in Mid-Nineteenth Century Massachusetts.* Boston: Beacon Press.

Knight, E.W., & C. Hall (eds.) 1951. *Readings in American Educational History.* New York: Appleton-Century-Crofts, Inc.

Lewis, C.D. 1937. *The Rural Community and Its Schools.* New York: American Book Company.

Mann, H. 1855. *Lectures on Education.* Boston: Ide and Dutton.

Manno, B.V. (ed.) 1989. *Rural Education: A Changing Landscape.* Washington, DC: U.S. Department of Education.

Martin, J.R. 1985. *Reclaiming a Conversation.* New Haven, CT: Yale University Press.

Marx, L. 1964. *The Machine in the Garden: Technology and the Pastoral Ideal in America.* London: Oxford University Press.

Nasaw, D. 1979. *Schooled to Order: A Social History of Schooling in the United States.* New York: Oxford University Press.

National Commission on Excellence in Education. 1983. *A Nation at Risk: The Imperative for Educational Reform.* Washington, DC: U.S. Government Printing Office.

National Education Association Department of Rural Education. 1960. *Improvement of Rural Life: The Role of the Community School Throughout the World.* Washington, DC: National Education Association.

Noddings, N. 1984. *Caring: A Feminist Approach to Ethics and Moral Education.* Berkeley: University of California Press.

Perkinson, H.J. 1968. *The Imperfect Panacea: American Faith in Education, 1865–1965.* New York: Random House.

Reeves, F.W. (ed.) 1945. *Education for Rural America.* Chicago: University of Chicago Press.

Reisler, R.F. 1981. "An Educational Agenda for the Eighties," *Phi Delta Kappan, 74*, 413–414.

Sanderson, E.D. 1939. *Rural Sociology*. Boston: Ginn and Company.

Sher, J.P. (ed.) 1977. *Education in Rural America: A Reassessment of Conventional Wisdom*. Boulder, CO: Westview Press.

Stern, J.D. (ed.) 1994. *The Condition of Education in Rural Schools*. Washington, DC: U.S. Department of Education.

Stuart, J. 1967. *Mr Gallion's School*. New York: McGraw-Hill.

Stuart, J. 1949. *The Thread That Runs So True*. New York: Schribner's Sons.

Stuart, J. 1970. *To Teach, To Love*. New York: World Publishing Company.

Task Force on Education for Economic Growth. 1983. *Action for Excellence: A Comprehensive Plan to Improve Our Nation's Schools*. Denver, CO: Education Commission of the States.

Taylor, W.R. 1961. *Cavalier and Yankee: The Old South and American National Character*. New York: Harper Torchbooks.

Theobald, P., & P. Nachtigal. 1995, October. "Culture, Community, and the Promise of Rural Education," *Phi Delta Kappan, 77*(2); 132–135.

Twain, M. 1959. *The Adventures of Huckleberry Finn*. New York: Signet Classics.

Tyack, D.B. 1974. *The One Best System: A History of American Urban Education*. Cambridge, MA: Harvard University Press.

Weber, M. 1958. *The Protestant Ethic and the Spirit of Capitalism* (T. Parsons, Trans.). New York: Charles Schribner's Sons.

Wiebe, R.H. 1967. *The Search for Order, 1877–1920*. New York: Hill and Wang.

Williamson, J.W. 1995. *Hillbillyland: What the Movies Did to the Mountains and What the Mountains Did to the Movies*. Chapel Hill: University of North Carolina Press.

Works, G.H., & S.O. Lesser. 1942. *Rural America Today: Its Schools and Community Life*. Chicago: University of Chicago Press.

RURAL LEADERSHIP: THE VIEW FROM THE TOP

CHAPTER 4

The Rural School Board

Both boards and superintendents need to be more forthright in their crucial relationship and decide there is a mutual responsibility to negotiate, develop, and sustain it.—Danzberger, Kirst, and Usdan, 1992, p. 97

Working with school boards to achieve the educational goals of a school district is a fundamental role for the superintendent and an important goal for all educational leaders in the district. This chapter is designed to address the issue of building positive working relationships with the rural school board. The information presented is based on the authors' experiences as school administrators, school board members, university professors, and K–12 educators; research studies that the authors completed during the past ten years; and, an extensive review of the contemporary literature related to superintendent-board relationships.

S CHOOL boards are enduring and vital components of public schools. Historically, the school board's role has followed Hunkins' 1949 definition: "A generally accepted principle of school administration is that the board of education should legislate the policies and appraise the results and the superintendents as the executives put the policies into operation" (p. 15).

Traditionally, state governments have delegated responsibility for the general supervision and administration of public education to local boards of education. Although state governments can and do delimit the prerogatives of local school boards through expressed powers assigned by statutory and administrative law, significant discretion and decision-making authority remain in the hands of local boards of education (Knezevich, 1984; Lunenburg & Ornstein,

Marilyn L. Grady, Department of Educational Administration, University of Nebraska-Lincoln; Bernita L. Krumm, Department of Educational Administration, Texas A&M University-Commerce.

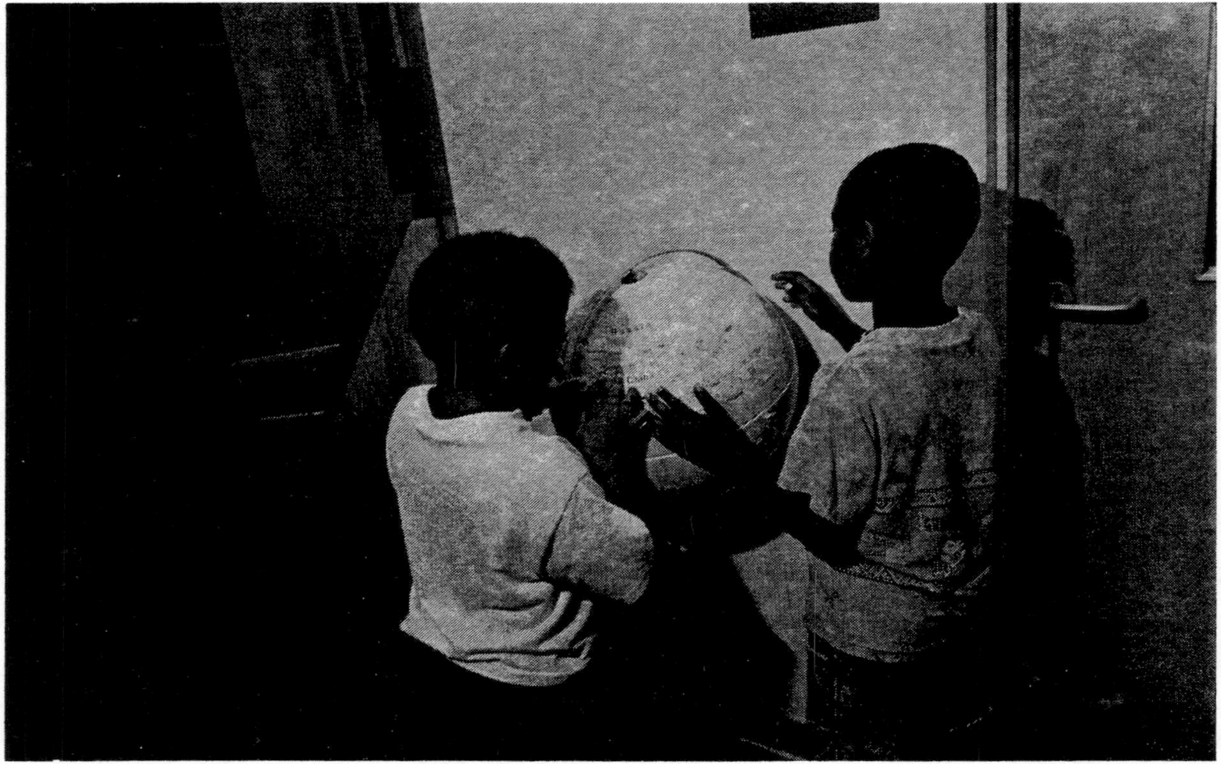

© Photo by Rob Amberg.

1991; Russo, 1992). Among the important functions performed by local boards of education are identification of the school district's goals and purposes, and acquisition and allocation of the resources necessary to fulfill district priorities (Danzberger & Usdan, 1992; Knezevich, 1984).

More recently, Denoyer (1992) delineated the board's role as follows:

> Boards should adopt policy, hire and fire the superintendent, and work with administrators to develop strategic plans for achieving educational goals. . . . In rural settings, boards have a powerful role. Rural school boards have a unique opportunity to impact education by involving teachers, administrators, and the community in policy development. To make policy an instrument of empowerment, policymakers should consider the following steps: (1) seeking information from any and all groups that the policy will affect to develop a statement about organizational growth; (2) write statements in the form of super-objectives giving a perspective of the individual roles in the total organizational setting; (3) distributing individual roles in the total organizational setting; (4) distributing policies and collecting suggestions for refinement from the school board; and (5) receiving thorough input on all organizational levels culminating in a formal policy statement by the school board. Policy development and revision involving all constituencies become the leadership role of the local board of education. (Van Alfen, 1992, p. i)

CRITICAL INCIDENTS: SUPERINTENDENTS

In a study completed by Grady and Bryant (1990), superintendents identified critical incidents they experienced in working with boards of education. The categories of critical incidents and their frequencies include: board members' families and friends, 36 (24%); board members' roles, 27 (18%); who is elected to the board, 17 (11%); superintendent not supported, 15 (10%); board itself, 14 (9%); athletic coaches, 10 (7%); community, 8 (5%); individual board members, 8 (5%); employee problems, 6 (4%); superintendent, 3 (2%); and finance, 1 (.6%).

FAMILY AND FRIENDS

The most frequently cited critical incidents related to school board members and their children, relatives, and friends. Problems with board members' children, especially their athletic participation, were common. Board member behaviors included threatening the superintendent, intimidating coaches, lobbying other board members, and, in one instance, having a basketball coach terminated because the board member's daughter was not "properly treated."

Other child-related incidents led to threats of termination or actual termination of school personnel. Board members sought special treatment, favors, or rule waivers for their children. Severe incidents involving board members' children included vandalism, stealing, drug possession, and convictions for driving while intoxicated.

Issues involving relatives of board members also produced conflict between the board and the superintendent. Hiring board members' relatives was a frequent issue. Superintendents described board members as vindictive.

Critical incidents also occurred because of board member friendships. Personal relationships influenced board decisions and exacerbated conflict.

BOARD MEMBER ROLES

The second category of incident related to board members' problematic interpretations of their roles. The superintendents described incidents of community members and long-term employees approaching individual board members outside board meetings about issues such as gym or football field use or other specific problems. Incidents of this nature are more likely to occur in a rural environment.

Superintendents described incidents of board members' involvement in administrative roles, including attempting to evaluate personnel, trying to terminate employees, assessing school bus driver performance, and purchasing items for the school without the superintendent's knowledge.

In these instances, according to the superintendents, the board members deviated from their formal roles, were susceptible to gossip, attempted to evaluate personnel and assumed other administrative functions. Board members operating outside their roles attempted to "get even" with teachers and to use their positions on the board for personal interests.

WHO'S ELECTED TO THE BOARD

A third category was "who's elected to the board." Dominant in this category were individuals elected to the board on a platform of firing the superintendent. Other cases included the election to the school board of ex-teachers, teachers from other districts, or fired district employees.

A simple description for this incident category would be individuals elected to the school board with an "ax to grind." The dominant "ax to grind" was attempting to fire the superintendent. Thus, of the seventeen incidents reported in this category, four resulted in the firing or resignation of the superintendent.

SUPERINTENDENT NOT SUPPORTED

A fourth category of critical incidents was "superintendent not supported." Incidents in which superintendents' recommendations for hiring were not followed by school boards were typical of this category, including school boards did not accept superintendents' maintenance recommendations or overturned disciplinary actions. Other incidents of superintendents not being supported included board members questioning the superintendent's decisions, questioning the superintendent's honesty, and questioning the handling of finances.

The tenor of these incidents was one that created a feeling of unpredictability. These situations made it difficult for superintendents to make decisions because of uncertainty about the board's response.

BOARD MALFUNCTIONS

The fifth category of critical incidents was board malfunctions. Board stagnation, the dissolution of standing committees, lack of an agenda, no control of the agenda, vying for the board presidency, and spending disagreements were noted as incidents precipitated by the board. These incidents, linked to the composition of the board and its behavior as a group, led to resignations in four of fourteen reported incidents.

In addition to these five categories that represent the majority (109/72%) of incidents reported by the superintendents, one other category of incident was directly related to board members.

INDIVIDUAL BOARD MEMBERS

Eight critical incidents (5%) emerged because of individual board members. These incidents involved problems arising from the idiosyncrasies of individual board members.

For instance, a board member with a master's degree in business administration tried to run a school's budget; one school board member ran her own school board meetings outside regular board meetings and conducted independent opinion polls. Board members also precipitated critical incidents through their persistent demands. A drugstore owner/board member expected purchases to be made from him regardless of cost.

CONSEQUENCES

As a consequence of these critical incidents, superintendents described their resignations and terminations. The superintendents reported resigning their positions in seventeen instances (21%). Two superintendents were terminated because of the incidents. Of the eighty superintendents, one reported resigning twice and another reported resigning once and being terminated once.

As an intangible consequence, the superintendents described the negative aura that pervaded their work and school districts after the incidents. The superintendents reported distrust, suspicion, and unpredictability as consequences of the incidents. Stress and strain, loss of friends and good will were other consequences of the incidents.

CRITICAL INCIDENTS: BOARD PRESIDENTS

Grady and Bryant (1991) completed research subsequent to their interviews with superintendents. They conducted interviews with fifty-nine school board presidents to identify incidents that were critical in their work with superintendents. The interviews provided a database representing seventy-five critical incidents school board presidents experienced with superintendents. The incidents were grouped into eleven categories of critical incidents and their frequencies were: communication/human relations, 28 (37%); staffing issues, 11 (15%); ethics, 8 (11%); competence, 6 (8%); personal issues 5 (7%); finance, 5 (7%); athletics, 4 (5%); credentials, 3 (4%); policy, 3 (4%); New Age Church, 1 (1%); and board member, 1 (1%).

COMMUNICATION/HUMAN RELATIONS

The most frequently cited critical incidents concerned communication/human relations. Twenty-eight of the seventy-five incidents (37%) were in this category. The board presidents described superintendents who were intimidating, reluctant to share information with the school board, publicly argumentative, and unwilling or unable to get along with people both in the schools and in the communities.

Fourteen of the twenty-eight incidents (50%) described as communication/human relations problems resulted in resignations or terminations of the superintendents. The incidents described by the board presidents were not discrete, well-defined situations. Instead, they were complex and reflected the cumulative effect of long-term poor communication and human relations skills.

STAFFING ISSUES

A second category of incidents concerned staffing issues and included eleven of the seventy-five incidents (15%). The school board presidents described instances of superintendents' personnel recommendations not being supported. In four incidents the superintendents attempted to terminate teachers without the support of the school board. None of the four teachers were terminated. In one incident the superintendent wanted to select three activities directors for the schools; the board authorized only two. In three incidents, superintendents ignored the directives of the school board in hiring selections. Two school board presidents described superintendents who were lax in their supervision of staff.

ETHICS

Eight incidents (11%) formed a third category labeled ethics. The school board presidents identified ethical issues ranging from "covering up mistakes" to removing $700 from a cash drawer. Two board presidents described incidents that emerged when superintendents did not report mistakes or errors to the school board. One superintendent, with the help of his secretary, advanced his own salary for several months before the situation came to the school board's attention. Another superintendent falsified reports to the Department of Education; a parent seeking testing data discovered the discrepancy. Five of the eight incidents described by the school board presidents as ethical issues resulted in superintendent resignations.

CONSEQUENCES

In addition to identification of critical incidents, the investigators inquired about school board presidents' perceptions of the consequences of those incidents. The school board presidents identified both tangible and intangible consequences of the incidents. As tangible consequences, the school board presidents described superintendents' resignations and terminations. Of the seventy-five incidents the school board presidents reported, 40 (54%) incidents resulted in superintendent resignations or terminations.

As an intangible consequence, the school board presidents described the negative aura that pervaded staff relationships and the school districts after the incidents. The board presidents also reported distrust and suspicion as consequences of the incidents.

CRITICAL ISSUES IN RURAL SCHOOLS

The most critical issues in managing and running small rural school districts according to Ferre et al. (1988) were finances, followed by regional economic conditions, state regulations, salaries, and providing an adequate variety of classes. In a study reported by Kennedy and Barker (1986), there were 93 usable responses from 28 states. Analysis of the responses showed that the major challenges confronting superintendents in small rural districts were those of securing adequate school funding and improving school curriculum. Of somewhat lesser concern were securing and retaining teachers and improving student academic achievement. School consolidation did not appear to be a major issue. The school board presidents felt that superintendents should be able to communicate well and work well with staff, students, parents, and community members.

SCHOOL BOARD CHALLENGES

The literature concerning school boards identifies board action and inaction that create problems. The critical incidents superintendents and board presidents reported substantiate that poor communication between superintendents and boards causes many of the problems they experience.

According to Danzberger et al. (1992), the critics agree that all too commonly:

- boards are not providing far-reaching or politically risk-taking leadership for education reform
- boards have become another level of administration, often micro-managing the school district
- boards are so splintered by their attempts to represent special interests or board members' individual political needs that the boards cannot govern
- boards have broad goals but lack the capacity for strong goal setting and planning to give direction to school systems
- boards are not spending adequate time on educating themselves about the issues or on educational policy making
- boards do not exercise adequate policy oversight, nor do they have adequate accountability processes and processes for communicating about schools.
- boards' actions are less impressive than their rhetoric in devolving decision-making to schools
- boards exhibit little capacity to develop positive and productive lasting relationships with their superintendents
- boards pay little or no attention to their governance performance and to their needs for on-going development of their capacity to govern
- boards in conflicted communities tend to make decisions in response to the "issue of the day" while boards in more stable communities tend to govern to maintain the status quo (Danzberger, Kirst, & Usdan, 1992, pp. 49–50)

Although criticisms prevail, locally elected boards deal with two of the most important elements in citizens' lives: their children and their tax dollars. Additionally, civil illiteracy about school boards and public indifference is not uncommon. This is manifested in the mere 5 to 15 percent of the eligible voters who participate in school board elections (Danzberger et al., 1992, p. 51).

Communication, public relations, interpersonal relations, and human relations were the dominant themes for improving board-superintendent relationships.

Danzberger et al. (1992) identified the following obstacles to board effectiveness:

- Public apathy
- Lack of public understanding of the policy-making role of the board
- Poor or sporadic relationships with state policy makers
- The need to improve teaching within the framework of collective bargaining
- Lack of time and an operating structure for focusing on education issues
- Discrepancy between time boards invest and their satisfaction with their accomplishments and ability to determine their priorities
- Difficulty in developing a "collection" of individuals into a policy-making board

- Reactive rather than proactive behavior
- Lack of strong links to other community sectors and government entities (p. 52)

SCHOOL BOARDS NATIONALLY

Grady and Krumm (1997) conducted a national study to identify the demographics of school boards in the United States and to determine whether there were differences in responses for rural and urban school boards. The following questions guided the study:

(1) What are the demographics of school boards in the United States?

(2) Were there differences noted in the demographics of rural and urban school boards?

Telephone interviews with the professional development specialists at 43 of the 50 (86%) state school board associations provided a rich database concerning school boards. The number of school districts per state ranged from a low of 1 district to a high of 1,046 school districts. Responses to a question regarding demographics of school boards revealed that in 17 of 43 (40%) states, all school boards were members of the state associations. In 16 of 43 (37%) states, between 95 and 99% of the school boards were members of the state associations.

In response to a question regarding number of members per board, a range of responses was reported.

Five and seven were the most frequently cited numbers of school board members. The range in number of board members was 3–14. In 32 states, there was a uniform number of board members per district. In 11 states, the number of board members per district varied.

In response to a question of whether board members were elected or appointed, 34 (79%) states reported having elected members and 6 (14%) states had both elected and appointed members. Three individuals provided no response to this question.

In response to a question regarding salary allowances, 31 states allowed salaries for board members.

In response to a question regarding expense reimbursement, 34 states allowed reimbursement.

In terms of age qualifications, eighteen years of age was the most frequently reported age qualification (16 states).

The study findings did not indicate differences in board demographics based on whether a school district was rural or urban.

INSTABILITY IN THE SMALL SCHOOL SUPERINTENDENCY

Educational Research Service reported 14,222 school districts nationwide with an annual turnover rate for superintendencies of 13.5 percent. Superintendent tenure was highly skewed toward fewer than five years. The greatest turnover of superintendents—16 percent—occurred among the smallest districts; fewer than 350 students. In comparison:

- Districts with 350–999 students had a 13 percent turnover,
- Districts with 1,000–2,399 students had a 12 percent turnover, and
- Districts with 2,500 or more students had a 13 percent turnover. (Anderson, 1990, p. 22)

Keeping these turnover rates in mind, one is reminded that a superintendent has to survive. Thus, the superintendent has to master survival skills (Jones, 1978, p. 221S). One of these skills is simply knowing when to fight, when to back off, and when to let someone else battle for you. No superintendent can lose too many battles (Jones, 1978, p. 221S). We have apparently reached the point where *survival* in the superintendency depends to a great extent on the Superintendent's political "savior faire" (Washington, 1989, p. 47).

McCurdy and Hymes (1992) listed factors identified by school board members and superintendents as responsible for destabilizing their relationships. Four were commonly identified by both groups:

- Board members often do not understand the differences between their roles and those of superintendents.
- Poor communication by both parties contributes to conflict.
- Board members often enter office with personal agendas.
- Board members and superintendents often fail to establish a necessary level of mutual trust. (Kowalski, 1995, p. 48)

KEY TASKS

The American Association of School Administrators and the National School Boards Association specify the following key tasks for positive working relationships between the board and superintendent.

First of all, those who govern and administer public schools must share a vision, a clear purpose, and the ability and courage to lead. The board and superintendent must work together to involve families, community organizations, and other public and private agencies for the benefit of the whole child and the entire community (AASA & NSBA , 1994, p. 1).

The board and superintendent must foster the highest possible performance by schools and students through means such as monitoring student achievement, placing program corrections into effect as necessary, keeping the public informed of the status of education programs and progress, ensuring that all teaching and learning fit together harmoniously, providing appropriate staff and board training opportunities, and otherwise fulfilling all governance responsibilities required by state and federal law (AASA & NSBA, 1994, p. 1).

Superintendents "should develop procedures for working with the board of education that define mutual expectations, working relationships, and strategies for formulating district policy for external and internal programs; adjust local policy to state and federal requirements and constitutional professions, standards, and regulatory applications; and recognize and apply standards involving civil and criminal liabilities" (AASA & NSBA, 1994, p. 3).

Superintendents "should know and be able to: (a) describe the system of public school governance in our democracy; (b) describe procedures for superintendent-board of education interpersonal and working relationships; (c) formulate a district policy for external and internal programs; (d) relate local policy to state and federal regulations and requirements; (e) describe procedures to avoid civil and criminal liabilities" (AASA & NSBA, 1994, p. 3).

SUPERINTENDENT RESPONSIBILITIES

According to the American Association of School Administrators and the National School Boards Association (1994), superintendents have these specific responsibilities:

- To serve as the school board's chief executive officer.
- To serve as the primary educational leader for the school system.
- To serve as a catalyst for the school system's administrative leadership team in proposing and implementing policy changes.
- To propose and institute a process for long-range and strategic planning that will engage the board and the community in positioning the school district for success in ensuing years.
- To keep all board members informed about school operations and programs.
- To interpret the needs of the school system to the board.
- To present policy options along with specific recommendations to the board when circumstances require the board to adopt new policies or review existing policies.
- To develop and inform the board of administrative procedures needed to implement board policy.
- To develop a sound program of school/community relations in concert with the board.
- To oversee management of the district's day-to-day operations.
- To develop a description for the board of what constitutes effective leadership and management of public schools.
- To develop and carry out a plan for keeping the total professional and support staff informed about the mission, goals, and strategies of the school system and about the important roles all staff members play in realizing them.
- To ensure that professional development opportunities are available to all school system employees.
- To collaborate with other administrators through national and state

professional associations to inform state legislators, members of Congress, and all other appropriate state and federal officials of local concerns and issues.

- To evaluate personnel performance in harmony with district policy and to keep the board informed about such evaluations.
- To provide all board members with complete background information and a recommendation for school board action on each agenda item well in advance of each board meeting.
- To develop and implement a continuing plan for working with the news media. (pp. 11–12)

If a superintendent is to provide vigorous leadership, the superintendent must know, among other things:

(1) The school board's plans, goals, and objectives for the district.
(2) How the district goals and objectives translate into duties and responsibilities of the superintendent. That is, what does the board expect to accomplish?
(3) How the board itself functions.
(4) How the board will evaluate the superintendent's work.
(5) How the superintendent will be rewarded.
(6) The superintendent's status with the board regarding continued employment. (Booth & Glaub, 1978, pp. 14–15)

PUBLIC RELATIONS

An essential component of the superintendency is public relations. In the critical incident reports, communication, human relations and interpersonal relations were dominant issues. A program of effective public relations might include the following elements:

- Policies that ensure open and honest communications and provide the human and material resources necessary for an effective public relations program.
- Regular formal and informal surveys of community members to determine their opinions, attitudes, and needs.
- Involvement of staff and community members in the decisions that affect them.
- Publications that regularly carry information, ideas, and opinions to staff and community.
- Identification and tracking of issues, trends, or conditions that could affect the ability of the school system to reach its goals.
- Training on how school people can relate to representatives of the news media, speak effectively in public, write in a way that members of the community can clearly understand, use appropriate listening skills and nonverbal communications techniques, and work effectively in a group. (AASA & NSBA, 1994, pp. 13–14)

Key elements of the communications program include working toward a sense of high mutual personal regard and respect, and developing a sense of trust and openness, a respect for each other's duties, a desire to address misunderstandings promptly, and a willingness to confront differences of opinion without acrimony (AASA & NSBA, 1994, p.14).

ONE DISTRICT'S PLAN

A useful model for clarifying superintendent-board communication can be found in the Tacoma, Washington, communication procedures.

(1) The Superintendent will meet with each Board Member on a regular basis to provide information and to respond to questions and concerns.

(2) The Superintendent and the Board will mutually agree upon a statement that details who shall be responsible for the District during the Superintendent's absences from the District. Prior to any absence, the Superintendent shall notify the Board and staff of dates of absence from the District and who is to assume responsibility during that period.

(3) The Superintendent shall provide an organization chart for the District that shows each position by title, the name of the person holding the position, and the date the person assumed the position.

(4) In case of emergency, the Superintendent and/or appointed representatives shall notify all Board Members of it and what action is being taken.

(5) The Superintendent will periodically send "Board Briefs" to the Board Members. These will provide, in summary form, information about a current issue or problem which the Superintendent feels a Board Member should know in order to discuss the issue at a Board meeting or to respond to constituent questions.

(6) In order to assure that Board Members receive requested information in a timely manner and to insure that no one staff member is unduly burdened by such requests, a "Board Request for Information" form will be used by Board Members when requesting information from staff. The form may be filled out by a Board Member or by the Superintendent's secretary in the event of a telephone request. The Superintendent then assigns the responsibility of responding to the appropriate staff member.

(7) The procedure described in #6 does not preclude calls from Board Members for quick data or fingertip information. Protocol dictates that the Superintendent be informed by staff of these calls. (Barna, 1996, p. 2)

TEAM APPROACH

Thinking of the board-administration as a "team" emphasizes the importance of establishing roles, goals, and priorities with board of education members while working as a team. Successful board-administrator relations depend on understanding the expectations and respective roles within the leadership team (Tift, 1990).

Harmonious working relationships among school board members result when members strive for cooperation rather than unanimity, engage in frank discussion, treat others with respect, identify someone who can promote compromise, involve the superintendent, and consider improving organizational self-evaluations, or attending retreats (McCormick, 1985).

CAVEATS

Given the tenuous nature of the superintendency, the following caveats are warranted:

(1) Don't underestimate the damage one board member can do.

(2) You inevitably will make enemies.

(3) Never spend a dime that you haven't receipted properly.

(4) Don't play favorites among board members.

(5) Don't sweep your mistakes under the rug.

(6) Never take any subordinate into complete confidence.

(7) Never count your votes until they are legally cast.

(8) Recognize the early warning signs of board displeasure.

(9) Remember that the school attorney works for the school board not you.

(10) Don't be afraid to say, "I don't know."

(11) When the battle is lost, retreat.

(12) Leave politics to the politicians.

(13) Losing your job is a bend in the river, not the end of the world.

(14) The press is not your friend when you're in hot water.

(15) Remember the properties of glass houses.

(16) Don't fool around with a district employee.

(17) An unattended school board might make decisions that can never be remedied. (Hagemann & Varga, 1993, pp. 37–38)

BOARD EXPECTATIONS

Washington (1989) reported the following ranking of board expectations in order of importance:

(1) Assistance with policy development and policy recommendation.

(2) Implementation of policy decisions.

(3) Effective communication and public relations.

(4) Effective management of the school organization.

(5) Facilitation of school-community relations. (pp. 45–46)

Similarly, Washington (1989) reported the following key suggestions for superintendents:

(1) Implement decisions of the board and not those of individual members

(2) Spend some time in executive session dealing with board member concerns

(3) Work closely with various board committees

(4) Encourage board members to not make promises without prior consultation

(5) Communicate—keep board members informed

(6) Be straightforward—"Tell it the way it is"

(7) Get board approval before acting on new issues and problems

(8) Let the board know your feelings on important issues

(9) Take frequent readings of the board's confidence level

(10) Use workshops to help board members improve their understanding of their role

(11) Avoid having personal relationships with board members (pp. 45–46)

FUTURE SUCCESS

The future success of the superintendent will depend on the following superintendent skills:

(1) Success will depend on the superintendent's ability to function simultaneously as politician, administrator, and diplomat.

(2) The superintendent will have to demonstrate the ability to get the most out of available human resources.

(3) Successful superintendents will be those who are able to involve people in the process.

(4) The superintendent will be expected to be more accountable.

(5) More of the superintendent's time will be devoted to improvement of instruction. (Washington, 1989, pp. 45-46)

STRATEGIES

Communication, public relations, interpersonal relations, and human relations were the dominant themes for improving board-superintendent working relationships. Programs focused on improving public relations, interpersonal relations, and human relations skills should be provided for superintendents. Emphasis on communication skills, both verbal and nonverbal, should be part of these programs.

Superintendents should have the skills to handle conflict. Preparation programs should include conflict resolution skills so that superintendents are able to resolve the critical incidents that occur in school districts. Additionally, superintendents should be able to assess community power structures. A number of critical incidents occurred because superintendents did not understand the power bases in the communities. The reported challenges or expectations were not related to the education of children. Superintendents who articulate a vision and clear goals for the education of children may be able to defuse incidents not related to the vision and goals of a school district.

Superintendents need to work in settings in which job descriptions, role expectations, and evaluation procedures are clearly established as part of district policies. Conflict may be avoided if expectations are clearly specified.

Two issues appear to dominate the tension between board members and superintendents. First, which decisions belong to professionals and which to local citizens is an issue that has teased generations of educational critics and produced an extensive discussion of school governance. The lay board is often partial and resists appropriate role definitions and separation of authority.

The second source of conflict, the training and socialization of administrators, promotes the administrator as the "person in charge." Leadership is akin to "riding a white horse in front of the parade."

Specific actions can be taken to improve the working relationship between superintendents and school board members. An initial step is to establish a clear procedure for conducting meetings. This includes: helping school boards conduct routine business meetings more efficiently, thereby improving their ability to reach constructive decisions and solve problems; organizing the new school board, electing officers, adopting policies, and appointing committees; planning the meeting and preparing the agenda; identifying duties and responsibilities of the board president, board members, superintendent, and school attorney; recording the meeting and preparing the minutes for distribution; dealing with the public at board meetings and handling complaints or criticisms, dealing with the news media—working with reporters, preparing for news coverage, handling interviews, and checklists for evaluating the school board meeting (Anderson, 1983).

The research and literature concerning superintendents and boards provides substantive guidance for creating positive working relationships. The work of the superintendent and board is essential to the education of our children.

A strong school board with a weak superintendent will not only set policy but administer policy. A strong superintendent with a weak board will not only administer policy but will set it. A weak board and a weak superintendent will neither set policy nor administer it. And that may mean that the citizens will step in to take things in hand—justifiably. But a strong superintendent and a strong board and informed citizenry happen to be the right elements for an education that can make the difference for our youngsters (Jones, 1978, p. 221S).

Those who will be successful in the superintendency should heed the recommendations found in the literature on superintendent-board relations.

REFERENCES

Anderson, S. A. 1983. Successful School Board Meetings. *A Special Edition for New Jersey School Boards.* Trenton, NJ: New Jersey School Boards Association.

Anderson, S. L. 1990. "How to Predict Success in the Superintendency," *The School Administrator, 22*, 24, 26.

Barna, L. 1996. Working Agreement Tacoma School Board and Superintendent and Activities of Individual Governing Board Members. A paper presented to the Tucson Unified School District in Tucson, AZ, November 10, 1995. Approved by the board February 20, 1996 (Policy 9100).

Booth, R. R., & G. R. Glaub. 1978. *Planned Appraisal of the Superintendent: A Performance-Based Program for School Boards and Superintendents.* Springfield, IL: Illinois Association of School Boards.

Danzberger, J. P., M. W. Kirst, & M. D. Usdan. 1992. *Governing Public Schools: New Times New Requirements.* Washington, DC: The Institute for Educational Leadership, Inc.

Danzberger, J. P., & M. D. Usdan. 1992. "Strengthening a Grass Roots American Institution: The Local School Board," In P. F. First & H. J. Walberg (Eds.), *School Boards: Changing Local Control* (pp. 91–124). Berkeley, CA: McCutchan.

Denoyer, R. A. 1992. *Response to the Task Force on School Governance.* (ERIC Clearinghouse No. EA 024 298).

Ferre, V. A., & Others. 1988. "Rural Superintendents View Their Role: Ranking the Issues," *Research in Rural Education, 5*(1), 33–34.

Grady, M. L., & M. T. Bryant. 1990. "Critical Incidents Between Superintendents and School Boards: Implications for Practice," *Planning and Changing, 20*(4), 206–214.

Grady, M. L., & M. T. Bryant. 1991. "School Board Presidents Describe Critical Incidents With Superintendents," *Journal of Research in Rural Education, 7*(3), 51–58.

Grady, M. L., & B. L. Krumm. 1997–98. "School Board Demographics, State Associations and Professional Development Activities: A National Study," *National Forum of Educational Administration and Supervision Journal, 15*(1), 19–29.

Hagemann, B., & B. Varga. 1993, March. "Holding On: Landing That Top Job Is Easier Than Keeping It," *The Executive Educator,* 37–38.

Hunkins, R. V. 1949. *Superintendent and School Boards: A Manual of Operative School Administration.* Lincoln, NE: University of Nebraska Press.

Jones, J. 1978. "What Superintendents and Boards Can Do," *Phi Delta Kappan, 60*, 221S–222S.

Kennedy, R., & B. O. Barker. 1986. Rural School Superintendents: A National Study of Perspectives of School Board Presidents. Paper presented at the Annual Conference of the Rural Education Association, Little Rock, AR, October 12, 1986. (ERIC Document No. ED 274 497).

Knezevich, S. J. 1984. *Administration of Public Education* (4th ed.). New York: Harper & Row.

Kowalski, T. J. 1995. *Keepers of the Flame: Contemporary Urban Superintendents.* Thousand Oaks, CA: Corwin Press, Inc.

Lunenburg, F. C., & A. C. Ornstein. 1991. *Educational Administration: Concepts and Practices.* Belmont, CA: Wadsworth Publishing.

McCormick, K. 1985. "Here's the Score on How Your Board Can Work in Unison," *American School Board Journal, 172*(6), 27–29.

Public Opinion About Kentucky School Boards: Results of a Statewide Survey. A Joint Study. 1987. Charleston, WV: Appalachia Educational Lab; Kentucky School Boards Association; Kentucky University, Lexington. Survey Research Center.

Russo, C. J. 1992. "The Legal Status of School Boards in the Intergovernmental System," In P. F. First & H. J. Walberg (Eds.), *School Boards: Changing Local Control* (pp. 3–18). Berkeley, CA: McCutchan.

Tift, C. 1990. *Rural Administrative Leadership Handbook.* Portland, OR: Northwest Regional Educational Lab (ERIC Documentation No. RC 017 809).

Van Alfen, C. 1992. *Policy as a Stimulant to Curricular Growth in Rural Education* (ERIC Document No. ED 354 133).

Washington, K. R. 1989. "The Superintendency: Reflections of Past and Present CEOs," *Education Canada, 19*(2), 44–47.

The Rural Superintendent: Succeeding or Failing as a Superintendent in Rural Schools

The job of the superintendent is highly complex and full of conflict, politics, and community input. This holds as true for the rural superintendent as it does his/her urban counterpart.—Ed Chance, 1997

The job of the superintendent is highly complex and full of conflict, politics, and community input. This holds as true for the rural superintendent as for his/her urban counterpart. Chapter 5 seeks the answer to two central questions: (1) What does it take to be a successful rural superintendent? and (2) What are superintendent behaviors and actions that most often result in superintendent turnover in rural schools? Practical information is provided that can assist one in being successful in the rural superintendency. When possible, superintendent and school board voices discuss issues of the superintendency.

IT had been snowing for three days. The January cold seemed particularly bitter as Jim Smithson prepared for the monthly board meeting. He had been superintendent of the Xerron school district for twenty-two years and knew his board and community as well as he did his family. Tonight he would be rehired unanimously by the board for his twenty-third year. Every board member had privately and publicly indicated their continuing support for him. They trusted him and had no doubt that he would get the school district through the current budget problems just as he had in the past. No one in the community had any complaints and everybody was happy with the direction of the school district. Jim appreciated everyone's support and was committed to the school district. In fact, he had never even thought about looking for another position since coming to Xerron over twenty years ago.

Edward W. Chance, Department of Educational Leadership, University of Nevada-Las Vegas.

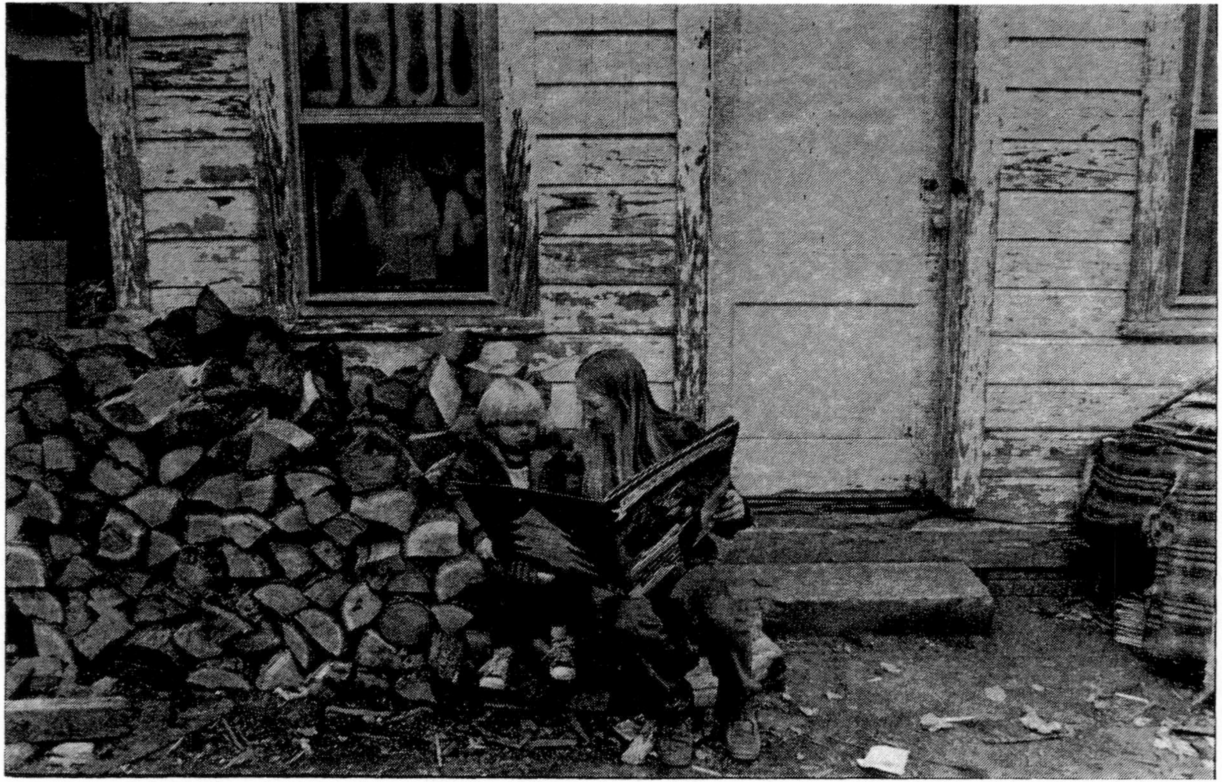

© Photo by Rob Amberg.

In a neighboring state, Susan Peters shivered in the same bitter cold as she got in her car to drive to the school board meeting. She was dealing with a mixture of strong emotions as she pulled out of her drive—anxiety, depression, and nervousness. She knew that in this third year of her superintendency in the Eagle Mountain School District she had "rocked the boat" perhaps too much. Several of the community leaders and the teachers had told her so. Her own school board had become tight-lipped about renewal, espousing some support for the changes she had initiated while indicating that she had moved too quickly in other areas. Susan had no idea how the board would vote tonight on her renewal as superintendent. She did know that it would either be a short meeting with her being rehired or a long, arduous night with an outcome she was dreading. She had tried to be philosophical about the situation, but at this stage it simply was not possible. The result of the school board's decision was too personal.

The two scenarios described above represent a unique ritual that many superintendents encounter each year either through an annual school board review or annual renewal of their contract. This yearly activity has the potential to positively or negatively impact an individual's personal life and professional career. But more than that, it has the potential to split a school district and/or community and destroy the educational process in the school district.

The job of the superintendent is highly complex and full of conflict, politics, and community input. This holds as true for the rural superintendent as it does for his/her urban counterpart. The major difference between an urban and a rural superintendent is that the rural superintendent may also be teacher, counselor, building principal, bus driver, and the total central office staff. The typical rural superintendent wears many hats and answers to a multitude of constituents on a daily basis. The stress of the superintendency is evident in the recent suicide of a superintendent in upstate New York after she endured two years of contentious interactions with the local school board (Thomas, 1997). The political nature of the superintendency is never far from the surface. "The very fabric of the schooling function in American society, because of the nature of that society, is essentially political . . . being a superintendent . . . is essentially a political activity, as are, of course, the mobilization of community support and the management of conflict" (Blumberg, 1985, pp. 46–48).

The superintendency has changed since its initial conception. It has evolved through four district roles since the first superintendent was appointed in Buffalo, New York, in 1837. These four roles, as identified by Carter and Cunningham (1997), are clerical, master educator, manager, and now, chief executive officer of the board. One thing is clear today, superintendents must be highly effective leaders who achieve established district goals (Leithwood & Montgomery, 1986; Manasse, 1985). They must have a clear vision of the future while managing conflict and supporting the democratic process, and must believe that schools can make a difference in the lives of children (Carter & Cunningham, 1997; Chance, 1992; Cuban, 1985). Certainly, these contentions hold true for rural schools.

But the questions remain, what does it take to be a successful rural superintendent? What are superintendent behaviors and actions that most often result in superintendent turnover in rural schools? The remainder of this chapter will seek to answer these two central questions as well as provide information that can assist one in being successful in the rural superintendency. When possible, superintendent and school board voices will discuss issues of the superintendency.

FAILING IN THE RURAL SUPERINTENDENCY

Surviving the superintendency is not easy. In fact, the simplest thing in the world is getting in trouble with one's school board, community, or staff. Although the majority of the conflicts between superintendents and their many constituents do not result in loss of their job, it is a very real possibility that every superintendent must confront.

In a significant study conducted by Grady and Bryant (1991), eleven reasons for superintendent turnover were identified. All of these eleven reasons focused on the area of relationships. The authors determined that the reasons for conflict between the superintendent and the rural school board/community were:

(1) Family and friends. Perceived or actual favorable or unfavorable treatment of family and friends.

(2) Employing relatives and friends. Either hiring or not hiring relatives or friends/relatives of influential people.

(3) Board members' roles. Board members performing in roles not part of their legal duties and/or micromanaging on a daily basis.

(4) Election with an ax to grind. One issue elections which increase or create conflict situations.

(5) Lack of support. Failure of the board to support the superintendent in critical situations.

(6) Board malfunctions. Board members behaving or performing in ineffective ways.

(7) Athletic coaches. Winning becomes more important than learning.

(8) Individual members. Personal problems or personality conflicts which hamper the function of the superintendent.

(9) The community. Pressure groups who have political, religious, or economic agendas.

(10) Contracts. Superintendent contracts and rights.

(11) Superintendents. The superintendent himself/herself creates the problem

through his/her inappropriate behavior (Grady & Bryant, 1991, pp. 23–24).

Many of the issues identified by Grady and Bryant concern school board-superintendent relationships. But, they can just as well represent the total school-community culture in which the rural superintendent must perform his/her daily duties.

Another major study, conducted by Chance and Capps (1992), sought to determine the critical incidents that most often cost rural superintendents their positions. In a study of school districts that had experienced excessive superintendent turnover (three or more superintendents in five years), it was determined that the dismissal of the superintendent was the result of four major reasons: communication problems, financial mismanagement, financial malfeasance, and immorality. A fifth minor category entitled "other" represented the few issues that did not fit the four broad categories.

Communication problems represented 37.2 percent of the reasons for superintendent dismissal. Open, unfettered, honest communication between the superintendent and the board, community, and staff represent a key issue in the success or failure of superintendents. Commonly heard comments that represented poor superintendent communication included ". . . he wouldn't take suggestions or advice . . ."; ". . . he would not tell the board what was happening in the school . . ."; he "could talk for 30 to 40 minutes and then the board would have to ask him if that was a yes or a no . . ."; and, "he was aloof and inaccessible to patrons or staff members . . ." Clearly, the inability to effectively communicate is a demonstrated way to lose one's position as a rural superintendent.

The second highest reason by which superintendents lose their positions was determined to be financial mismanagement (30.5 percent). In these days of tight budgets and increasing concerns for the viability of rural schools, a rural superintendent must be a financial expert. In this study (Chance & Capps, 1992), financial mismanagement referred to the act of spending money on nonessentials, hiring staff that were not needed, and failing to maintain an adequate budget or records of expenditures. Examples relating to financial mismanagement included examples such as purchasing "$10,000 in supplies" that were not needed; reducing the cash reserve of a school district by hiring extra coaches in order to win athletic events; and not maintaining adequate cash flow so that the staff could be paid. The majority of the problems in this category represented the superintendent's inability to deal effectively with district financial considerations. Financial mismanagement really means financial incompetence.

The area of financial malfeasance represented 25.4 percent of the reasons for superintendent dismissal. Financial malfeasance does not imply the incompetence of financial mismanagement, but rather issues ranging from theft to lying regarding school finances. In fact, one individual stated that "experience just gave the superintendent the know-how to legally steal." Many of the issues reported here could have resulted (and perhaps should have) in the criminal prosecution of the superintendent. Examples uncovered in this study included using district gasoline for a personal car, boat and truck; using a district credit card to pay for "bar bills"; giving oneself a salary increase and trying to hide it from the board; and illegally giving away surplus school property to local patrons.

Several people in this study indicated that they had "always held the superintendent in high esteem and [were] shocked by his actions of dishonesty." One individual, when discussing rural superintendents, stated that "some have lost sight of why they're in education." Examples of financial malfeasance not only cost the superintendent involved his/her position but also negatively colored future relationships between superintendents in the district and the school board, community, and staff. These actions did more than that, they hurt the students in the school.

The fourth major category was immorality, which represented 5 percent of the reasons for superintendent dismissal. Immorality most often dealt with sexual issues, such as having an affair with a teacher or a student. Accusations of affairs or actual affairs inevitably resulted in a superintendent losing his or her position. School districts and communities expect the superintendent to possess unreproachable morals. In a rural school district one's daily behaviors and actions are under a constant community microscope and viewed by everyone. Thus, any unacceptable behavior by community standards is immediately observed and commented upon.

The final category, "other," represented only 1.5 percent of the reasons a superintendent would lose his/her position. A mixture of reasons were found in this category, ranging from religious affiliation to personality conflicts, to community fit. Clearly, superintendents may lose their positions for very real, substantive reasons but they also may lose them for any reason if the community and school board so desire.

Thus, it appears that a superintendent's career can be tenuous and that it is easy to lose one's position if certain board or community expectations are not met. The areas that represent difficulties for the rural superintendent include issues of communication with both internal and external constituents; financial issues related to malfeasance and mismanagement; and finally, immoral or unethical behaviors. Rural communities expect the best from rural superintendents and hold them to high performance standards, both personally and professionally. The rural superintendent who meets these standards/expectations can have a long fruitful career while those who do not meet community expectations will move from rural school to rural school. On the way, they manage to hurt all who care about the education of students and rural communities.

SUCCEEDING IN THE RURAL SUPERINTENDENCY

Many who decide to become rural superintendents are very successful and have long careers in one or two schools. These long-term successful rural superintendents are able to blend community expectations with school district needs. Their schools are best represented by stability and progress as opposed to ongoing chaos, unmanaged change, and mistrust.

Norton, Webb, Dlugosh, and Sybouts (1996) indicated that "superintendents need scholarly credentials . . ., an orientation towards action . . ., and an understanding of human dynamics combined with business acumen and, equally important, high visibility in the school and community" (p. 58). This view was supported by Carter and Cunningham (1997) when they stated "the superintendency requires 'fire in the belly,' physical stamina, leadership skill, vision, and a strong desire to improve the lives of children" (p. 4). They also noted that "the keys to being a successful and responsive superintendent, then, are open communication, integrity, hard work, positive direction, core values, sound judgment, and effective decision making" (Carter & Cunningham, 1997, p. 36).

But beyond somewhat nebulous platitudes, what are the traits of a long-term successful superintendent and what skills are necessary to survive in such a stress-filled position for an extended period of time? A study by Copeland and Chance (1996) investigated long-term rural superintendents in order to determine what made them successful. Four rural superintendents who had between twenty-one and forty-one years of experience were selected for an in-depth qualitative study of their abilities, their rural school districts, and their communities.

In a review of the activities of these successful rural superintendents, certain actions and behaviors immediately became obvious. All superintendents were born and reared within 100 miles of the school district they led. Thus, they understood regional values and beliefs. They were extraordinarily visible at all school district activities and events. They were viewed as "people"-oriented and saw leadership and guidance of people as more important than the management of things. They listened carefully to community patrons and their staffs, often choosing to rely upon traditional approaches yet supporting worthwhile innovations. All four rarely socialized with board members away from the school and did not formally communicate with board members outside the monthly board meeting. However, informal communication with board members often happened on a daily basis.

A list of characteristics and attributes of the successful rural superintendent was determined from a detailed analysis of the data. This list is found in Table 5.1.

As can be seen from the table, most of the characteristics and attributes represent various leadership aspects as well as an astute view of the rural school community. But what does this really tell one about these successful rural superintendents? Surprisingly, no single style of leadership emerged. In fact, regardless of the type of leadership exhibited, this study confirmed Clark, Lotto, and Astuto's (1984) assertion that "the key to effective leadership was due to the interaction within the system by the people who populated the school dis-

TABLE 5.1. Characteristics and Attributes of Successful and
Effective Long-Term Rural Superintendents.*

1. Sound Financial Manager	16. Christian
2. Fair in Dealings with Others	17. Pride in School and Community
3. Involved in the Community	18. Provided Stability
4. Hired Quality People	19. Conscientious and Hard Worker
5. Available and Accessible	20. Genuinely Cared for Others
6. Deliberate on Decisions	21. Accepted as One of the Community
7. Related Well to Others	22. Supportive of All School Activities
8. Mutual Respect	23. Made Adequate Provisions for Staff
9. Mutual Trust	24. Happiness with Job
10. Progressive	25. Well Organized
11. Good Listener	26. Delegated Authority
12. In Charge and in Control	27. Assertive
13. Good Interactions with all Stakeholders	28. Knowledgeable
14. Good Personality	29. Marketed School and Programs
15. Student-Oriented	30. Granted Professional Freedom

*Items included in this table are not rank ordered.

trict" (p. 43). Indeed, the level of interaction between the various components of the school district and its greater community was a direct result of the leadership manifested by the rural school superintendent. The effective, successful rural superintendent provided a district and community wide stabilizing force that allowed for the development of a concerted focus on students' success and performance. The most obvious result was the creation of a rural culture that encouraged trust, respect, and believability. This confirms Hersey and Blanchard's (1995) conclusion that leader's behavior within the school community either directly or indirectly influences the school system's output.

The successful rural superintendent strives to develop consistent quality-laden interactions with all of the stakeholders of the school district. One superintendent indicated that "people look at the school and are very proud of the school and its accomplishments." Another indicated that "you ought to be a very strong part of the community . . ." He further stated, "I take a lot of pride in the school . . ." Another shared, "I enjoy working with students. I enjoy interacting with them. I like to see them grow and mature." This same superintendent further stated that "I really enjoy interactions with all of the stakeholders of the school district."

When staff members, community leaders, and just "plain" citizens were asked about these rural superintendents, they responded with enthusiasm and directness. One staff member, thankful for a stable environment in the school, indicated, "Like in a household you need stability . . . I really think it affects the student body. There's not that settledness and that atmosphere that's conducive to learning when turnover often occurs." One community leader was especially pleased when he stated that the superintendent "doesn't tell the school board what to do and the school board doesn't come up and tell him what to do. They all run the school through compatibility and unity." A patron shared, "the people in the community all respect the superintendent . . . If he didn't have the respect of the people in the community, I don't think he would have been here this long." And finally, a staff member stated, "I think he's just involved . . . He cares about the community, the school, the children, his church, his family. He's just everywhere."

When one looks at successful rural superintendents, it becomes obvious that they fully understand the political realities of rural schools and rural communities. An overriding attribute needed to deal with the political realities of rural schools is a high degree of tactfulness, fairness, and integrity. A board member supported this contention by stating "he is tactful with those community people that want to be the decision makers . . . he has a strong level of trust with everyone. What he says goes." Another board member indicated that "the board has confidence in the superintendent . . . He tries to be fair . . . I think everybody within the community knows that." A staff member supported the theme of fairness when she indicated of her superintendent that "he is very fair to every school program and department . . . Our superintendent has been very successful in this community because he is involved."

When these successful rural superintendents discussed the political realities of rural schools, invariably they mentioned the importance of knowing what was going on in the community and the necessity of being visible to school patrons. They also described the difference between being visible and involved and sitting at the "local coffee shop listening to idle gossip." These rural superintendents expounded on the importance of knowing the community and what the community's values and expectations are for the school district. As one superintendent stated, "They [the community] don't want the school taking off on any wild tangents." "Knowing the pulse" within the community was a theme repeated by several. Although many of the successful rural superintendents were political forces to reckon with in their individual communities, all of them understood the importance of providing a political base for school patrons and community leaders in discussing the school district. They understood the nature of local politics and attempted to ensure that they were seen as part of the political, religious, and educational milieu of the rural community. This is one of the basic reasons for their long-term, continued success.

Finally, there is one additional area in which these successful rural superintendents excelled and that was their ability to serve as good financial custodians of the district's often limited resources. Conversely, one the primary reasons for the failure of the rural superintendent was his/her inability to do so. The successful rural superintendent also exhibited sound knowledge of facility management. His or her district was well maintained, reasonably modern, and viewed as more than adequate for the instructional program.

> The successful rural superintendent exhibited an impressive repertoire of leadership attributes and mannerisms necessary to successfully lead the school district. There was little question regarding who had been hired by the school board to run the school.

The successful rural superintendent exhibited an impressive repertoire of leadership attributes and mannerisms necessary to successfully lead the school district. There was little question regarding who had been hired by the school board to run the school. As one superintendent succinctly stated, "I will listen to everyone but the final decision is mine." A staff member echoed this view by indicating that "he is frugal but that doesn't mean he will just respond in the negative . . . He weighs what is right for students. Then he makes the decision." If there was a problem or issue that needed to be addressed by the school board, it went on the rural school district's board agenda where the rural superintendent "lets the board make the policies . . . and decide on the big issues." This was most usually completed with "a suggestion" to the school board from the superintendent.

SURVIVING THE RURAL SUPERINTENDENCY

The successful rural superintendent is an individual who effectively addresses the needs of a complex and mixed constituency that includes the rural community, the school board, the school staff, and the students. The manner by which he or she accomplishes this is most often indicative of various leadership characteristics and attributes that basically represent a genuine interest in the success of the rural school and those within it. People skills are perhaps more important than managerial skills although these are needed for the continued maintenance and attainment of district goals.

The rural superintendent, in order to survive a multitude of perils and pitfalls, must be scrupulously moral, an excellent communicator, a good listener, diligently seek to hire the very best individual for the task at hand, and allow others the freedom and responsibility to perform effectively in their position within the school district. The rural superintendent must also know how to effectively and efficiently use his/her power. That means one must be able to collaboratively address issues confronting the school without abdicating all decision-making processes.

Recently, Brunner (1997) identified some important concepts of collaboration of which a successful superintendent should be cognizant. The most relevant of these concepts were that "collaboration is not delegation," "include everyone in the decision-making process," and "share all information, and communicate with everyone" (Brunner, 1997, p. 9). She aptly determined that the superintendent of today must involve as many as possible because this increases the ownership in any decision for everyone in the organization. This collaborative use of power may be difficult for many trained and educated in the "old" ways of leadership, but collaboration should be seen as an approach that does not result in the relinquishment of anything but the development of a greater community sense and pride for the rural school.

A rural superintendent can taken some very important steps when he/she begins the process of collaborative decision-making and developing a community that fully supports the rural school district. These are:

(1) Be a good listener;

(2) Create an ongoing process for input;

(3) Seek input from all constituents not just the usual supporters of the school;

(4) Provide alternatives to decisions for the school;

(5) Don't ignore obstacles, address them;

(6) Avoid educational jargonese and superior attitudes; and,

(7) Communicate productively (Wadsworth, 1997, p. 152).

These steps reinforce the necessity of establishing a culture that values others and actively shares power with them by seeking their input. The successful rural superintendent must be viewed by the school district's stakeholders as an individual who is patient, trustworthy, and credible. These are not items that one purchases at a local convenience store, rather, they are representative of the very core of the rural superintendent today. They come from values, beliefs, and vision, and are exhibited through daily actions. Those who are successful as rural superintendents inherently understand the importance of such behaviors. Skills related to management, finance, and curriculum can be taught and learned, but those things most important for a rural superintendent represent intrinsic abstractions that cannot be procured cheaply or fabricated sufficiently by those who do not possess them.

Ultimately, the rural superintendent must be able to manage change within the rural school district. Such change may be the result of changes in school demographics, state reform mandates, or changes in the community's expectations for the school district. A rural superintendent must create an organizational structure that promotes school improvement and sustains the change process. The one thing that becomes evident in looking at successful long-term rural superintendents is that they know how to manage change and understand the difference between constructive change and change for change sake, which often equates to the educational fad of the week. These rural superintendents recognize that some type of change is inevitable but establish parameters for school decision-making that promotes change as a process, not a singular event.

Ennis (1997) suggested that the superintendent work diligently with his/her board of education to increase board members' acceptance level for change. School district policies should be reviewed and revised as necessary to support the change process. The school board also is encouraged to provide the adequate resources for staff development to support the change in the school district and any goals developed relevant to this change. School principals should be actively involved in any change process in addition to teachers, support staff, and even students. The key to managing any change is to communicate with all stakeholders concerning any changes being contemplated or implemented. Throughout any change process, it must be understood that in a rural district change impacts not only the educational institution but the total community. Finally, the rural superintendent must carefully monitor the progress of any district change. The successful rural superintendent needs to support school based change only when deemed necessary and not just for the sake of change. He/she must also involve others in any change process and fully communicate such efforts to all internal and external stakeholders.

Throughout this chapter the importance of communication between the rural superintendent and the district's stakeholders has been emphasized. The successful rural superintendent diligently utilizes certain approaches to maintain his/her relationship with those in the school district but most importantly with the rural school board. He/she does the following:

(1) Remains focused. Decisions should always address the needs of students and the district's vision.
(2) Provides information in a timely manner to board members, the media, and district stakeholders.
(3) Prepares carefully for all board meetings.
(4) Communicates with board members in an appropriate manner providing them with the right amount of information thus avoiding unnecessary surprises.
(5) Communicates prior to board meetings with board members and other relevant district stakeholders.
(6) Provides the same level of information to board members before, during, and after board meetings.
(7) Deals with conflict effectively and does not hold grudges over anything said in the "heat of the battle."
(8) Constantly evaluates his/her personal and professional behavior in all interactions with district constituents and his/her relationships with various district stakeholders (modified from American Association of School Administrators, 1997).

CONCLUSION

The rural superintendent today, as in the past, is an individual who must serve the dual masters of the rural school district and the rural community. More than that, however, the rural superintendent must be able to function in a multifaceted position that requires one to be CEO, financial manager, human relations expert, change facilitator, politician, power broker, and educational specialist. The ability to handle so many roles and tasks at one time is not a simple act.

Today's successful rural superintendent is required to possess a depth and breadth of skills that his/her predecessor perhaps did not exhibit. The rural superintendent must be both competent manager and conserver of limited school and community resources while being an excellent human relations expert (i.e., communicator, facilitator, and encourager). He/she must focus on students and their well-being while also taking into consideration the larger, politically charged venue of the rural community and rural school district.

The successful rural superintendent strives through interactions with all of the district's stakeholders to create a culture that supports the educational process for rural students. The rural superintendent must be the ethical, emotional, and transformational leader of the school. He/she must be able to determine focus and direction while creating a climate that nurtures learning and success for all. He/she must be a superb communicator and collaborative leader who involves a multitude of constituents in shared decision-making strategies. The rural superintendent must be able to flourish in the chaos of expectations and demands that often represents rural schools and their communities.

Finally, rural superintendents must exhibit the vital characteristics of wisdom, courage, common sense, and a willingness to learn throughout their career. And, they must never forget the children they serve and represent. Rural students deserve the best education possible and the rural superintendent is responsible for providing the leadership to achieve this goal.

REFERENCES

American Association of School Administrators. 1997. *The Leader's Edge, 1* (1).

Blumberg, A. 1985. *The School Superintendent: Living With Conflict.* New York: Teachers College Press.

Brunner, C. C. 1997. "Exercising Power: A Study Differentiates Authoritarian and Collaborative Decision Making Among Superintendents," *School Administrator, 54* (6), 6–9.

Carter, G. R., & W. G. Cunningham. 1997. *The American School Superintendent: Leading in an Age of Pressure.* San Francisco: Jossey-Bass.

Chance, E. W. 1992. *Visionary Leadership in Schools: Successful Strategies for Developing and Implementing an Educational Vision.* Springfield, IL: Charles C. Thomas.

Chance, E. W., & J. L. Capps. 1992. "Superintendent Stability in Schools," *National Forum of Educational Administration and Supervision Journal, 9* (2), 23–32.

Clark, D. L., L. S. Lotto, & T. A. Astuto, 1984. "Effective Schools and School Improvement: A Comparative Analysis of Two Lines of Inquiry," *Educational Administration Quarterly, 20* (3), 41–68.

Copeland, M., & E. W. Chance. 1996. "Successful Rural Superintendents: A Case Study of Four Long Term Superintendents," *The Rural Educator, 18* (1), 24–28.

Cuban, L. 1985. "Conflict and Leadership in the Superintendency," *Phi Delta Kappan, 67* (1), 28–30.

Ennis, E. 1997. *An Examination of Superintendent Behaviors Related to School Based Change.* Unpublished doctoral dissertation, University of Oklahoma, Norman.

Grady, M., & M. Bryant. 1991. "School Board Turmoil and Superintendent Turnover: What Pushes Them to the Brink?" *School Administrator, 48* (2), 19–26.

Hersey, P., & K. Blanchard. 1995. *Management of Organizational Behavior: Utilizing Human Resources.* Englewood Cliffs, NJ: Prentice Hall.

Leithwood, K. A., & D. J. Montgomery. 1986. *The Principal Profile.* Toronto, Ontario: Ontario Institute for Studies in Education.

Manasse, A. L. 1985. "Vision and Leadership: Paying Attention to Inattention," *Peabody Journal of Education, 63* (1), 150–173.

Norton, M. S., L. D. Webb, L. L. Dlugosh, & W. Sybouts. 1996. *The School Superintendency: New Responsibilities, New Leadership.* Boston: Allyn and Bacon.

Thomas, R. J. 1997 (June 25). "The High Cost of Incivility," *Education Week,* 41.

Wadsworth, D. 1997. "Building a Strategy for Successful Public Engagement," *Phi Delta Kappan, 78* (10), 749–752.

CHAPTER 6

Personnel and Human Resource Functions in the Rural School District: Some Insights and Directions

Positive people will make the difference!—Robert Jordan, 1992

What is needed in rural schools is a fresh perspective on democratic leadership that maximizes the strengths and minimizes the weaknesses of rural and small town schools. This chapter will focus on that model as it pertains to the human relations/personnel functions of school administration in the rural district. By focusing on the democratic style as a structure of personnel and human resource activities, it is hoped that a direction for making the rural school truly a collaborative structure can emerge. Out of such a collaborative structure could evolve initiatives for revitalizing the educational, economic, and social life of rural and small-town America.

After focusing on organizational factors that promote positive human resource development, the chapter turns to more traditional personnel functions of rural schools. Finally, changes occurring in America's rural schools are reviewed.

IN Donald Warren's *American Teachers: Histories of a Profession at Work,* small-town life and problems associated with schooling in rural America are thoroughly investigated. One insightful statement by Warren about rural or country schools is worth mentioning. When he discusses the heart or essence of rural education he notes:

> The small school and the opportunity for individualized instruction; the lack of supervision and freedom to experiment with teaching methods that worked; the intimate knowledge of the students and their backgrounds; the close ties between the people and the school; the appreciation and support of the parents—those

Robert C. Morris and Les Potter, Department of Educational Leadership and Foundations, State University of West Georgia.

characteristics of country-school teaching that made it rewarding—were largely lost, no doubt forever, for the sake of efficiency and the large school. (Warren, 1989, p. 114)

In this type of community setting the *school is the community* in many rural towns. The school is the entertainment center; in small towns school sports play a major role. Sometimes, usually with the leadership of one person whom everybody knows, there are also offerings in music and drama. The school band is a valued activity for many small-town and rural communities, from marching in the 4th of July parade to enhancing community productions. In addition, the school is often the only place large enough to conduct town meetings. Although the students provide entertainment for the community and the school buildings are open for community use, often school superintendents or principals do little to engage their community in any direct way. They see the school as an extension of the community but not the community as an extension of the school. The local community and business leaders are often the ones who have the vision to incorporate the school into the community. In many ways community members are estranged from their own school's curriculum. This is not a subversive attempt by school officials but an old paradigm that the school's curriculum is determined by educators. Educators usually cannot see the connection between the curriculum and the community's needs. Superintendents and principals do little to engage their community in productive ways to better serve their students. With "professional authority" these administrators have eschewed citizen involvement and participation, creating a professional distance that separates life in school from life in the community. Often when parents attempt to give support or become involved in school activities they are met with suspicion and skepticism by the educational community. The only exception is usually PTA/PTO and booster clubs. And these "funding" groups typically have little or no impact on the school's curriculum and the needs of the community. While school administrators report despair about lack of parent involvement in the schools, they simultaneously are suspicious of, or reject, such involvement. Their belief in parent-community involvement is at best limited. It is easier to complain about school-parental involvement than to try and improve it. An interesting dichotomy of community and school has evolved, and has had tremendous impact on rural education.

Ideas about what is appropriate administrative leadership for schools have changed over the years, the prevailing model at each period has been unitary across the nation. As Owens (1990) has chronicled, the model of scientific management championed by Frederick Taylor gave way during the 1950s to a human-relations emphasis. Then the 1970s called for educational leaders to engage in building political coalitions—so aptly captured in Cuban's *Urban School Chiefs Under Fire* (1976). Whatever we decide upon, it is obvious that the predominant focus in national attention to schools and schooling is on the urban and suburban districts. Scientific management, the human-relations movement, and administration as coalition building all grew out of our national concern for industrialization and political stabilization in our urban centers. The community of professors of education and the textbook publishers also contributed to the view of school administration as constituting a list of concepts and skills that would be applicable in all school settings with little reference to the rural school. And every successive wave of school reform during the 1980s completely ignored rural schools.

Thus, one of the considerable shortcomings of traditional study of administrative leadership in schools is that it is decontextualized (unmindful of the sociological complexities within the context of leadership) and, by default, aimed primarily at middle-class white America. This kind of study group does not accurately portray students from urban school settings. More recently, preparation programs are taking side glances at urban settings. More and more, we can realize that administrative leadership in suburbia or the inner city is not an appropriate model for educational leadership in small and rural communities, where the school is an intimate part of the community. In small towns the superintendents and principals are public leaders, at center stage. They are in a position, therefore, to contribute not only to educational enhancement but to community enhancement as well. They have much more potential power for community change and leadership than do their urban counterparts.

As early as 1840, when most schools were rural, Horace Mann, Massachusetts' first State Superintendent, argued for centralization and state control of school districts. The prevailing organizational model of the late nineteenth-century school was Max Weber's top-down bureaucracy, with a professional administration and a very rigid division of labor with specialized teaching functions. The model also included the principle of universalism, that all students should be treated alike, with each child receiving a standardized curriculum modeled after European/Asian education. Although the nineteenth-century model is not particularly functional in the late twentieth century, and even as some urban schools are attempting to more away from it by empowering smaller decision-making units at school sites, the bureaucratic model of the nineteenth century unfortunately prevails today in many rural school districts. Whether they are aware of it or not, small-town educators seem to be mimicking an old-fashioned mass-production model of academic life that many of their urban counterparts are striving to give up. The single best model, the democratic style, designed at the turn of the century under the influence of Frederick Taylor and later by the human-relations and political-coalition models, serves as a template for most small-town schools. But what is needed is a fresh perspective on democratic leadership that maximizes the strengths and minimizes the weaknesses of rural and small-town schools. This chapter will focus on that model as it pertains to the human relations/personnel functions of school administration in the rural district. By focusing on the democratic style as a structure of personnel and human resource activities, it is hoped that a direction for making the rural school truly a collaborative structure can emerge. Out of such a collaborative structure could evolve initiatives for revitalizing the educational, economic, and social life of rural and small-town America.

A PICTURE OF HUMAN RESOURCES

L. Dean Webb's 1994 definition of human resources includes a number of insights and perceptions about the activities surrounding the human resources processes.

> Those processes that are planned and implemented in the organization to establish an effective system of human resources and to foster an organizational climate that enhances the accomplishment of educational goals. This view emphasizes human resources administration as a foundational function for an effective educational program. The primary elements of the human resources processes, implied in the definition, are recruiting, selecting, and developing staff, as well as the need for establishing a harmonious working relationship among personnel. Although this definition emphasizes the significance of the human element, it also states that the purpose of human resources administration is focused on achieving the goals and objectives of the system. This focus includes a major concern for developing a healthy organizational climate that serves toward the accomplishment of school goals and the meeting of the personal needs of the school's employees. (Webb, Montello, & Norton, 1994, p. 51)

In developing a clearer understanding of how the above insights, processes, and beliefs can be actuated by the human resources administrator in a rural setting, a group of organizational factors will be discussed as elements of success. These factors include: climate, collaboration, compromise, serving customers, interpersonal relations, and leadership. As one dissects this listing, a design or pattern for meeting the needs of teachers and students in the small town setting is created.

1. Climate. *Here the emphasis of the personnel function is to endorse and help develop a positive climate among students, faculty, staff, and the community.* Experienced administrators can walk into a school and sense the climate of the building within a few minutes. A climate within an organization is built over time and is composed of countless factors and conditions. Successful administrators do not let a climate develop or exist without direction, but assume a responsibility for creating a climate that is supportive of people, programs, and educational improvement. A high school principal from rural New England might describe how he/she carries out the function of positive climate in a school by discussing the kind of real impact he/she can have by believing firmly in climate as a school goal. For instance, by decorating the walls of the building with beautiful art prints that can be purchased inexpensively from galleries and stores, a whole new climate for a building can take place. Community volunteers can frame them, and very quickly school hallways can be transformed into a beautiful art gallery of prints of the most famous paintings in the world. Or considering the negative messages of today's heavy-metal and rap music artists, what about instituting a program of playing classical music softly over the public address system in the hallways, cafeteria, or offices? The music could even be selectively played in individual classes under the guidance of the teacher. The mellow effect of classical music will be soothing to everyone as well as exposing students to outstanding music.

2. Collaboration. *The notion that the personnel direction (principal) of a rural school works alone in his/her job is unrealistic in today's effective school. Today's successful administrators know they have certain identified responsibilities that only they can perform, but they are also quick to acknowledge that they cannot be absolute despots.* They cannot manage a school only their way and to their ends. The collaborative style of management involves all who will be affected by decisions. Effective principals use a collaborative style of leadership to move their schools forward. School improvement programs that reform and restructure education begin with the premise of collaboration.

3. Compromise. *Henry Clay was the master of compromise and the art of politics is reputedly based upon compromise. Perhaps the art of school administration is also based upon compromise.* The notion here is that one consider making reasonable compromises when making decisions. Sometimes it is better to have "half of a loaf than none." Therefore, judgments as to whether a compromise position is worth pursuing or not often have to be made. Being able to reach a point at which two parties admit that they agree to disagree is valuable. Likewise, for most disagreements an acceptable solution can be found, providing enough energy and communication is put into the search for the solution. The people involved must truly want to find a solution, and most problems are not easily solvable. The idea is not to exert undue pressure upon an opponent but be willing to gracefully back away from a proposal for the good of the students.

4. Serving Customers. *Much of the literature concerning today's administrator deals with innovation and quality in meeting the "customers' (students, parents, and community) needs."* Successful school administrators in rural situations recognize this possibly better than any other group. They know that they need to satisfy their customers. By inviting parents, business persons, and "mere" taxpayers into the design and management of our schools, we are doing no more than serving our customers. By opening the doors to the school, the rural administrator is linking himself to the community—his/her survival is secured. By knowing the community, schools can better serve the needs of the community. Pedagogy cannot survive in a vacuum. Society demands more and more services from the public schools in more diversified aspects of life. Few of the issues that plague us can be answered through traditional instructional processes. There has to be input from varied sources. That input needs to be accepted in a spirit of genuine appreciation. This includes learning to understand and value the diversities that strengthen our nation.

5. Decision-Making. *Shared decision-making, participative management, and similar ideas need to be embraced and utilized by rural administrators throughout the country.* The contributions made by parents, business and political authorities, as well as teachers and other school personnel are staggering. Regardless of one's administrative/teaching style or philosophy of education, one should not expect everyone to agree with them all the time. Some groups will agree with certain decisions, just as other groups will disagree with those same decisions. But support is needed to make important decisions. Specifically, administrators need the support of and encouragement from parents, business leaders, and community leaders as well as their understanding of the aims, purposes, and objectives of American education. The influence of administrators in different sectors of the community is most valuable in communicating the intent of the school.

When adequate authority and/or leadership is given at the school level, many important decisions affecting scheduling, personnel, curriculum, and the use of resources can be made by the people who are in the best position to make them, those who are most aware of the problems and needs. Only by meaningfully involving educators in their own professional destiny, by involving parents who are stakeholders, as well as students who are the recipients of these efforts will real concern, creativity, and initiative be stimulated.

6. Interpersonal Relations. *If decision-making can be accepted as the nature of administration, then perhaps a corollary is that decisions are made about, with, and through people.* The effect of good decision-making is not limited to the authority of an administrator to make decisions but is greatly affected by how others perceive administrators' actions regarding decisions. Today's school leaders must be able to build effective interpersonal relations with all people, relationships characterized by fairness, openness, honesty, and trust. The key things are:

(1) Demonstrate respect of people for who they are and where they have been in their life.

(2) Take time with people, by showing an interest in them and listening to them.

(3) Make a concerted effort to do what you say you are going to do, and follow through. This creates predictability and builds trust, even if the person disagrees with you.

(4) Share personal stories and aspects of your life in professional relationships, which demonstrates vulnerability and humanness and reduces power inherent in formal roles and positions in organizations.

(5) Always try to make sure that a person never "loses face" when dealing with

sensitive personnel/human issues. Try to keep in mind how you would want to be treated, remember the "Golden Rule."

(6) Value diversity and the richness that cultures and ideologies, political thought, and perspectives bring to organizations and communities. Honor and respect all people as human beings regardless of their culture, socioeconomic status, age, or race. People, no matter what their position in life or where they come from, want to feel they are valuable and respected.

A final point worth mentioning here is a picture of lifelong learning. By constantly trying to understand and comprehend through workshops, classes, readings, and so on, we are constantly encountering experiences that stretch us beyond our comfort zone and cause us to grow. As rapidly as our world changes and information bases are changing, we must come to realize that as soon as we begin to feel comfortable and start to seek comfort at the expense of embracing new thought and the ways of doing things that stretch us, we will have begun the journey to ineffectiveness.

7. **Leadership.** *In terms of personal communication and style of approach, the heart of productive and meaningful leadership appears to be based on two principles: (1) helping students learn and (2) engaging all members of administrative units in working toward a common goal.* Asking the "right questions" can encourage the "right answers." Many times in the restructuring or organizations the same old questions are asked and, as a result, the same old answers are given. It is more important to make sure that the right questions are asked. For example, in reforming schools it is not the question, "How should we restructure our schools?" It is, "What should we be restructuring about education?" Sometimes it is a matter of asking questions in the right order to get to the core of an issue or problem. The questions that should be driving leadership in educational reform today are: (1) What should students learn? and (2) How do students learn best? If these two questions are not being asked then leadership is not taking place.

Developing a leadership style often has to do with believing in the abilities of people to make good decisions. This hinges on the belief that there is not just "one right way" to do things, and a belief that people who have sufficient information do not usually act in self-interest but will act for the greater good of others. The issuing and timely communicating of information is important here. When a staff is customarily uninformed about issues concerning their school, then being told what happened long after the fact, it destroys the staff's morale. Information sharing is always appreciated by staff and students.

Finally, obtaining first-hand experiences is a great way to "educate" aspiring administrators. This can be done by putting those individuals who show interest or potential in administration into administrative tasks. As a result of the practical knowledge and experiences they obtain in the program, administrative aspirants are able to reach a valid decision as to whether they possess the requisite skills to function as an educational leader. Those individuals who have been involved in this kind of activity often feel strongly about the experiences gained. And they see them as vital factors in their successful candidacy for a leadership position. For the rural administrator, it is a means for developing and maintaining a talented pool of potential individuals who will become the future leaders of the district.

RURAL EDUCATION AND THE PERSONNEL FUNCTION

Personnel procedures in the rural school districts of America mimic those of their larger urban and suburban cousins in most areas. Although the format and functions are essentially the same, there are a few differences. Generally, there is less formality in rural districts because of the smaller size and scale of the personnel department. Large districts are very bureaucratic by nature. They may have an assistant superintendent of personnel who is not involved with the induction process at all. This job may require the assistant superintendent to work with union problems, negotiations, strategic planning, grievances, reports to state educational bodies, and reports to the local school board. This person may never see or speak to a teaching candidate.

There may be a director who manages all of the departments in personnel and oversees the day-to-day operation of the program. He/she may act as a mediator for simple disputes, write the various job description, and manage the total personnel operation. The functions of the personnel department would be divided into two sections and the personnel department itself divided into two sections and led by a supervisor for each section: one for the certified staff (teachers and administrators) and one for noncertificated (bus drivers, secretaries, custodians, maintenance workers, etc.). Then there may be a team of subordinate administrators to handle interviewing, staff development, induction process, and compensation and benefits. Secretaries are used to handle the enormous amount of phone calls, filing, data collection, certification checks, correspondence, and other mundane tasks.

When the job candidates have proceeded this far in the process, their names and folders are sent to principals as openings occur. When a candidate is selected by a given school site, his or her name is sent back to personnel. The superintendent has little input in the overall process. Superintendents receive the list of potential candidates from the assistant superintendent, but normally this is just a formality. Then the list is presented to the school board several weeks before its next meeting. Board members are given the courtesy of reviewing the names but the great majority of the names are unknown to the members. District policies are generally specific about board members' micro-managing and interfering in the daily operations of the school district. If all the correct bureaucratic procedures have been followed, there is no need to interfere in the hiring process by the board.

In rural areas these procedures are either shortened or eliminated. For instance, in the interviewing process, in many rural districts the personnel department is limited to one administrator (this could be a separate entity such as a director of personnel, an administrator who wears several hats, or the superintendent) and a secretary. Here, the process could be shortened to the initial screening by someone in the central office with the interview conducted at the site only. In rural districts, the only administrators may be the superintendent and the principals. They would have to divide the personnel tasks among them and the process.

DISTRICT FUNCTION: STRATEGIC PLANNING

Rural districts' needs are generally similar to urban ones. Numbers of applications and openings will be fewer but the diversity of positions can be the same. Developed by visionary superintendents is the strategic planning team that looks at the immediate and the future requirements of the school district. The number of members varies and almost anyone can be asked to serve. Planning teams have one mission: to review the entire educational system, from top to bottom. Smaller committees are assigned to specific areas, such as personnel. The committees can include personnel/school administrators, teachers, and community members. They examine the immediate needs and the future needs of personnel, taking into account financial concerns, staffing openings, growth (or lack of) in the district, and the personnel process currently being used. The committee makes recommendations to the superintendent who works with his/her cabinet and the school board to implement a vision and any necessary policy changes for the personnel department and its processes.

DISTRICT FUNCTION: RECRUITMENT AND SELECTION

Districts with few needs and a small budget have limited opportunities to search. Any openings will hopefully be filled locally. If not, then from the immediate region. It is expensive to advertise in the media and to send recruiters to far-flung universities. However, this is being done more often as rural districts have to compete for minorities and critical-need teachers such as special education and math/science. With a limited recruiting budget and the difficulty of rural districts finding teachers, it is imperative that the district locates and hires good people who are going to stay. The job descriptions are written, updated, and posted as necessary. Job descriptions must meet all local/state/federal guidelines for nondiscrimination. The teaching applications the candidates complete are usually generic. Potential K–12 teachers complete the same form. In the smaller schools administrators are looking for teachers who can teach more than one subject and even teach their minor. A history teacher, for instance, may have several preparations—U.S. history, geography, world history, and economics. Candidates would be wise to include in their resumé and the application their ability and interest in various extracurricular activities as they are likely to sponsor or coach one or more after-school programs. Sports, cheerleading, band, and other activities are extremely popular in rural areas.

Once a teacher has formally applied for a position with a resumé and application, the secretary will create a file (usually this process is not totally computerized) and send out the necessary forms to request references and transcripts. If there is an opening in the district, the administrator will contact the applicant. It is time consuming and expensive to create a "pool" by interviewing candidates for anticipated openings. As a result, many districts are creating a pool of potential employees by doing telephone interviews. This is cheap and simple and lets the candidate know that the district does have an interest, even though it may not be immediate. If the candidate is brought in for an interview, then all the form filling, meetings, and questions take place in one day. Districts do not reimburse job applicants for travel or any incurred expenses. The interviews may be done by a central office administrator or by the principal. If the candidate is a serious choice, the principal will double-check the references. If the principal wants to recommend the candidate for employment, he/she calls central office and notifies them. The secretary will make sure that the candidate's paper work is in order.

A difference between urban and rural districts occurs at this stage as the rural district is very concerned to make sure the candidate will fit in with the school and the community. Being "different" as an employee is not tolerated in rural communities as it may be in other areas of the country. With smaller numbers of employees, the oddball staff member is easily noticed and becomes a persistent problem for the administration. Principals must be very concerned about public opinion. Whomever the principal chooses will be a reflection on the superintendent and the school board. Sometimes, at this stage the superintendent and board members get involved. They may want to discuss the candidate with the principal or even interview the person themselves. But however the process is done, the final decision to hire is up to the school board.

DISTRICT FUNCTION: INDUCTION

The induction process of rural schools is again simplified. Most districts cannot afford and do not need elaborate orientation programs for new employees. This process begins during the preplanning days prior to the opening of school. If done at all, the new hires may experience part of a day at the central office listening and filling out forms. The rest of the induction process is handled by the principals. This can be as intensive and productive as the principal makes it. If the new hire is lucky, he/she may spend several days in orientation meetings, inservice, and department meetings, reading handbooks, receiving textbooks and a student roster, planning for the first day and decorating the classroom. The new teacher is loaded down with myriad "stuff" that must be read and digested before the opening of school. If the district is smart, the planning days take place before the weekend. This will allow the teacher to work in the building on Saturday and Sunday on his/her own time.

DISTRICT FUNCTION: STAFF DEVELOPMENT

In the smaller rural districts staff development is a daydream. If they can, several districts will combine their limited inservice monies to better utilize their resources and develop a mutually agreeable staff development program. However, inservice is usually conducted by the principal with help from the central office. These programs are often limited and almost always informational. Little time is spent in monitoring what the staff has learned or if it is being used in the classroom. Because of the lack of resources and the haphazard planning of many staff development programs, the teachers are often resentful of the intrusion into their time. Many districts require a certain amount of time to be used in this manner. It is disliked by both the administrators and the staff. To have effective staff development programs requires a lot of planning.

Large districts may have the services of a full-time staff development administrator, who works with principals concerning their needs, helps allocate the necessary resources, and designs the program. First, the school and the district arrive at a vision of where they want their district to be. Then the central office staff development person works with the individual schools to design an effective strategy to ensure the best approach for the training. Usually the sessions stretch over a long period of time where teachers have opportunities to try out what they have learned. And what they are practicing is being monitored. In small rural areas this cannot happen to the same extent.

DISTRICT FUNCTION: EVALUATION

One of the key factors in determining teacher performance, which will decide how students are learning, is the evaluation process. This part of the personnel function is the least popular and most difficult to administer. All districts use a formal method of evaluating staff, generated either at the state level or locally. Either way, principals and staff usually have little input into the form. Personnel offices are very clear concerning the deadlines and the procedures that need to be followed in the evaluation process. Principals are called in for their own evaluation orientation meetings early in the school year. They subsequently receive memos and notices reminding them of due dates. Principals spend many hours working with teachers at their schools on the nuances of the process. How effective the process is depends on the principal's commitment to observations, teacher supervision, classroom visitations, staff development, and evaluations. As busy as principals are handling everything but curriculum and instruction, small attention is paid to the evaluation process. In smaller schools with little teacher turnover, the principal can spend more time with the new and problem teachers. Also, in smaller districts there are fewer central office experts who can help the principal in this process.

Beginning principals suffer if they are not supported in this endeavor by competent central office staff. This is especially true in high schools where the principal cannot be content knowledgeable in all subjects. For example, principals with a physical education background can feel helpless observing a French class. They can observe the pedagogy/classroom management, but it is difficult to assess the teacher's subject matter knowledge without additional help.

DISTRICT FUNCTION: COMPENSATION/COLLECTIVE BARGAINING/LEGAL ISSUES

Rural districts are not alone in their desire to attract and hold the best employees possible. And rural districts can attract quality educators. They can sell their remoteness, warm weather, lower taxes, cheaper housing, mountains, skiing, and so on, but salary will probably not be a selling point. Most districts "front load," that is, they will offer very competitive salaries to start. However, in paying for teachers' experiences and additional education the salary scale is not very encouraging. Rural districts hope to lure candidates for the abovementioned attributes and then "hook" them once they arrive. If a new teacher enjoys the surroundings, has a family, buys a home, gets involved with the community, enjoys the quality of life, then he/she is less likely to leave for higher wages. The financial benefits that can be offered are less attractive in a rural area than in other places as could be expected.

The nature of the collective bargaining process in rural areas depends on the state. In strong union states this is a very important part of personnel. In other states there is no negotiated contract between staff and the school board. Educators must take what they are offered. In states with collective bargaining, the personnel office, superintendent, and other administrators are very involved. In other states, little if any energy is spent in this process.

For legal issues, larger rural districted will have a school board attorney on a retainer. The district will pay for these services as they are needed. In smaller and less affluent districts this is a luxury that is not available. Attorneys are used only in dire emergencies and the district hopes that it has enough money in their contingency account to pay for legal fees and any legal retribution.

THE CHANGING RURAL SCHOOL SCENE

For the rural school to become a more powerful component in community life, particularly in facilitating economic and social development, administrators must become democratic leaders in their schools and democratic models in their communities.

Today's rural school, often invisible to the urban eye, is for the most part eco-nomically depressed and in social decline. Changes required to alleviate the ever-changing problems of rural schools—their hard-pressed teachers and their at-risk youth—must go beyond what the small towns can do for themselves. State and federal policymakers must seek innovative ways to help small town schools become a launching pad for economic and social development. John Goodlad said it best: "Futurists have a tantalizing way of describing the year 2001 as though being there has little to do with getting there. The future arrives full blown. But it is the succession of days and years between now and then that will determine what life will be like. Decisions made and not made will shape the schools of tomorrow" (Goodlad, 1984, p. 321). Public policy can influence human behavior. Lawmakers may not be able to guarantee that all children will learn, but they can allocate resources in ways that either foster or limit the possi-bilities for learning.

Given the changing rural and small-school landscape that contributes to put-ting many families and students at-risk, and the lack of social and other support services in rural communities, it would seem that one of the first priorities for rural and small-school districts would be social and economic revitalization of the local community.

To work toward this end, policymakers must consider issues and possible so-lutions associated with school consolidating; the current status of teaching in rural schools; the role of school administrators; and the responsibilities of preparation programs, professional associations, and the state and federal gov-ernment. The local rural school, regardless of size, should become more of a center for local economic and social development than it is today. Community revitalization is less likely to occur when the local school has been removed as its centering point, lost in consolidation efforts.

The small-town school can be a source of emotional support and involve-ment so often missing in the urban context, but its curriculum must also help youngsters to assist their own communities in entering the twenty-first century productively. Thus, it must include much more than support for football, the band, and other forms of community entertainment.

The internal governance of rural and small-town schools in most instances follows an outmoded administrative theory and is frequently authoritarian and traditional, pitting teachers and administrators against one another. Because of staff and student numbers, many rural and small-town district organizational structures are more decentralized than the layers of hierarchy found in most ur-ban districts. Rural and small-town school administrators need to take advan-tage of this structure. For the rural school to become a more powerful compo-nent in community life, particularly in facilitating economic and social development, administrators must become democratic leaders in their schools and democratic models in their communities.

Finally, the focus of change must go beyond what rural and small-town educators can initiate by themselves. Economic and structural limitations run too deep; assistance must be provided at state and federal levels of government. Jonathan Sher (1988) argues that rural schools do not get their fair share of education funding. He believes that a combination of low property taxes, a political preference for addressing urban problems, funding formulas allocated on a per-capita basis, and a low national priority for education all work against adequate funding for rural and small-town schools. Consider the possibilities when state and national incentives are created to increase educators' access to state-of-the-art strategies and tools in teaching and administration. This could include: cooperative learning, entrepreneurial opportunities, school-business partnerships, peer coaching, organizational development, student government, and team teaching. Such incentives can only encourage teachers and administrators in rural areas to become unstuck from their hierarchical patterns. These and other incentives could be administered through state departments of education and should be designated specifically for staff development programs in the rural areas of a state. Exchange programs with other educators engaged in economic and social development programs within their schools and communities, both within and across state lines, are also to be encouraged. In sum, the varied areas of concern within rural schooling are extensive, but not as far-reaching as those of administrative leadership and policy development.

As our nation moves closer to a centralized system of accountability—through national goals of education, national assessment measures with overtures toward a national curriculum, and possible, sweeping policies such as school choice—rural and small-town schools must be remembered and included during the development of policy mandates. It is hoped that representatives from rural and small schools become an integral voice at every level of educational policy-making. The voices of millions of rural and small-town students and community residents deserve to be heard. A concerted national effort to address rural and small-town education with the inclusion of rural experts could result in more vigorous rural and small-town communities, as well as a more uniform and just system of education in this country.

REFERENCES

Cuban, L. 1976. *Urban School Chiefs Under Fire.* Chicago: University of Chicago Press.

Cuban, L. 1990. "Reforming Again, Again, and Again," *Educational Researcher, 19*(1), 3–13.

Goodlad, I. 1984. *A Place Called School.* New York: McGraw-Hill Publishers.

Owens, R. 1990. *Organizational Behavior in Education.* Englewood Cliffs, NJ: Prentice-Hall.

Sher, J. 1988. "Why Rural Education Has Not Received Its Fair Share of Funding: And What to Do About It," *Journal of Rural and Small Schools, 2*(2), 31–37.

Warren, D. (ed.). 1989. *American Teachers: Histories of a Profession at Work.* New York: Macmillan Publishing Co.

Webb, L.D., P.A Montello, & M.S. Norton. 1994. *Human Resources Administration: Personnel Issues and Needs in Education.* New York: Merrill, imprinted by Macmillan Publishing Co.

CHAPTER 7

School Improvement

The worst and best thing about being a teacher is that, ultimately, what you're trying to do is to make yourself unnecessary.—Wallace Fowlie, Duke University

It is easier to know what to do, than it is to do.—Old Chinese Proverb

This chapter focuses on school improvement and instructional outcomes. While rural schools can be isolated, they do not have to out of the stream of new ideas and instructional practices. This chapter is based on the assumption that the principal is the central lever for instructional improvement at the local level; therefore, the focus of new ideas and practices needs to center on the principal. Additionally, this chapter aims to conserve two resources—time and money—so the principal's efforts at school improvement may be efficient and fruitful. The chapter is divided into two parts: (1) school improvement for rural central office leaders and (2) school improvement for rural school leaders. While the ideas in each part are designed for typical leaders in those settings, they may be of use to any leader wanting to improve the outcomes of a given school. Additionally, there are "idea boxes," which present unique ideas for school leaders.

THERE is a small, K–8 weather-worn school in rural New Brunswick, Canada, that straddles windswept Keswick Ridge, far from the nearest town of Fredricton. Down the narrow road to the school the last sign says "Moose Crossing." Approaching the school, the first impression is that of a tattered, old building with no visual appeal. Upon entering the school, the visitor first notices a line of shoes, perhaps a hundred pairs, carefully tucked along one central hall wall. Tile lines the floor, old institutional paint adorns the walls, yet the inside of the school is alive with the world of children. Why are so many shoes

Richard M. Haynes, College of Education and Allied Professions, Western Carolina University.

China Grove Elementary School, China Grove, NC. © Photo by Rob Amberg.

lined up? The principal brightens, saying "You haven't been here during bad weather. These are outdoor shoes. As the students leave school they get out of their indoor shoes to put on the outside ones to wear home."

Keswick Ridge School certainly meets any definition of "rural school." While the outside of the school bespeaks the harsh winters in which it exists, the inside is warm and filled with the work of children. The first classroom entered is a kindergarten. The thirty students never notice the visitors come in, they are too engaged with someone who is teaching them how to make hand-churned ice cream. The only one who notices the visitors is one child who pulled on a pant leg, declaring "My shoe isn't tied." And his foot is then extended. With the shoe quickly tied, his warm smile beats any other thank-you possible. He hurries back to the group. The school is busy, yet friendly, thanks to children who say "excuse me" as they shuttle past adults during class changes. One classroom was filled with computers. Another, actually three classrooms with the inner walls knocked out, was brimming with students in grades six to eight. One hundred twenty-five of them were purposefully engaged. A hum filled the room, and computers and televisions were scattered about the class.

Two teachers were moving among the study groups, almost like honey bees going from flower to flower. In one corner students maneuvered on the Internet, reaching worldwide. The setting was rural but the students were cosmopolitan. The learning environment was world-class.

Such rural schools do not occur by spontaneous combustion. They are deliberately crafted by gifted leaders such as Keswick Ridge's David Neilson and the Department of Education's innovation team leader, Tom Hanley. Together, central administration and local principal share a clear vision of a continuously improving school. Such a vision is possible in your school as well.

PART ONE: CENTRAL OFFICE RURAL SCHOOL LEADERSHIP

School improvement can begin at the central, or district, office level. Leaders at this level need to end their own isolation as a first step. This could begin by studying the *design* of the curriculum, and extend into the *delivery* of that curriculum. It is assumed the reader has organized a district curriculum council; if not, that should be the first step.

ESTABLISHING THE CURRICULUM

In the United States, there is a major effort to create a national curriculum as most other developed nations in the world already have. U.S. leaders of the effort are uncomfortable with that label, stating they are creating voluntary frameworks. While the standards are voluntary, a framework differs little from a curriculum, as the California curriculum frameworks demonstrate. New Zealand has had a national curriculum since the 1870s. The last draft of the curriculum (in 1993) became a "framework." When asking New Zealand educators what the difference was, the author was told they wanted to use current terminology, but there was no real difference.

The third international assessment of student achievement in science and mathematics revealed that the United States had made limited progress since the second international assessment in 1992, remaining in the middle. The third international study compared over forty nations among which the United States ranked generally in the middle. Larry Suter explained: "The United States' curriculum is a mile wide and an inch deep" (Suter as quoted by Lawton, 1996, p. 1). Explaining the need for a well-understood curriculum, Senta A. Raizen explained: "The 5th grade teacher doesn't necessarily know what the third grade teacher did" (Raizen as quoted by Lawton, 1996, p. 9). Some well-articulated, taught curriculum is needed to start the process of school improvement.

If the reader's district follows no state curriculum, it is suggested that the national frameworks be used. In the United States, the oldest, and best conceptualized curriculum is the national framework in mathematics. It includes grade-level mathematics competency guidelines, suggestions for assessment, and recommended methods for mastering the competencies. Other national frameworks are in varying stages of development at this writing, including frameworks in science, language, the arts, history, geography, civics, and physical education. The standards are being written by the national associations in each area (for example, the language standards include reading, writing, and speaking skills and were cooperatively developed by the National Council of Teachers of English and the International Reading Association), funded by the United States Department of Education.

It is recommended that central office curriculum personnel become familiar with the national frameworks and use them as one standard for curriculum design. At this writing, the easiest access to the national frameworks guidelines is via telephone (1–800–USA–LEARN) or via the Internet ("www.ed.gov"). Another means of getting the materials is to contact the respective national association (i.e., national frameworks in science are available through the National Science Teacher's Association).

The reader is advised to follow the work on the national frameworks regardless of the reaction a national curriculum begets (generally negative). After all, college-bound students take either the ACT or SAT, both of which are national tests of a presumed national curriculum. Most standardized tests, such as CAT and ITBS, also imply a common curriculum upon which the standards are set.

There must be some standard against which schools develop their curriculum. In addition to the national frameworks, a second source for a well-conceptualized curriculum is the Wisconsin Curriculum Guides, which have been widely followed in states where no state curriculum is provided. When it comes to establishing a curriculum standard, the *last* means for doing that should be the textbook. Granted, most textbooks are nationally marketed, presuming a common curriculum, but the text becomes the curriculum only in the absence of some better standard.

CURRICULUM AUDITING

Once the curriculum is established for the district, a curriculum audit may be in order to determine *what* teachers are, in fact, teaching and *how* they are delivering the curriculum. A curriculum audit basically is a report by teachers about what they are teaching. There are many possible forms a curriculum audit may take, but the following suggestions may assist the reader in designing the audit for the district:

- The audit is most reliable when teachers do not feel they are being evaluated. Therefore, the audit's results should be reported anonymously. This author's experience with audits found that grade level or course (i.e., Algebra 1) needs reporting if several schools are involved in the audit, but individual teachers' names are not necessary.
- The audit should be kept brief. Results can be tabulated and returned in a group meeting. If the leader starts to point out practices that are good, teachers will quickly turn to those needing improvement. That makes change the teacher's idea, not the leader's.
- There are many sources of audit questions. Some are:
  —The national professional association in a given teaching area
  —The California State Department of Education (P.O. Box 271, Sacramento, CA 95802–0271) will send a copy of its publications guide free; materials are sold at state cost. Out-of-state purchase orders are not accepted; send a check. They have produced some excellent handbooks such as "Handbook for Planning an Effective Writing Program." Watch the age of these publications, however. The handbooks average around forty pages of effective schools research on the area, and a ten-page audit.
  —Metropolitan school districts may have audits they are using with an area specialty (such as mathematics). These systems tend to be generous when asked if they would share a copy.
  —Whatever standardized test the district uses should be a source of audit questions. For example, as an assistant superintendent of instruction in a rural eastern North Carolina school district, the author scrutinized standardized test results in biology, knowing his teachers were excellent and well-equipped for teaching a laboratory-based course. Yet test results were only at the 50th percentile. An audit revealed that the test was split evenly between the plant kingdom and the animal kingdom. The teachers, however, devoted five of six

grading periods to the animal kingdom. A simple adjustment saw test scores jump to the 72nd percentile the following year.

An audit may be conducted in a matter of minutes although it takes time to create. The work of Larry Frase, Fenwick English, and William Poston (1994) is recommended for the instructional leader who wishes to read further in this area. As explained below, the audit results allow teachers to determine where changes need to be made.

INSTRUCTIONAL SELF-APPRAISAL

An instructional self-appraisal is, as the name indicates, a means by which a program of instruction may be reviewed specifically to improve the content or procedures used in an effort to increase the learning outcomes of the course. The effective schools movement has provided many good sources of such standards. Instructional self-appraisals can be complex, long-term reviews of all aspects of a program of study, or they can be as simple as an individual wanting to assess his/her teaching against some standard of excellence.

The most valuable form of instructional self-appraisal perhaps lies between these two extremes. The best time to conduct an appraisal is when a course of study is undergoing a change any way, such as when new testing is mandated or when a new basal text is being adopted, because teachers are going to be most interested in change at such a time. The instructional self-appraisal has the additional value of being positive in its impact, because the teachers are involved in it rather than having change mandated from above.

The steps in the process of conducting an instructional appraisal include:

(1) Conducting a comprehensive review of the literature on school excellence practices indicating what features are common in the highest-achieving programs in a given area. Fortunately, many professional organizations and the California Department of Education provide documents that synthesize and simplify the research so that it is often, but not always, readily available.

(2) A curriculum leader (such as an area supervisor, or lead teacher) becomes familiar with the research on effective programs of study in the target area. The same person becomes familiar with the system's current course of study that is to be appraised, along with the textbooks and techniques most commonly used, plus any testing that impacts on the target area, along with an inventory of currently available instructional resources for the area targeted. For example, when the social studies curriculum is reviewed a map and globe audit of the available maps and globes, along with their ages, should be conducted.

(3) The curriculum leader then develops a brief assessment instrument that can

be used to self-appraise (assess) the program as it is reported by the teachers who actually teach it. In developing the instrument, the curriculum leader needs to include questions about: (a) the practices most commonly used in high-achieving programs, (b) areas of diagnosed weakness based on low areas of test scores, and (c) areas that have been of concern to those involved in the appraisal. Audit questions are often asked on a five-point, Likert-type scale, ranging from "frequently used," "seldom used," "not sure," "used rarely" to "never used" responses. Examples of questions could include, if mathematics instruction is being assessed, the availability and frequency of use of manipulatives; in the elementary grades the amount of time generally reserved daily for mathematics instruction, access to computers; and soon. Test score data should reveal questions about the frequency of exposing students to word problems, estimating, and soon. The appraisal instrument needs to be relatively simple, and clearly written, probably no more than three pages long requiring about fifteen minutes to complete. The appraisal can be given to teachers and a modified form given to students, parents, or any other interested party. A good practice is to have the appraisal instrument reviewed by a curriculum specialist within the school system, from another school system, or by an area university. The specialist can serve as an editor as well as serving as a content specialist.

(4) The curriculum leader then distributes the appraisal instrument. Normally the instrument includes both instructional questions (how are you teaching, are you teaching) and curriculum questions (what did you teach, how much time did you devote to this) in order to understand the complete instructional program.

(5) The curriculum leader collects and tabulates the data gathered from the assessment. System results are returned and compared to the mandated curriculum, what is tested, and what high-performing programs are doing. The comparison generates discussion without accusation to see what changes need to be made, why they are needed, and how they will improve the results of instruction. It also reveals what is currently being done well that should be retained. Teachers take ownership, selecting the new directions and changes in instruction or selecting new materials needed.

(6) If the instructional appraisal is tied to another change (for example, new state-mandated testing) then the results of the appraisal can direct the alignment needed. For example, if a new basal textbook (or series) is to be selected, then the textbook adoption/rating decision can include reviewing the textbook for support of the changes textbooks could provide if they are carefully selected. An example in mathematics education would be as follows: If the appraisal disclosed a need to stress problem-solving and daily work with word problems, then one of the ways that the mathematics books could be assessed would see if they had a clear, regular program of problem-solving and daily exposure to word problems.

(7) If the instructional self-appraisal is related to the writing of a new curriculum guide (a recommended practice), then the results can be used to include new practices as the curriculum is redesigned. If the appraisal found a need to increase the teaching of mathematics for a set amount of time on a typical day, that needs to be in the guide; if testing dictates that a certain chronology needs to be followed, tie it to a recommended teaching calendar so that the time is provided to balance the curriculum as needed. Be sure that teachers understand why this is being done and why the improvements should get results.

When writing a curriculum guide, put it on a computer and produce it in a draft form first. Have the teachers responsible for teaching it use the draft for a year and review the instructional self-assessment results with them at the end of the year. Meet a few times during the year to learn how the guide can be improved. Then, following the year-long field test, revise and distribute the completed curriculum guide. Finally, approach curriculum design assuming a finite life-span, so the district has a routine curriculum review/revision process. Ideally, all aspects of the curriculum should be reviewed every five years, keeping the entire curriculum in line with the latest concepts in effective teaching and learning.

Additional uses of the instructional self-appraisal include reporting to the school community changes that will occur and why. Also, tying the appraisal results to new teacher selection (example: If you need more word problems taught in mathematics and there is a vacancy, select the teacher who is likely to do that). Use the self-appraisal's results (and accompanying curriculum guide teaching calendar if developed) to orient new teachers to the curriculum as it should be taught. The findings of the instructional self-assessment can also become the basis of long-term staff development activities, which have an increased likelihood of success because the goal of the inservice is understood. In addition, classroom observations and a review of lesson plans can be used to monitor the effect of the change. The leader may want to give the same self-appraisal instrument a year later to compare the results of both appraisals, helping the teachers see what changes they have reported on themselves and what measurable effect that may have had on test scores.

An instructional self-appraisal is as valuable as the quality of the work that goes into creating and conducting it and then using the results to truly change an instructional program for the benefit of its recipients.

CURRICULUM GUIDES

Whenever teachers meet, a common question is "what do you teach?" and the answer is usually a curriculum one, as "I teach French." But how is a teacher, particularly one who is new to the district, to know what to teach? A curriculum guide should be short, accessible, current, and useful to the teacher.

The old cumbersome guides that listed measurable, behavioral objectives are *passé*. Mercifully. A curriculum guide should be written by teachers with experience teaching the curriculum as intended. It is recommended that at least one special educator be involved in writing the guide for two reasons: (1) the special educator may not know the content as well as a specialist, but such people normally know much more about teaching and learning than a content specialist knows; and (2) the curriculum needs modifying for inclusion programs that should be part of curriculum design.

The curriculum guide should be short. The audience should be someone who is brand-new to the system. When teachers can exchange thoughts about the curriculum and their teaching with a high level of understanding about the curriculum, you have an *articulated curriculum*. The curriculum guide should answer these questions:

- At what pace should I teach, i.e., "If I teach United States' history and 50 percent of the time should be devoted to the twentieth century, am I on pace if I reach the Civil War half-way through the course?" This calls for a "teaching timeline" or a "teaching calendar."
- In what order should basic topics be presented?
- If there is a standardized test at the conclusion of the course/year, what is on the test that should be taught?
- How can the textbook and other teaching supplies be used to support the curriculum?
- What does effective schools research say about teaching this content?
- How is reinforcement and reteaching to be provided?
- What materials are available to support teaching the curriculum?

Two sources of information about the curriculum include: (1) High-achieving, high-growth school districts must have some efficient means of letting new personnel understand the curriculum; call such a district and ask to see what they give new teachers to put them "on board" effectively; (2) the Mesa, Arizona schools have colorful, effective wall charts that outline their curriculum most effectively. A clearly articulated curriculum has another advantage: It allows teachers to explain what they are teaching and what the standards are when parents seek information.

Further information and sample curriculum guides can be found by conducting an ERIC search.

TEACHER EDUCATION AND STUDENT TEACHERS

An often overlooked source of curriculum instruction ideas is the teacher education program in a nearby university or college. If your district is not affiliated with a teacher education program, call the nearest one and ask to become involved. Some rural districts offer assistance with housing and related expenses to bring student teachers to the area. It is a great way to entice new personnel.

If your district is in a multicultural setting or has a minority population many schools of education will be interested in placing student teachers there. If a teacher education program either has, or is seeking, national accreditation, it must meet NCATE (pronounced N-CATE) standards. Among those standards is "field experiences" (which includes student teaching), which should include experiences in a multicultural or minority setting. Colleges cannot report to NCATE that such a population is too far away, making distance a moot point. Therefore, your interest and multicultural setting can be an asset.

Most colleges do not pay schools to take student teachers. Among those that do pay, a tuition-free course is often provided. If no incentive is mentioned, request help with staff development. Student teachers should arrive with new knowledge about the most effective teaching techniques for their subject, which makes them a source of new ideas. Additionally, particularly if the district is far from campus, ask the university supervisor to provide after-school inservice. If the faculty member is seeking tenure (called "tenure-track" as opposed to "fixed term"), which normally takes seven years before tenure is conferred, he/she may be seeking a way to work with local schools at no charge, since faculty members are expected to provide "service" to local schools as well as the university. Asking for inservice is a compliment and a benefit to the faculty member.

PROBLEM-SOLVING WITH ACTION RESEARCH

Most school systems use strategic planning to direct long-term school improvement efforts. Writing the strategic plan is something akin to Will Rogers' comment about ending the German wolf pack menace during World War II. Asked by the press if anything could be done, he replied: "Certainly! I know exactly what to do." Stunned, the reporters asked what he'd do. "Simple," he boomed, "I'd heat the Atlantic until it boils and then pick subs off as they bubble to the surface!" When asked how he'd do that, Rogers replied: "Look, I'm into ideas, using them is a problem for the administrators!" Hopefully, strategic plans are better conceived than that.

Moving from desired changes to solving problems may require action research (AR). There are many forms of action research, one of which is explained below. If the reader wishes to look further, ASCD has an excellent video training program and guide for establishing action research teams.

AN INTRODUCTION TO ACTION RESEARCH

This is a brief introduction to action research that may be used for problem-solving by supervisors. Action research may take many forms, but it is ideal for site-based management where teachers are viewed as intelligent professionals.

The author first used action research with a five-school inquiry team that wanted to raise reading and mathematics test scores. Five middle schools all had significant percentages of students from identifiable groups whose mastery of basic skills was eroding while other students' skills continued to grow. The main purpose of action research is to unite educators in a site-based search for solutions to problems. This cooperative effort has several advantages: (1) it takes research "into the trenches," (2) it turns those who are affected by the problem into the researchers with a vested interest in solving it, and (3) when there is proprietorship with the solution, there is a greater chance of success than if something is mandated from above.

FORMING THE AR TEAM

After a particular problem has been targeted for AR, the first task is forming the AR team. Usually this consists of five people: the supervisor (content specialist if possible); a local school content specialist(s) (such as a reading teacher, LD teacher, etc.); the building principal (if different from the supervisor); and classroom teachers who work with the students manifesting the problem. The AR team is front-loaded with teachers so it is not a central office team. Each member is on equal footing, with the supervisor serving as a facilitator. Each school has its own team.

The team sets regular meeting dates, keeps minutes, and may call on other people as needed. The team must make periodic reports to the faculty so everyone is aware of the team's efforts and is involved in the actual work. If the team can be given some release time and a small pool of funds, all the better. Local grants may be used for this purpose. Should time and money not be available, the team can still function.

AR is not "pure" research. It is done in the field, which makes it flexible enough to solve an actual problem, so the solution is inductively reached rather than rigidly formatted.

STEP ONE: IDENTIFICATION OF THE PROBLEM

All factors that bear on the problem must be open for analysis—often this involves test scores, dropout rates, teacher assessments, community feedback, and so forth. The data are studied by the AR team so a problem statement may be drafted. The ability to state exactly what is wrong, rather than manifestations, is not easy. Often questionnaires are used in beginning this step. Personal anxiety may cloud the problem, and that needs to be considered. Once a succinct statement of the problem has been prepared, it should be taken to the whole faculty for review and input. A final draft of the problem statement is then written.

STEP TWO: PROBLEM ANALYSIS

The data generated in Step One is distilled into a research format. The search in this step is for a cure to what is causing the problem. The supervisor assumes a collaborative mode as a creative researcher (also know as a "go-fer"), who provides nonbiased research at the AR team's disposal. Unworkable solutions are set aside with explanation in case they need further review later. This step often begins a paradigm shift by the AR team. What results is an establishment of parameters of the problem. Then the focus is on solutions.

This step must be approached with a "can do" attitude expecting the problem will be solved. The team needs to focus on cause and effect, and existing assumptions should be checked for validity because an incorrect assumption can be part of what causes the problem. Sacred cows and problem-shifting need to be recognized for what they may be—excuses for not solving the problem. The team must recognize its own biases and the administrative biases as well—the more autocratic the latter, the more threatening change is. As solutions begin to emerge, they should be prioritized from "most likely to work" and "most possible to do" on a guide for planning. Those that are "most likely" on both lists should be used first. Nothing succeeds like success. Tackle more difficult problems after building credibility.

STEP THREE: FORMULATING HYPOTHESIS

Scientific guessing comes into play. Possible solutions should be "held up to the light" one at a time (using the prioritized list above) with an eye toward: (1) the economy of effort, (2) priority ranking with the most useful ideas listed first, (3) cost (both time and money), and (4) feasibility. Team morale goes up at this point.

This is a transitional process from problem analysis to hypothesis setting. The team needs all available research at this stage. The supervisor provides that research. The funding to make calls to places that appear to have solved similar problems and to bring in a consultant facilitates this step. The focus is on getting sufficient research on other solutions—practically no problem is totally unique.

The hypothesis should be accompanied with a plan of action and presented to the general faculty for response and review. This is best done on a scheduled workday so the proposed solution(s) and plan of action can be methodically and reflectively reviewed while teachers are relatively fresh. Once the hypothesis has been studied, the focus needs to be on accepting a most-likely solution.

STEP FOUR: EXPERIMENTATION AND ACTION

If at all possible it is best to take two or three "most-likely" solutions and try them with volunteers for an experimental tryout. Study which solution gets the best results, and why the result occurred. Remember, the idea is being put on trial, not the volunteer! That clarification reduces pressure and allows the solution to be better studied. Once the best solution is found, there will be greater faculty confidence because someone on the staff has already succeeded with it.

STEP FIVE: EVALUATION

This is traditionally the weakest step in AR work—and the one that causes failure the most often. Most teams want to subjectively reflect on the result and pronounce the problem fixed. The team needs to go back into the data that led them to this solution to be sure a real solution is at hand. That will help other AR teams that will be studying the work of this team, and it will give a real understanding of what worked and why it did.

AR is a vital, dynamic process that facilitates true site-based management and treats teachers like the intelligent professionals they are. Try it!

CREATING A CONSORTIUM

Small school systems are at a disadvantage compared to large urban districts, which have large sales volumes. But that can be changed. If several rural school districts establish a consortium, the advantages of volume purchasing can result. Since school districts are usually configured similarly and they are all in the same business, serving similar clientele, there are many ways in which a consortium can benefit everyone.

The assistant/associate superintendents or director of instruction can contact counterparts in other rural school districts to discuss a consortium (or Curriculum Council). Natural ways in which a consortium can work include textbook adoptions, technology repairs (computers, media equipment, etc.), and curriculum/instruction exchanges. Depending on the technology available, a consortium can function electronically via interactive television, cutting down on travel time for meetings. As a result, face-to-face meetings might only be needed quarterly.

In states where with a state textbook adoption cycle, coordinating textbook adoptions is simple. In states where no such cycle exists, an early function of the consortium should be to establish a cycle. With enough coordinated textbook adoptions, booksellers will be willing to provide services the larger school districts take for granted: donating class sets of textbooks and materials to "trial teach" as part of the adoption process, guaranteeing the lowest price at which books will be sold, bringing in textbook consultants to offer free training on the use of the new materials, and "freebies" such as video disks, workbooks, and so on. One rural school district of 2,000 students cannot get such things, but a ten-district consortium of 20,000 students can. To determine what the large school districts routinely get, call the central office of a large district to learn what to expect. With one class set of donated books to "trial teach" for an adoption, a lead teacher from one district can report to the consortium about the utility of the books; the lead teacher could also meet with teacher teams to discuss books prior to adopting them. Rotating trial sites among the consortium districts is recommended.

A district consortium can also be a great way to exchange best ideas for teaching techniques. The consortium can bundle staff development funds together and bring in well-known presenters who would be out of reach for an individual system, simply based on cost. The consortium can write competitive grants to meet districtwide needs, and it can bring in specialty programs such as those from the National Diffusion Network (see below).

IDEA BOX

Rural schools need to avoid reinventing the wheel to solve instructional problems others have already solved. Four suggestions are made below.

(1) Be aware that federally funded education projects that are unusually successful go through a rigorous process of validation, which proves that the project really works and that it is transportable among school districts. Once validated, these projects are available for distribution on the National Diffusion Network (called "NDN"). Because these programs are federally funded, dissemination is provided *at cost*, far less than copyrighted materials cost from for-profit companies. There are many dozens of NDN programs, covering every area of the curriculum including adult education. The programs are explained in a publication, *Education Programs That Work*, produced by Sopris West Inc., 1140 Boston Ave., Longmont, Colorado 80501. The programs usually provide videotaped explanations and program coordinators are listed for contact. The book is not produced by the government so there is a charge for it, but this writer has found it to be very valuable. Another means for learning about NDN programs is via the United States Dept. of Education watts line mentioned earlier.

(2) Maintain a synthesis file or notebook. This author is a long-time member of ASCD, and *Educational Leadership* for years has provided synthesis papers about education issues (grouping, homework, grade retention, etc.), each of which is filled with the most up-to-date research on an educational issue. I simply keep a copy of all of the synthesis papers in one notebook,

knowing that I have the best research available on dozens of topics I need to be an expert on. Give me thirty minutes and I can become an expert on almost any problem!

(3) Fund a rotating professional library. Buying a quantity of professional materials is expensive and it normally comes from limited library funds. Why have each school in a district—or consortium—buy its own books when they could be rotated among teachers on a regular basis. By setting aside a nominal sum from each library budget (1–2%) and rotating the collection, teachers can be exposed to a variety of new ideas at a fraction of the expense of providing them for each school. If administrators share journals the same way, another advantage occurs.

(4) Create a mobile teacher idea center. Having the funds and staff to create a teacher idea center may be beyond the financial reach of a single school, but not several schools working together. One person—perhaps paid on a teacher assistant salary—could rotate among several schools on a regular basis. The person could pick up teacher requests (make a board game about this, transparencies for that, a bulletin board on a certain topic, etc.) on one visit, returning with the materials made on the next. If an old school bus was filled with letter-making dies, teacher idea books, and materials for making teaching products (as for "make and take" workshops teachers love and some short-sighted administrators dislike), an entire teacher center could visit schools on a set basis. It cuts down on the redundancy of needing supplies in each school that are used occasionally, and it keeps a flow of new ideas arriving at the school. Teachers with good ideas and limited artistic ability can be supported as well. This same concept can be used for audiovisual repairs and computer repairs, too.

PART TWO: LOCAL SCHOOL LEADERSHIP

Local rural school leaders should benefit from good directions and ideas from the district level, but the lynch pin of a rural school is the principal who is the instructional leader day in and day out. No one else can suddenly step in and provide that leadership.

COMMUNITY SURVEYS

The effective rural school leader both *knows* and is *known* by the community. While attendance at community events is part of being known, the school leader might consider conducting a community survey to assess the community's expectations and evaluation of the school. A community survey should be tailored to the school and what it needs to know, including issues of curriculum and instruction. The results of the survey should be shared with the school's leadership team and the community. Areas of assessed need should be prioritized and put into annual school improvement plans. Action on those issues should be reported at community meetings.

STRUCTURING THE DELIVERY OF INSTRUCTION

As the instructional leader of the school the principal should give teachers something specific to follow. If the school does not have teacher-developed teaching calendars, that is a good place to start. The purpose of a teaching calendar is to provide both pace and sequence to the instructional program. The old adage that "the search is the treasure" holds true with this activity. To construct teaching calendars teachers must have time to deliberate about the amount of time devoted to teaching each segment of the curriculum, the pace at which the curriculum is presented, and the alignment of the teacher's lessons to the stated curriculum of the district, state, or national frameworks. The end product is far more than an annual calendar, it is a guidance system that informs teachers if they are teaching what is supposed to be taught. The principal develops a teaching calendar as follows.

During a staff meeting, the principal should ask questions about what teachers are teaching, how they know if they will get the mandated curriculum taught, and how they are preparing students for required testing. It is not unusual for seasoned teachers to experience such a conversation for the first time. Then the idea of a teaching calendar should be presented. In very small schools (where there is one teacher per grade or high school academic area), place teachers in natural groups such as K–2, 3–5, or at high school into humanities and science/math and enrichment groups. In a larger school, grade-by-grade and subject-by-subject groups work best. The teachers need to focus on *what they teach* and *what they depend on others* to teach. Discussions should focus on the unit plan level, on the objectives of whatever curriculum they follow, and on standardized test areas. Once there is consensus about what each teacher (or teachers with common classes) should teach, teachers are ready to start working on the calendar on a monthly basis (as, in November we'll teach . . .").

The principal should inject questions about time on task as the groups work. In elementary grades a teacher who "loves" science may spend four times as much instructional time on science as someone who feels weak in that area. Anderson (1993) studied elementary mathematics instruction and time on task; he found some teachers devoting sixteen minutes of instruction daily while others spent as much as fifty minutes *per day* yet they ostensibly taught the same curriculum. Part of the teaching calendar should be a statement of average time per week devoted to teaching certain skills.

Once the monthly teaching calendar and time-on-task targets take shape, the teachers can study the curriculum from the district, state, or national frameworks and place appropriate objectives in various months. Expect some changes of month-to-month plans at this point. When the author was conducting this activity in his former school district, it made a tremendous impact. A new textbook adoption in social studies was coming, so a survey of the North Carolina curriculum was conducted. Teachers who had been teaching the fifth grade had always used a United States history book; a new book, also United States history, was on the adoption list. When the teaching calendar was provided, it showed that a geography of the western hemisphere was expected in the state-mandated curriculum. Teachers looked at the curriculum outline and asked: "Why hadn't anyone ever told us? Is this new?" The curriculum was over twenty years old but no one had ever focused on it before.

BUILDING SEQUENCE CHARTS TO SHOW THE ENTIRE CURRICULUM ON ONE PAGE

If the school lacks a fundamental curriculum and if there is none forthcoming from the district office level, the principal can lead the faculty in designing a learning sequence chart. These charts may supplement anything coming from the district office. This is a modification of an idea from the Mesa, Arizona, public schools, mentioned earlier. During the 1980s Mesa was one of the most rapidly growing school systems in the United States, with an average of one thousand new students added annually. That meant the equivalent of an entirely new school and staff annually, so some means needed to be found to orient the new teachers quickly. The sequence charts were the result. At this writing they have been updated, and continue to be used.

The purpose of a sequence chart is to organize, by grade, the fundamental curriculum on a matrix with each curriculum strand (i.e., reading, mathematics, social studies, etc.) creating a vertical column starting with the lowest grade at the top, and the grade levels listed on the left-hand margin, in order. For example, kindergarten, grade one, grade two, and so on, could be listed on the left-hand margin with each grade given a row that can be read across the chart from left to right. The curriculum strands are listed across the top, with each curriculum area filling a column. Anyone can read the social studies curriculum column from top to bottom, seeing at each grade level how the curriculum builds on previous knowledge. Also, the chart may be read as a grade row, so that the curriculum for grade four, as an example, may be read for social studies, reading, math, and so forth, to see what is taught and what is mastered at that grade level. Figure 7.1 shows what a fundamental learning sequence chart looks like for elementary grades. Note that time on task is listed for each curriculum area, again to help teachers identify not only *what* to teach, but also *how much time* to devote to teaching it.

The development of learning sequence charts can begin by the principal taking the lead. Particularly in small rural schools (with a staff of ten or less), each

Hours per Week of Instruction
Using 5.5 Hour Day

	Reading	Writing & Language	Math	Science	Social Studies	Art & PE
K						
1						
2						
3						
4						
5						

This chart can be drafted on newsprint. Each grade team should write each block (as "science" in 3rd grade's block) with no more than 6-7 basic objectives per block. Teachers need to exchange blocks with teachers at lower & higher grades. This will help align the curriculum as well. Once a single strand, like K-5 Mathematics, is prepared all teachers should read it from K to 5 together, checking for sequence flow from grade-to-grade and to be sure each objective is targeted as written. Keeping the chart void from "teacherese" makes the chart useful to parents and older students. If a high school print shop or local newspaper will print them, cost is minimal. What a great tool for parent conferences.

Figure 7.1 Learning sequence chart (kindergarten–5th grade).

teacher must provide expertise in a given area for the whole school. One teacher needs to be assigned leadership for each curriculum area, with the teachers using the lead teacher as an expert on both the curriculum and the testing of it. To become an expert on one curriculum area, the teacher could to do three things: (1) talk to the district office curriculum specialist about the curriculum expectations, focusing on content, sequence, and the curriculum's relationship to standardized testing by the district; (2) locate a curriculum coordinator in a large school district that teaches the same curriculum and uses the same standardized testing as your school (the author found that large systems were generous about sharing the curriculum structure used); and (3) if there is standardized testing in that curriculum area, contact the publisher of the tests to request all materials available about the test, its structure, and the curriculum upon which it is based. It is not unusual for calls to test publishers to reveal that a test manual is available at a nominal (normally under $25) fee; the likely benefit from studying the manual will offset the cost.

As the teacher is becoming an expert on the curriculum area assigned, it is helpful to learn what accessible school district (using the same curriculum and test) has the highest scores and to call a specialist in that district to learn what they have done to get such results. If your local district has a test coordinator, ask that person to come to the school, meet with the curriculum leadership team, and discuss testing results for the past three years. Then have copies of test results, released questions, and any other teaching materials left for the local teachers to use. Scheduling an annual meeting with the coordinator and the curriculum leadership team is strongly recommended.

STRUCTURE THE CURRICULUM TO FOLLOW STUDENTS FROM GRADE TO GRADE

Once the teaching calendar takes shape, the principal should devote time to review the feeder curriculum. In other words, the kindergarten teacher(s) could explain what skills students should have developed by the end of kindergarten to the first grade teachers, who will then explain how they will review those skills at the beginning of the year with the new first graders, and what skills they will have developed to feed into second grade and so on. This activity helps teachers understand each other better and makes for smoother transitions between grades. It also builds a sense of cohesion when standardized testing occurs at some grade levels and not others so that when, for example, third-grade results are returned, the K–3 teachers should approach the results as a collective measurement of their teaching.

One simple way to facilitate this process is through the use of student portfolios. Each student's work can be added to a separate file with entries made monthly. Progress can be shown in each area the teacher is responsible for, with some form of final examination or final assessment added to show the mastery of each student at year's end. The mastery instrument should be drawn directly from the stated curriculum, with all students taking the same test. The construction of the test can be a central office responsibility or a local school project. Obviously, when a commercial test is used, those results can supplant the locally made test.

It is recommended that the sending teacher provide a narrative about the student's progress and any extenuating circumstances that may have affected student performance on the final test. If a half day of inservice time can be provided within the school, grade transfers can be accomplished with sending and receiving teachers going over individual files. When students' school campuses are changed and significant distances are involved, a full day of portfolio exchanges may be needed. It is suggested that a regular rotation between sites be planned annually, so fifth-grade teachers, for example, go to the middle school to deliver portfolios one year, and middle grade teachers come to an elementary school the next year. Prior to starting the portfolio exchanges, a brief program led by the principal and leadership team can be provided to the guest teachers, with an overview of changes in the curriculum, new materials (such as computer technology), and a review of the school improvement efforts so teachers understand each other and the programs the students are co-dependent on.

ACCOUNTABILITY TESTING

Schools are measured in terms of accountability—namely, comparative standardized test results. School boards, newspaper reporters, real estate agents, and so on, all understand the bottom line on testing—"How well did you do compared to . . . ?" However, how to improve test results often is not well understood, and that is the job of the local principal.

The first steps in improving test results are outlined above—*the tested curriculum must be the primary part of the taught curriculum.* While there is concern about "teaching to the test," the only fair test is one for which students have been prepared (i.e., taught about). Therefore, the only fair standardized test is one for which the students have been adequately prepared. The role of the principal is to ensure that teachers are adequately informed about the curriculum and the mastery test of it. Teachers must provide structured time on task for students to learn the skills for which they will be tested. The following suggestions come from a study of successful schools which have faired well on standardized tests:

(1) Successful schools use some form of criterion-referenced test (CRT). The SAT/ACT test preparation guides include test questions that are actually old released questions or questions written to mimic the actual test questions. People who are renewing their driver's license also expect to see sample questions which are like the ones they will face. Those are CRTs. Check to see if the test manufacturer or the school district has such questions. They can be used as shown below.

(2) Successful schools know that CRTs need to be used within reason. If the test is given at the end of the year (or near the end), there are two ways to use CRTs, either:

   a. Do CRT testing two or three times during the year with the test format, conditions, content and style as much like that of the test that students will take as possible to prepare students for testing conditions, formats, and the mastered content. Overdoing the frequency of CRTs can be counterproductive.

b. Use CRT testing as part of regularly scheduled testing throughout the school year. This should involve testing on a regular basis (say, once every six weeks if one uses six-week grading periods). Part of the regular, teacher-made tests should be labeled "CRT" and the students should take the test as if it were the standardized test (particularly for early elementary this may mean learning to transfer answers onto a scan sheet and bubble in the correct answer). When these tests are returned, the CRT section should be reviewed with the students to tell them how well they would have done on the standardized test.

One word of caution. Many school districts like to buy "test banks" of questions to prepare for standardized tests. The sales people who call usually will tell you their test bank is specifically designed to match the text to which you are accountable. The book sales people tell you the same thing about their books and the teacher's edition that goes with it. This author can tell, from personal experience, that a teacher's edition for a public school textbook he wrote has his name on it and he did not even know there was a teacher's edition until he was at a conference and saw one on display! Test banks may be wonderful, but check them out with school systems that have bought them to see if they really did raise tests scores. There can be two questions, both in the format of the test your students take, and in the same style, yet they can be vastly different questions. There is a big difference in what students need to know to answer these two questions: Did Columbus discover America vs. How did Columbus discover America? Test banks may have the right format and content, but do they ask mastery questions that really reflect what our students are taught?

The final step in increasing test scores means changing a long-held norm: Teacher tests are private property. Why? Test grades are not. Standardized test scores are not. Why should teacher-made tests be like something only the teacher gets to see? In many Eastern Pacific Rim countries, teachers plan together collectively help each other polish lesson plans, and write tests together. And when they are done teaching, they reflect together on how well their common plans went. Rural schools can fight teacher isolation by making tests open for the principal to assess and for common test results with CRTs to be shared.

IDEA BOX

If there is a spare room in the school, could it be converted into a teachers' room? This is an idea from world-class schools, designed to break the isolation that teachers commonly complain about. Move the teachers' desks into the teachers' room, rather than creating teacher isolation by putting one desk in each teacher's room. Group the desks by grade level or subject so teachers who share common responsibilities are in an area where they can talk with each other.

Make the teachers' room professional the same way doctors do, by having teachers bring in their diplomas, framing them, and hanging them on the wall. Do the same with their teaching licenses.

Borrow an idea from Japan—use black and white photos of each teacher, and write a biography of where they went to college, certifications held, special areas of interest, and school responsibilities. Then make a school directory that can be produced on a mimeograph or photocopier to be sent to each parent the first day of school. Instead of having the only description of the teacher and staff come from a child, parents can look up the staff members who will work with their children, attaching a face to the name and skills to the teacher. Include others like teacher assistants, guidance personnel, and secretaries.

Finally, consider investing a few dollars to expand your computer, buying business card software and business card, pre-cut stock. Having a card that says "Jane Smith, Professional Educator, XYZ School" not only makes the teacher feel like a professional, but it makes the school *look* the same way.

MEETING THE REMEDIAL NEEDS OF STUDENTS

One of the biggest problems faced by schools involves slow students who fall behind. Leaving them behind without remediation condemns such students to a spiral of failure in which they fall further and further behind. In rural settings there may be fewer resources available to meet a variety of remedial needs and transportation home becomes a significant factor if after-school work is needed. This requires the leaders and the staff to be creative with the time available.

Communication with the student's home is essential. There should be a clearly understood calendar for progress reports to be sent to any student failing to do "C" work in the middle of the grading period. A telephone call to a parent who can be reached while the student is in school can ensure that the parent is aware of the academic problem while ensuring that the notice is actually delivered. The interim report should be specific, delineating what the problem is (a checklist is not recommended as it encourages minimal communication with parents). Teachers should make the office personnel aware of midterm reports for two reasons: (1) it allows the office to verify the teacher's efforts to communicate home, and (2) it allows the principal to look for excessive notices being sent by one teacher. The latter may signal a teaching problem rather than a learning problem. When dealing with parents who habitually check their child out of school early, one possibility would be to suspend early check-outs for students who get progress reports sent home.

Parents should be encouraged to become involved in meeting the remedial needs of their children. One rural school, Fairview School in Jackson County, North Carolina, organizes evening meetings monthly during which a pot luck dinner is served. Some parenting tips are provided, and parents work with both teachers and student teachers who are providing help for students who are behind.

The school day may be audited to find time for meeting the needs of remedial students, with the lunch period being a time to examine. If students were released from class for lunch one minute ahead of others they could be first in the lunch line. An abbreviated lunch period can be followed by time spent in remediation. Teachers (and administrators) can volunteer to provide help on a bi-weekly, rotating basis. Twenty minutes a day of intensive remediation in small groups yields over three extra hours of learning time every two weeks for students who need the assistance. The time can be found and there is no cost.

Should after-school time be available, the teacher assistants of Haywood County, North Carolina, offer an excellent example of an effective way to offer intense, one-on-one remediation. The county president, Dianne Haynes, had the idea of starting APPLES, as part of North Carolina's accountability drive "ABC" plan ("ABC" stands for Accountability, Basics, and Local Control). To the teacher assistants in APPLES, "ABC" stands for "All Because we Care." Mrs. Haynes asked teacher assistants to volunteer two hours a day, two days a week (Tuesdays and Thursdays) to work intensively with elementary students who were struggling with basic skills in reading and mathematics, the curriculum areas the teacher assistants specifically target in their classrooms. The school supplied a snack and a drink for each student, and parents signed a permission form for the students to participate. The children were either to get picked up by a parent or sent to the after-school program until parents could pick them up (the latter program was paid for by the parents). Teachers were asked to identify students with the greatest needs in those basic skills, no more than two students per teacher's room, limited to the grade level where standardized testing ended the year. Assistants worked with very small groups—usually no more than four students each—with a curriculum the assistants knew well. Results were incredible—students who had been failing suddenly saw their self-esteem jump and grades often went from "F" to "B." Test scores also went up. Not bad for the cost of a snack and a drink.

CONCLUSION

School improvement takes time, teamwork, and clear communication. It is hoped that the combined efforts of district offices and rural school leaders can provide the best education possible. After all, the schools house our only "next generation." They deserve no less than our best.

REFERENCES

Anderson, L. W. 1993. "What Time Tells Us," *Timepiece: Extending and Enhancing Learning Time*. Reston, VA: National Association of Secondary School Principals.

Brophy, Jere. 1997. As reported in *Curriculum Development*. Madison, WI: Department of Public Instruction.

Chalker, D. M., & R. M. Haynes. 1994. *World Class Schools: New Standards for Education*. Lancaster, PA: Technomic Publishing Company.

Frase, L. E., F. W. English, & W. K. Poston. 1994. *The Curriculum Management Audit: Improving School Quality*. Lancaster, PA: Technomic Publishing Company.

Haynes, R. M., & D. M. Chalker 1997. *World Class Elementary Schools: Agenda for Action*. Lancaster, PA: Technomic Publishing Company.

Raizen, S. A. As quoted in M. Lawton, "Math, Science Curricula Said to Fall Short," *Education Week*, October 16, 1996.

Suter, R. As quoted in M. Lawton, "Math, Science Curricula Said to Fall Short," *Education Week*, October 16, 1996.

WEB SITES

American Educational Research Association. Washington, D.C. *www.aera.net*.

American Federation of Teachers, Washington, D.C. *www.aft.org*.

Appalachian Educational Laboratory Inc. *www.ael.org* (linked to nine other education research laboratories).

AskERIC. ERIC Clearinghouse on Information and Technology. Syracuse University. *http:/ericir.syr.edu*.

Association for Supervision and Curriculum Development. Alexandria, Va. *www.ascd.org*.

Center for Social Organization of Schools. Johns Hopkins University. *http://scov.csos.jhu.edu*.

Consortium for Policy Research Center. University of Wisconsin at Madison. *www.wcer.wisc.edu/cpre*.

Education Commission of the States. Denver. *www.ecs.org*.

Education Research Service. *www.ers.org*.

Education Testing Service. Princeton, N.J. *www.ets.org*.

Electronic Solutions for the Research and Education Community. *//web.fie.com*.

High/Scope Educational Research Foundation. Ypsilanti, Mich. *www.highscope.org*.

National Commission on Teaching and America's Future. Teacher's College, Columbia University. *www.tc.columbia, edu*.

National Education Association. Washington, D.C. *www.nea.org*.

National Goals for Education, U.S. Department of Education, Washington, D.C. *www.negp.gov*.

N.C. State Department of Public Instruction, Education Reform Pages. *www.dpi.state.nc.us?edreform*.

North Central Regional Educational Laboratory, Oak Brook, Il. *www.ncrel.org*.

Parents as Teachers National Center. St. Louis, *www.patnc.org*.

RURAL SITE-BASED LEADERSHIP

CHAPTER 8

Leading Rural Schools:
Building Relationships and Structures

To be successful, rural school reforms must be led by principals who demonstrate the power to get things done, not power over people.—Gehring and Bailey, 1997

Recent discussions of School Reform suggest that we use "site-based management." When applied to rural schools, however, this term carries little descriptive power. By their very nature, rural schools are often small, isolated, autonomous, and self-sufficient. Also, by their very nature, rural schools are unique in the ways they manage themselves. Therefore, a more descriptive way to discuss rural school management and leadership is to explore the unique relationships and organizational structures that are essential to effective rural school leadership.

THE RURAL SCHOOL INFERIORITY COMPLEX

A S students introduced themselves during the first class of my Foundations of American Education for college sophomores and juniors, two young women revealed that they were graduates of a small, K–12 school in an isolated region of the Appalachian Mountains. I and the other students reacted sympathetically.

As the semester went on, however, sympathy changed to curiosity, interest, and finally envy. During class discussions of the problems and issues confronting many American schools, these students reported that the negative social and educational situations described in our readings never surfaced in their school. By the end of the semester students from suburban and metropolitan schools were asking these two students to explain how problems like teacher autonomy and professionalism affected their school. The two women said things like,

J. Casey Hurley, Department of Educational Leadership and Foundations, Western Carolina University.

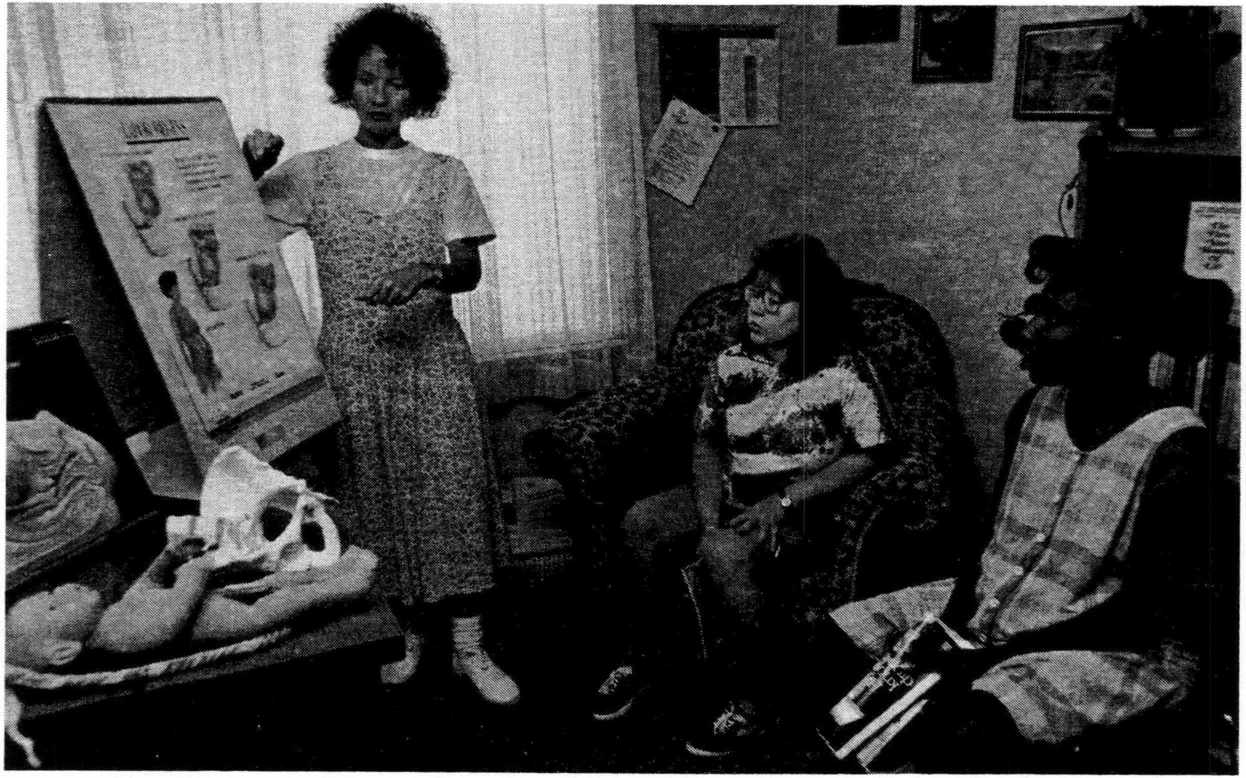

© Photo by Rob Amberg.

"We knew and respected our teachers." "Teachers were our guides." "We all got along real well." The looks on the faces of the other students told me these sentiments did not match their experiences in large, comprehensive schools.

My own beliefs about these two students' K–12 education also changed during the semester. After they introduced themselves on the first night of class, I expected them to be shy, socially naive, and poorly prepared for college. In fact, they were among the best students in class, often making insightful observations about the issues confronting students and teachers in American public schools.

In retrospect, I realize my surprise was because I had just come from being an administrator in three different high schools—one suburban and two rural. And the most subtle, yet pervasive issue confronting the two rural high schools was the desire to be more like the suburban schools that were winning conference championships. It seemed that both parents and teachers wanted to be associated with schools that were larger, more diversified, more cosmopolitan. Gregory and Smith (1987) also recognize that some small schools develop an inferiority complex. According to them,

> Status influences the course of education in many ways. Schools arrange themselves in a pecking order; small schools have sought to emulate large high schools. In recent decades, a school was immediately on the defensive if it did not have all the facilities and specialized personnel that a large school had . . . Small schools—those with graduating classes of less than 100 students—were considered inherently inferior because they could not offer as many foreign languages or advanced science courses . . . If consolidation was not feasible, one did what one could to emulate a large school's organization and curriculum. (p. 61)

This is an important issue because it reminds us that trying to make all schools like our largest ones may be disadvantageous to small schools. The "one best system" of education envisioned by many businessmen and lawmakers may be counterproductive to producing effective small, rural schools. When organizational members of small schools strive to become like large schools, not only do they develop an inferiority complex, they also lose sight of their strengths—their potential for developing positive relations among adults and students, for attaining a sense of community, for developing relevant educational programming, and for knowing students so well they do not need to be labeled.

By sharing their experiences in a small, K–12 school, these two college students, convinced many of us that, small schools are not necessarily weak schools. In fact, it seems to me, now, that rural schools are some of our finest American educational institutions. Instead of being unfortunate institutions in regions too isolated to be harvested by the consolidation combine, small, rural schools are often places where educational excellence flows naturally. Instead of being weeds in the educational landscape, rural schools are often vines that bear rich fruit and healthy nourishment for young people.

The purpose of this chapter is to illustrate how rural schools that build on their strengths become fertile environments for children. The chapter provides evidence that educational opportunity and excellence have more to do with meeting students' needs in a communal setting than with providing comprehensive curricular and extracurricular programs. Some rural schools are true educational communities; this chapter reports how several of them harness the power behind that idea.

Although the purpose of this chapter is not to criticize large schools, it is important to point out that many educators are beginning to realize that "bigger is not better." After years of making schools large enough to be "cost effective" (a business concept misapplied to education because it assumes a concrete, desired outcome and a way to measure it), and then passing state laws that require all schools to conform to the structures needed to operate these large institutions, educators are beginning to realize the limitations of large schools and large school districts.

For example, in a keynote address at an education summit in Asheville, North Carolina, George Wood said, "If the principal can't stand in front and know every kid's name every day, something is wrong, period. A teacher can't know 150 kids a day—who's idea was that?" (Dryman, 1997, p. A10). Gregory and Smith (1987) have also made a strong case for the "smaller is better" high school.

Furthermore, recommendations from groups advocating reform of high schools, middle schools, and elementary schools include calls for smaller schools. For example, in *The Basic School* Boyer (1995) writes:

> School size matters, too. "If all the research on the best environments in which to . . . educate children could be boiled down to three words, they would be Small Is Beautiful," notes educator Winifred Gallagher. Small institutions encourage community. And while no arbitrary line is drawn, we suggest as a rule of thumb, that the Basic School be small enough for everyone to be known by name—perhaps with no more than four to five hundred students. Larger schools might be organized as schools within a school. (pp. 16–17)

SITE-BASED MANAGEMENT IN RURAL SCHOOLS

Recent discussions of School Reform suggest that we think of schools as unique, autonomous educational organizations, not as interchangeable parts within larger educational districts or state systems. The term most often associated with this idea is "site-based management." When applied to rural schools, however, this term carries little descriptive power. By their very nature, rural schools are often small, isolated, autonomous, and self-sufficient. Also, by their very nature, rural schools are unique in the ways they manage themselves. Therefore, a more descriptive way to discuss rural school management and leadership is to explore the unique relationships and organizational structures that are essential to effective rural school leadership. This chapter describes the ways several rural school leaders have developed strong relationships and effective organizational structures in their communities and schools.

The logo of the Maine Network of Small Schools shows a schoolhouse cracked down the middle and falling apart as long-stemmed flowers burst through the roof. According to Gordon Donaldson, Director of the Maine Academy of School Leaders (MASL):

> [the] logo symbolizes both the breaking away from the structures of schooling and the flowering of the best child-centered teaching from Maine's educational past. The Network seeks to move beyond the artifice of imposed structure and in its place nurture educational processes and practices that will bring the talents and human capacities of our children into bloom. (Donaldson & Marnik, 1995, p. xvi)

Similarly, in my conversations with rural school leaders, I heard that rural schools are different. They do not fit into neat categories. Instead, they are extensions, or even centers, of diverse communities. They are places where parents are connecting with students, where teachers and staff go beyond the call of duty, and where everyone pitches in to help the kids.

In order to describe some of the rural schools that are "breaking away from the structures of schooling," I solicited the names of rural school leaders who are proud of the ways they build on their unique strengths. I contacted the office of the Annenberg Rural School Challenge, and I used the Internet to find rural school leaders who would speak with me for thirty minutes over the phone.

I interviewed fourteen rural school leaders in twelve states—Alabama, California, Idaho, Maine, Missouri, Nebraska, New York, North Carolina, Ohio, South Dakota, Virginia, and Washington. Seven of these school leaders are men, seven are women. Three work in K–12 schools, three in high schools, one in a middle school, and seven in elementary schools.

One of the schools is a comprehensive high school enrolling more than 900 students. The other thirteen schools have much smaller enrollments. One of the high schools is 98 percent African-America, two elementary schools and the middle school are racially mixed. The other schools are predominantly white.

First, I asked these principals and assistant principals to share any experiences that led to positive relations with members of the community. Second, I asked them to describe the formal and informal structures created to accomplish goals. Third, I asked them to explain how they build on the unique strengths of their rural setting. National rural educational leaders call this idea "pedagogy of place" (Sher, 1995). Fourth, I asked if there were any state initiatives that were either getting in the way of or assisting rural school educators in their state. Finally, I asked what advice participants would give someone going into a rural school principalship.

These fourteen rural school leaders related some interesting stories. This chapter includes contributions from each of them. Their stories and descriptions start with a headline that captures unique elements of their situations.

RELATIONSHIPS WITH COMMUNITY MEMBERS

Three principals told stories about early experiences that set the tone for later positive relations in their communities. The first story is about a challenge to an elementary school guidance program. The second is about a principal who decided he was going to confront the "gruff man with the mean dog." The third story is about a new principal who was viewed with suspicion until he stopped at the local roadside grocery to participate in the local farmers' mid-morning discussion session.

"AN EPIPHANY"

"It was the early 90s, and I had been principal for just a short time. The church attended by most of the upper class students and parents had a new minister. This minister mounted a parent challenge to the guidance program in our elementary school. I think it was sort of a power play by him because, when I met individually with him, he was very adversarial.

"Parents started objecting, and they had some printed material from the Eagle Forum. So I decided to hold a meeting for parents. Fifty or so showed up. As I listened to them, I realized they wanted us (educators) to know that, 'this has to do with my kids.' I saw this and I had an epiphany.

"Usually I considered these kinds of objections as flag-waving; but, in this case, I saw parents with real concerns and worries. They demonstrated thoughtfulness and care for their children and the place of the school. I hadn't seen this in the other rural schools where I worked. Maybe it was because, in this case, these were friends.

"I found out that deeper personal relationships lead to having more at stake. This situation also helped me see the individual impact of programs and policies on kids. I am now more aware of how parents think about the impact on their own child. This is beyond political pressure, this is about shared responsibility."

THE "GRUFF MAN WITH THE MEAN DOG"

"We were going to have students in our K–8 school march to the town square for an anti-drug rally. I was new, and I had never met the 'gruff man with the mean dog,' as he was known by some in the community. He owned most of the property on the town square, including the local feed store. Nobody was going to ask him if we could rally at the town square.

"I said, 'I'll do it.' So I went down to the feed store one school day. My normal approach would be to get to the point as quickly as possible and get back to school. I ended up spending three hours getting to know him. We developed a strong relationship, and he said we should go ahead with the rally. We even drove to his house where he wanted me to see some of the things that were important to him. He turned out to be a terrific resource that we didn't have before.

"Spending time with this man opened doors that had previously been closed. A lot of it was that more things were available on the town square. He was well-connected and he was a key person among several influential groups in town. After that, every couple of months I went down to the feed store to sit and talk awhile. I truly enjoyed my visits and considered them time well-spent; and sometimes, if I took my time, the mean dog would let me pet him."

"CHECKING THE BUS ROUTES"

"When I first became an administrator in this school, I was a new assistant principal. One of the veteran elementary school principals took me aside and gave me a talk that I needed. He told me, 'Be aware of your community and be approachable. See your folks.'

"One summer day he came by and told me to get in the car with him to 'check the bus routes.' Our first stop was a roadside grocery—your typical rural summertime gathering place. It had two benches and two gas pumps outside. He introduced me to the tobacco farmers gathered there. We proceeded to talk with these people, and I could see they were suspicious of me because I was from a large city in a different part of the state.

"I got their attention, though when I took my Coca Cola and opened it and poured a small pack of peanuts into the bottle (a ritual of these tobacco farmers). They smiled and asked where I learned that.

"This tore down walls and started a conversation about tobacco farming. I talked about tobacco farming where I grew up, and they were interested in the different methods used in different parts of the state. They ended up talking about how good their kids are.

"After we left the grocery store, we went into a nearby community center and talked to some people there. That was a real significant time and I didn't appreciate it until later."

How do these stories illustrate unique aspects of rural school leadership? Several things can be learned. First, it is not enough to call meetings. Rural educational leaders must sincerely listen to their community. The first principal understood better how the parents felt once he saw these parents as neighbors and friends. Only then could he see that, "This is beyond political pressure, this is about shared responsibility." Sincere, open discussion is essential in rural communities. This principal also told me that, by acknowledging the sincerity of the people, he gained their trust. In contrast, they rejected the leadership of the minister who soon left the community.

Second, it is not enough to deal only with community members who come to the school. In the second and third stories we learn the benefit of getting on community turf. Effective rural school leaders break down walls between the school and the outside community. Rural educators must have an attitude different from those who say, "if they cared about their kids, they would come to the school." Effective rural school leaders reject this idea and reach into even the most inhospitable environments to break down barriers between the school and adults in the community. This same idea is reinforced in other stories later in this chapter.

CREATING ORGANIZATIONAL STRUCTURES

When I asked one principal about structures created to achieve school goals, he said, "I'm not big on structure. We tend to break structure down and go one-on-one with each other." As we went further in the discussion, however, he described a faculty book club, and he explained that the male teachers had a standing poker game during days when the school was closed because of snow.

> Instead of searching for models that work elsewhere, rural educators need to creatively think about the possibilities unique to their location and community. Rural school leaders need to look inward more than outward.

Organizational structures can be formal or informal. It is especially important for rural school leaders to recognize, create, and nurture informal structures. In rural situations, it is often the informal structures that can be effective in achieving specific purposes. The following stories illustrate a cross-fertilization of formal and informal structures.

"THAT WAS THE BUILDING BLOCK FOR A PARTNERSHIP TO BE FORMED"

"The school district was trying to build a new school in 1991. The community and even the faculty were split on the need for a new building. We needed to build a partnership among school district people and members of the community. Those against the building formed the Concerned Taxpayers Group. Another group favored the new school because they wanted an improved community center. They tried to pass a bond but it failed miserably. They needed a two-thirds majority for passage.

"There was a lot of misunderstanding between the two groups, so we formed Patrons for Better Schools, consisting of faculty, students, clergy, and community members. We held cottage meetings around town, with five or six people, sometimes in a home. Two or three of us would answer questions about school district plans and program ideas. I think the students changed more minds than anyone. That was the building block for a partnership to be formed.

"After one year we ran a bond to see where we stood. Our share increased from 30 percent to 50 percent. We decided that persistence was needed, so we just kept at it. Then we decided we had to visit people who were "anti." We asked them to tour the 1936 building. We eventually ran five more bonds, one every six months. We got 66.7 percent on the sixth bond.

"The biggest thing we had to overcome in the community was this divide—many years of mistrust and disharmony in the community. And this really brought that to an end. One individual didn't want the school at all. He was a fierce opponent, but he was also a building contractor. After the bond passed he offered to pour the concrete for free.

"We were only able to bond for 1.1 million of a 1.5 million dollar building. So community members pitched in to do the grading and landscaping. Some people who showed up with their trucks were ones I thought sure had voted 'No.' But when people saw all these people trying to save money, that changed their minds about the school."

"A REAL COMMUNITY HAPPENING"

"One thing we have done for many years is a big Halloween carnival. This is not just a school carnival, it is a community event. We have six to eight hundred people attend each year. I organize it through the PTO. We try to bring every aspect of the community in. Businesses support it, ads are sold, parents and community members volunteer time to cook and serve food and run carnival games.

"The money is used to maintain the school. We have the best-kept school. Our community is proud of how the school is kept; it's always clean.

"All kinds of people attend—high schoolers, middle schoolers, and elementary school students. Parents and grandparents come. It is a real community happening. Even if we would not make any money, it serves a purpose."

"A DIFFERENT CLIMATE FROM WHAT WE HAD"

"The kind of climate I wanted to build with my staff was a different climate from what we had. As a doctoral student and PE teacher I knew about teamwork and coaching. I had read about effective schools and about organizational models in business and industry. So I developed a model that we could use in our school.

"We moved from administrative-driven meetings to staff-driven ones. We developed horizontal teams and had inservice on empowerment. We increased communication and collaboration among teachers and staff. We eventually got to where teachers and staff no longer looked to me for direction.

"Each team selects a representative to a monthly meeting. We meet during the school day, and coverage is provided from 2:45 to 4:00. I wanted to call it a Leadership Council, but they (teachers) didn't see themselves as leaders. We call it the Team Representative Meeting.

"The support staff also have their teams, which led to a conflict in the very beginning. The teachers were interested in doing away with holiday parties. Instead, they wanted to have celebrations based on curricular themes. The noncertified staff came out in full strength. They were mainly the mothers, grandmothers, and neighbors of the students. They said, 'Let kids be kids.' With everybody having an equal vote, the decision was to leave things the way they were. Later on, one of the teachers said to me, 'I just wish you would have made the decision.'

"I don't want to have a major uproar in the community over parties. We can live with this for the next several years. We put it to bed for this year, but it may be an issue that will come up again."

What do we learn from these descriptions of organizational structures in rural schools? Two were built to achieve financial purposes, one focused on instruction and operation of the school. Couldn't these same stories be told in large, suburban and urban districts? Upon closer examination, the answer is, "Probably not."

First, the key to successful passage of the bond was going into people's homes in small groups, and the principal hypothesized that students played a major part in convincing community members to increase their taxes to build a new school. This personal approach is rarely, if ever, tried in larger districts because passage of a bond involves too many houses. In this situation, educators teamed with students to do more than pass a bond referendum; they brought to an end "years of mistrust and disharmony in the community."

I have never heard such a claim made after a bond referendum campaign in a large district. Instead, bond campaigns in large districts remind me of a boxing match, with educators in one corner and taxpayers in the other. Counting the ballots represents the end of a round, not the healing of a community.

In the second story the principal was not exaggerating when she said the Halloween carnival involved almost everyone in the community. We get a picture of an annual event that pulls people together. As she said, "Even if we would not make any money, it serves a purpose." Fund-raising carnivals in large districts may involve many people, but not the percentage of involvement described in this rural setting. Furthermore, using the proceeds to maintain "the best-kept school" is an example of a rural school rallying behind a cause rarely seen in large districts, where school cleanliness is primarily the responsibility of the custodial staff. As the principal told this story, it was clear that the community takes great pride in the appearance and cleanliness of its school. The point is that the community sees a need to rally around this cause each year; and because they do, everyone shares in the work and everyone feels proud of the school.

The third story is about the development of a horizontal team structure. Isn't this something that even large corporations and school districts have implemented? Yes, but rarely with such a total rejection of hierarchy. Even in the name they gave to their organization, the school staff displayed an egalitarian spirit. "I wanted to call it a Leadership Council, but they (teachers) didn't see themselves as leaders. We call it the Team Representative Meeting."

Further, the whole idea of one person, one vote was a key to the outcome of the conflict. Although one of the teachers wished the principal had decided the matter, the principal knew that would have destroyed the integrity of the teams. The principal went on to explain that the issue may emerge again, but the process had worked so far, and the process would be invoked again if teachers wanted a change.

This is clearly different from most large school districts, which operate with the central office staff at the top of the professional hierarchy, the school administrators at the next level, followed by the teachers, and the support staff at the bottom. Even where I have seen horizontal teams tried, this hierarchy is preserved because we believe that certain educational professionals should have a larger part in making educational decisions. Isn't this why they earn higher salaries?

If this story leaves educators a little uneasy, let's remember the epiphany of the principal in the first story: "This is beyond political pressure, this is about shared responsibility." The good news is that shared responsibility among parents, staff and teachers is possible in small, rural schools; and, when it is achieved, schools become healthy environments for our children.

PEDAGOGY OF PLACE: BUILDING ON THE UNIQUE STRENGTHS OF RURAL SETTINGS

When I started planning this chapter, I contacted Alan DeYoung, who has written extensively on rural schools. He suggested that I find out how rural school leaders build on the unique strengths of their rural settings. For too long rural schools have been expected to adopt the same structures, follow the same rules, and achieve the same goals as larger, urban and suburban schools. Many rural schools simply follow along. They end up becoming, as one interviewee said about a middle school he worked in, "This school could have been anywhere as far as I was concerned. It was a school with rural kids, but not a rural school."

One purpose of the Annenberg Rural Challenge is to encourage rural schools to build a distinctive "pedagogy of place" that rejects standardization and provides direct benefits to rural students and communities. This same idea is suggested in the logo of the Maine Network of Small Schools—break away from old school structures so the learning of children can flower.

In my conversations with principals I found several who embraced this principle. Some were part of the Annenberg Rural School Challenge, some were not. Four examples follow.

"AND THIS IS HIGH QUALITY LEARNING"

"We've created the Rural Resource Center in the high school. It is a place for everyone in the community. We have an Internet-accessible computer and tables for conferences. Three women from the community decorate the room each month according to different local themes: 'The Hunt,' 'Veterans,' 'Local Church Histories'—which were written by the students. Local ministers meet there too.

"Adults are there, and students go in and out because they have decided to look back and study their place, who they are, and where they come from. We're part of the Rural Challenge, and a few teachers have done some things so kids are more interested in their home, not just wanting to find the big city.

"The 'study of place' doesn't just affect the kids. The teachers, too, sat down and read 'Broken Heartland' together. It talked about the farm crisis of the mid–80s. We sat down and discussed chapters. We could relate the book to our community. We got into issues of teacher pay and lowered expectations for students. Some teachers even admitted they were guilty of that, right in front of me.

"We wanted to get everybody to do something concerning 'study of place' in their classroom. Even if they didn't, they took a hard look at themselves and where they live.

"In junior English class the students also read 'Broken Heartland.' Students saw themselves and their parents in the book. They saw the future, if things kept going. It hit on everything they see on Main Street here.

"This led into students studying monopolies and injustices toward Native Americans. They read three books in nine weeks. This is unheard of, but that is what happened because we made use of our rural circumstances.

"The kids also did a community cash flow project. They determined that an increase of 10 percent spending in the county would boost the economy by over 2 million dollars and increase taxable sales by 27 percent. The kids did spreadsheets, mailings, newsletters, etc.

"And this is high-quality learning. It's not the project, it is the process. The process has made the students initiators and the teachers learners. That is when you are successful."

"THE ALTERNATIVE WAS CONSOLIDATION"

"We have the luxury of being in a state park. Eighty percent of our budget comes from state taxes. But our enrollment had fallen from 400 to 60 because we have been in two 'boom and bust' cycles—first mining, then logging.

"We had some classes with two or three kids. Simultaneously, the state was raising curriculum standards. These two factors became real stressors on a small district, and it motivated people to become involved. The alternative was consolidation.

"We began looking for ways to excel and become a pilot school for a new state choice initiative. We developed a magnet program for the purpose of doing research on the Adirondack Mountains, where we are located. We wanted private school parents to become clients, and we considered building a boarding facility to increase enrollment. As it turned out, we formed partnerships with the local state university and a state interpretive education center on the Adirondacks. With the university we developed an ecology program, and our students did several research projects with university faculty.

"Research and information gathered in the outdoor labs gave our students a sense of pride in our environment, and the project has attracted students who would otherwise go to other schools. We also increased expectations for students to the point where it concerned some local parents. According to them, we had too much reading and writing.

"We do two projects each year. Graduates used to come back from college and report that they were uncomfortable talking in large groups, so our students make a public presentation of their research. Our challenge was to take a state initiative and use it to address a local problem. At least now I don't have teachers worried about closing because our enrollment is up to seventy-eight, with fourteen magnet students."

"WE'RE STILL TEACHING SCIENCE, BUT MAKING IT PERSONAL"

"I used to be in a school of 1,200 students. Being in a small school is a completely different experience. A small school is just good for kids in general.

"We have an agricultural community, and it is important for us to stress our agricultural basis—growing rice. We have begun to tour rice farms and talk about what you do with rice. We're still teaching science, but making it personal.

"Our elementary students go to high school and see what the FFA students are doing in their projects. There is a big push to celebrate diversity, but education has a habit of doing pendulum swings. We should not lose sight of things that bring us together."

"WE HAVE CHICKENS THAT BELONG TO THE NEIGHBOR BUT LIVE ON OUR CAMPUS"

"Our school is on a beautiful, 13–acre site. The curriculum is tied to our rural environment and agriculture. We have chickens that belong to the neighbor but live on our campus. We celebrate the harvest between Halloween and Thanksgiving, and we study agricultural processes.

"We also have a nationally registered waterway on our property. We work with the Department of Natural Resources to monitor water quality, measure fish, and analyze the creek.

"We operate much like a family. We have cross-age tutoring, and a reward for positive behavior is to allow older students to help in the preschool. This is an old-fashioned place—we have kids help other kids.

"We also get a lot of intergenerational help—brothers, sisters, aunts, uncles, and grandparents. We have about twenty grandparents who volunteer on a regular basis, and elderly people living near the school volunteer. The school is kind of the center of life.

"We work closely with the high school FFA. They partner with our elementary students. They develop good relationships and provide good role models."

These are just a few of the schools utilizing their unique rural settings. It is important to point out that, unlike much educational literature, these stories are *not* told to illustrate some of the things that should be tried by other rural schools. These are *not* models to be copied or transplanted. The point of the Annenberg Rural Challenge is to ask schools to become the best school possible, given their unique environment and community.

With this in mind, and with these four stories as examples, it is important for rural educators to identify the strengths of their situations and simply think about ways to build on them. Instead of searching for models that work elsewhere, rural educators need to think creatively about the possibilities that are unique to their location and community. They need to look inward, not outward.

The next section illustrates why this admonition is necessary. State legislatures often make laws and policies that treat all schools the same. Legislators see it as their job to ensure consistency across the state. This is not ill intentioned, but the effects can damage rural schools (Howley, 1997).

Even in states with a tradition of local control, we see a trend toward more state control. For example, a principal in Maine explained that, even though local control is valued in his state, a statewide testing initiative began ten years ago. Similar initiatives have taken root in almost every state, and this is the topic of the next section.

STATE INITIATIVES AND SMALL, RURAL SCHOOLS

Getting a complete picture of the ways different states address rural school issues is difficult because every state is unique in its control and operation of school districts. After working with rural schools in two different states and talking with these fourteen rural school leaders, however, it is clear that the 1980s and 90s are a time when states are moving toward greater control and what they call "accountability." The following four stories illustrate this trend and put it in perspective for rural schools.

"GET OUT OF OUR WAY AND LET US TEACH"

"Our state (Washington) has a lot of initiatives. They are even discussing eliminating small schools. One bill recently passed says that, by the year 2000, every school will realign its curriculum with the state benchmarks in grades 4, 7 and 10. They have identified outcomes in math, reading, writing, social studies, science, problem solving, and technology. They are currently designing and testing the tests for these.

"Local control is a real concern around here. Teachers and parents on the Site-Based Council are wondering about this law. We spend all our release time working on this. The next step is teacher accountability and new evaluation standards for teachers. Parents are concerned about the grade 10 graduation test. This is high stakes for their children.

"I am not so concerned. I see that we are already beyond this. I just want the state to get out of our way. The older teachers see past state initiatives sitting on the shelf, so they tend to ignore it, too. Some of the younger teachers see this as an opportunity to do some things better. What we are really saying is, 'Get out of our way and let us teach. You guys have no idea how much money and time is needed to do this. It is difficult to stretch those dollars in a small district.'

"In this district teachers have to do both—planning and teaching. Teachers spend a lot of their summer designing this stuff. The curriculum committee is the staff, which is also the group that chaperones and everything else.

"Many people think that, if you are good, you are in a big city. Those people have no idea of how good things are in rural schools."

"THAT CAN'T BE DONE IN A SMALL SCHOOL"

"I don't set the state (Missouri) up as the enemy, but I covertly use them to challenge the staff. When the teachers sense a challenge and say, 'We can do it anyway,' I let them go after it. I ease it in so it is not something required, but a challenge. Typically, they rise to the occasion.

"Our state asked for proposals to get funding to become A-Plus schools. I heard large-school administrators say, 'that can't be done in a small school.' In the meantime, our teachers did it. We have the same curriculum as the 3-A school down the road. Our kids get the same materials.

"We've done it on our own. Six miles away they got grant money to study and present a proposal. In my school, two teachers and I sat down and did the same thing—realigned and redesigned the curriculum to integrate the arts. We put it in. We're selling it to the parents, and we're making it work.

"Because we are small, I have to be accessible. People say, 'Richard, I need to talk with you.' When I do the evaluations I don't jump through all the hoops the state wants us to. If I don't know what is going on in the classrooms, I am not doing my job."

"THIS COULD ACTUALLY PUT SMALL DISTRICTS OUT OF BUSINESS."

"One new idea (in California) that is a real hot topic is the 95/5 initiative. The legislature wants to reduce administrative costs to 5 percent or less.

"This could actually put small districts out of business, or force consolidation. If you have 900 kids, you still have to have a superintendent and a principal for the elementary school, middle school, and high school and cover other administrative costs and supplies. They want 95 percent of the budget to go directly to the classroom.

"They are doing this to try to improve how funds are spent in the big city districts. The irony is that the big districts will be able to comply much easier than we will."

"NOBODY WANTS TO GO ON ALERT, OR BE PUT ON ACADEMIC CAUTION"

"We (Alabama) now have standardized testing in grades 3–11. We don't mind testing and accountability, but they take away from the human things we need to do.

"We are part of the PACERS program, which has been a source of tremendous school improvement over the last five years. Through some of the PACERS projects at our school, we gathered more alumni support and received more support from the district office.

"We now have a community music celebration, in addition to the student newspaper we started three years ago. People in our community were excited about the children performing and writing songs. The songs came from the elders in the community who came in and told stories about how it 'used to be' here. The students then wrote songs from these stories.

"We do special programs like this as part of PACERS, and these projects require documentation. Now the teachers are afraid to stick with the projects because this takes time away from preparing students for standardized tests. And nobody wants to go on alert, or be put on "academic caution" by the state.

"We just completed our testing for this year, and the students and teachers are tired. With the projects we do for PACERS the children can be creative, especially in the elementary school. We want to be accountable, but who is benefiting by leaving out some of the human element?"

In how many states would we hear similar stories from rural educators? The main point is that we need to think differently about rural schools. Paul Nachtigal (1996) writes,

> The one thing that we are sure about is that rural schools and rural communities have not been well served by the industrial model of education. This model, with its centralization, specialization, and standardization has decontextualized education. The agenda for public education has been moved further away from the local community. So, a central premise of a genuinely good, genuinely rural school is that it values local culture and is grounded in the local context. (Nachtigal, 1996, personal correspondence)

We need to remind state legislators that rural schools may be the models they should be holding up for others. Instead of promoting centralization, and standardization, they ought to recognize the benefits of localness and cultures that nurture children. At least, as one principal put it, the state should, "Get out of our way and let us teach."

This may be a good time in educational history to push for more acceptance of school diversity and localness. The Council of Chief State School Officers (1996) recently reported that "we are hearing strong rumblings that community-focused and caring-centered conceptions of schooling will increasingly compete for legitimacy with established notions of school organizations as hierarchies and bureaucracies" (p. 6).

Evidently, even people working to standardize the licensure of school leaders recognize a rising dissatisfaction with bureaucratic educational organizations. (There may be some irony here; but we will have to see the Council's final recommendations before we know the depth of their understanding of the importance of "community-focused and caring-centered conceptions of schooling.")

On the other hand, rural educators should recognize that the most powerful educational movement in America today contradicts the spirit of local control. Almost all states are involved in establishing standards for student achievement (Johnson & Farkas, 1997). State-established standards may help some schools, but locally established standards fuel the development of genuinely good rural schools. Three of the stories in this section illustrate that local standards are powerful motivating forces for program development and student achievement. One school is able to provide the A-Plus School program because the teachers in this small elementary school are challenged by the idea that their school is too small. In one school students are writing and performing songs about local history. In another rural, K–12, magnet school, where the teachers wish the state would stay out of their way, the principal reports that they are a nationally recognized model for technology in schools. According to her, because they have embedded technology in the school, "We have gone from a textbook, teacher-centered approach to an experiential, hands-on approach. This has affected how kids look at education, teachers' expectations, and what parents think about education. I continue to ask kids how things are going and involve them formally and informally in discussion about educational directions. In our student survey we ask what is working well. These kids have embraced this so thoroughly that they are even analyzing their own ability and suggesting things that work well for them. They're very much involved and so are their parents. The parents have told me, 'If you did not provide this kind of program, I would have to send my kids elsewhere.' "

As these stories suggest, locally established standards are powerful motivators of students, teachers, and parents. We also see that state standards can get in the way of local ones. When teachers shift their attention from the projects that have improved the school to preparing students for standardized tests required by the state, who benefits? who loses? As an assistant principal said, "We want to be accountable, but who is benefiting by leaving out some of the human element?"

THINKING ABOUT ACCEPTING A RURAL SCHOOL PRINCIPALSHIP?

Several of the school leaders interviewed for this chapter spoke eloquently in their advice to someone thinking about becoming a rural school principal. The advice of all fourteen interviewees was similar. As might be anticipated, they primarily spoke about the need to build positive relationships with the people in the rural community. Their suggestions can be divided into four categories: (1) become part of the community, (2) focus on people and relationships, (3) move sincerely but slowly, and (4) expect to work hard.

These "words of wisdom" also help to conclude this chapter by focusing on important aspects of rural school leadership. Anyone considering a rural school principalship should consider the following advice—*Become Part of the Community.*

One principal suggests, "If you are going to be an administrator in a rural area, live in the community, become a part of the community. Trying to be a principal and live elsewhere can be destructive."

Another advises, "You need to develop a sense of being a part of the community—attend community events, church, NAACP meetings. Otherwise, your job will be uphill. Some people in administration come from rural places and understand the system. It helps to be like that."

A third principal puts it plainly, "I would say, immerse yourself in the community. Learn about it; become part of it. Most administrators fail in small communities because they do not become part of it. Therefore, they have little or no support system."

But we hear a word of caution from a fourth principal who said, "Parents feel like this is their school. It is the center of the community. They feel they own it. As an administrator you are only a guest."

Taken together, these are sound suggestions for someone moving into the rural school principalship. We are reminded not only of the importance of becoming part of the community, but also that, depending on the circumstances, an administrator hired from outside the community may always be perceived as an outsider. In my discussions with these school leaders, I learned that some of them had become integral members of their communities, but others felt they would never be "one of them."

FOCUS ON PEOPLE AND RELATIONSHIPS

One principal stressed the need to have good interpersonal skills. She advised, "They need to know their community. In the rural community there is a lot more 'people' focus than there is 'business' focus. The school in the rural community is still a respected institution.

"The principal should understand who the key players are, and what the issues are. You need to be an extremely good listener and listen to the patrons of your district and know where they are coming from. Community people really feel that, if the school leaves their town, their town will die. The principal needs to listen to this.

"Small town people like the idea that their kid can walk to school. Many of our people have chosen to live here, where they went to school themselves."

Another principal believes that building positive relationships is the foundation for the school program. She said, "First, you have to be willing to accept people like they are and look for their strengths. Second, I think relationships are the key to working in a rural school. Third, you have to make your curriculum incorporate the strengths of the community. Make sure students can use the concepts you teach them in the life they live."

A third principal shared his suggestion for building relationships with students. He said, "Build trust. Develop a genuine concern and caring attitude toward your community. Place yourself in situations where you go to them, and they don't always have to come to you. Get on the school bus, and that will tell you about the kids. A school bus is a second class mode of transportation. When kids see you there, they see that you care."

Finally, one principal put it simply, "Try to deal with the people, not with policies, rules, and regulations. This is a people business. When you reduce people to something less than what you are, you reduce yourself, too."

BE SINCERE AND MOVE SLOWLY

One principal suggested a sequence to follow in establishing yourself. He said, "Get to know your people as quickly as you can, but don't make any major decisions to change things. That sends the message that, 'What you do is not good. I know better.' Then (after relationships are built) you can slowly focus on the things that need changing, but first get their buy-in."

Similarly, an assistant principal advised, "Develop an agenda slowly. Develop support for it, and make sure it does not stray too far from community values. Your direction must be consistent with community values, or you will be gone. Effective rural school leaders are the ones who can put new ideas in context with the old—make bridges between them.

EXPECT TO WORK HARD

One principal promotes not only working hard, but making sure the community recognizes you are working hard. He said, "Plan to work hard. You can't delegate. They already have their jobs, and they are working their guts out. A person who comes into a small town and works hard will gain their respect. For their money, they expect to see somebody working. In farm communities they work close to their homes—working some place else is foreign to them. They have a place-bound philosophy. When I go in to work on the weekends, I park my truck right in front so they know I am there."

Another administrator reflected on the amount of time and energy that are required. She said, "Be involved, but not too intimate. You have to have a good sense of self. You have to be able to take the hard knocks. You also have to be a high-energy person. I followed my husband for many years. Now that he is retired the district gets all of my time, about sixty hours per week."

Finally, one principal pointed out that rural schools often expect their principals to be servant leaders. He said, "The rural folks are quick to judge you on approachability, your word, your handshake. They don't agree with appointments. They have time off, you are a servant of the county, and they expect to see you."

CONCLUSION

This chapter illustrates some of the ways that rural school leaders are building on their unique strengths. My hope is that rural school leaders who read this chapter will be inspired to recognize the strengths of their communities so they can create more schools with fertile environments for children.

REFERENCES

Boyer, E. L. 1995. *The Basic School: A Community for Learning.* Princeton, NJ: The Carnegie Foundation for the Advancement of Teaching.

Council of Chief State School Officers. 1996. *Interstate School Leaders Licensure Consortium: Standards for School Leaders.* Washington, DC: Author.

Donaldson, G., & G. Marnik. 1995. *As Leaders Learn.* Thousand Oaks, CA: Corwin Press.

Dryman, S. 1997. "Innovator: Schools Are Communties—Principal Transforms Small, Rural School into a Model of Achievement," *Asheville Citizen Times,* March 23, A10.

Gregory, T., & G. Smith. 1987. *High Schools as Communities: The Small School Reconsidered.* Bloomington, IN: Phi Delta Kappa Educational Foundation.

Howley, C. 1997. Studying the Rural in Education: Nation-Building, "Globalization," and School Improvement. Educational Policy Analysis Archives. (http://olam.ed.asu.edu/epaa/)

Johnson, J., & S. Farkas. 1997. *Getting By: What American Teenagers Really Think About Their Schools.* New York: Public Agenda.

Nachtigal, P. 1996. Personal correspondence.

Sher, J. 1995. *The Annenberg Rural Challenge: An Introduction and Invitation.* Granby, CO: The Annenberg Rural Challenge.

CHAPTER 9

Southern Schools, Southern Teachers: Redefining Leadership in Rural Communities

Teaching is not what I expected. When I grew up in rural West Virginia and went to school, I remember what teachers did and I remember the role that they played. There was pride in teaching. High school teachers were looked at as leaders in the community and people that you looked up to. Those days are gone. People feel, and I didn't realize this until I was teaching, it's kind of degrading to say, "I'm a high school teacher." You have to say it under your breath. I used to think people had a lot of respect for high school teachers, but I feel that they don't anymore. It's just a guy who wants to teach school is just the attitude I get now. That's kind of an embarrassment to me because I do enjoy it.—High School Teacher

This chapter discusses attempts to redefine the roles and responsibilities of teachers working in leadership roles in southern schools. The context for this discussion is by necessity shaped by the prevalence of rural poverty and notions about the deficits inherent in rural communities in the South. Teachers as leaders is presented as a metaphor for school improvement while simultaneously addressing issues related to teacher dissatisfaction with the profession.

INTRODUCTION

TEACHING has traditionally attracted individuals who come to the profession for the right reasons but find the public schools are the wrong institutions for their dreams and aspirations. Teachers express dissatisfaction with the profession for many reasons, but most focus on the dissatisfactions associated with

Eleanor Blair Hilty, Department of Educational Leadership and Foundations, Western Carolina University.

© Photo by Rob Amberg.

a "lack of autonomy, self-esteem, and extrinsic rewards" (Newman, 1994, p. 11). Efforts to empower teachers have generally focused on site-based management or other collaborative efforts to share decision-making responsibilities between teachers, parents, and administrators. At a professional level, these efforts have also taken the form of proposals for mediated entry into a differentiated profession as well as mentoring programs and merit pay schemes. Efforts to recognize the various levels of skill, education, and expertise of teachers open the door to opportunities for teachers to assume important leadership roles beyond the classroom; roles that may challenge traditional notions of school leadership. Nevertheless, these proposals offer teachers few meaningful opportunities for "real" change or impact on the shape and direction of school programs, and on the professional status of teachers.

Teachers, given their front-line responsibilities have always played some of the most significant roles in schools; however, issues surrounding the "feminization" of the profession have limited a serious consideration of teachers as leaders; for example, teaching is seen as a semi-profession with few opportunities for advancement, increased levels of responsibilities or pay; a profession that allows for easy entry and even easier reentry after extended periods of unemployment outside the home. And yet, in earlier times, schools were small, and particular teachers often assumed the key roles of both teacher and principal. Even today, as secondary programs consolidate and expand, teachers are given opportunities to assume the roles of department head or lead teacher in various curricular or program areas. These shifting responsibilities have seldom been explored or considered phenomena worthy of discussion, and yet, it seems that teachers should be some of the most important participants in any discussion of school effectiveness and the changing aims and purposes of schools. If we truly want to meet the challenge of public schools for a new century, teachers must guide our vision of where we are going, and most importantly, how we can get there.

The past decade has produced numerous national reports that have called for reform of American education. These reports have reflected the depth of public dissatisfaction with the schools. Public schools are most often perceived as institutions that no longer "work"; a significant portion of young people fail or drop out of school each year and good teachers either leave the profession or "burn out." Critics of American education argue that the welfare of this nation is in jeopardy if the public schools do not commit to meaningful change in this decade. These concerns, while treated as generic to all schools, ignore the important differences that set apart schools in urban, suburban, and rural school districts. In fact, efforts to talk about *all* schools or *all* communities are flawed due to the organization and structuring of schools in the United States where states and local education agencies have tremendous autonomy with regard to the rules and regulations that govern their public schools.

Attempts to "re-form" or restructure the schools in a new image have most often lacked an ideology that informs or shapes the direction of these efforts. While questions about curriculum, tests, and the merits of site-based management are central to recent attempts to make the public schools more amenable to the needs of society, even these issues require the leadership of a core of individuals guided by a set of beliefs that reflects a commitment to equity and excellence while valuing the sanctity of the relationship between school and community. Calls for action are, most often, general and provide little direction for the restructuring of schools that include a reconsideration of the roles and responsibilities of those professionals who work in these institutions.

CONTEXTUALIZING THE CONVERSATION: THE SIGNIFICANCE OF RURAL COMMUNITIES AND SCHOOLS

It is not possible to discuss school leadership issues in rural communities and schools without considering the significance of both geographical and economic forces that provide an important context for such a discussion. For example, rural schools and rural school districts are characterized as having qualities that taken together set them apart from their urban and suburban counterparts:

- Rural schools and rural school districts usually enroll small numbers of pupils (i.e., fewer than 1,000 pupils per school district).
- Rural school districts commonly are experiencing significant enrollment decline.
- Rural residents report incomes significantly less than their urban and suburban peers.
- Rural school districts usually employ school buildings that house smaller numbers of pupils.
- Rural school districts typically are sparsely populated.
- Due primarily to small numbers of pupils generally located in large geographic areas, per-pupil transportation costs for rural school are inordinately high.
- Due to the absence of significant trading centers, rural school districts often are nearly exclusively dependent on real property taxation for their local revenue. (Stern, 1994, p. 48)

Discussions of rural communities and schools by necessity focus our attention upon some of the core values and beliefs that shape rural life. DeYoung and Lawrence (1995) quote Stern:

> The family, the church, and the school have been at the heart of rural communities since this country was settled. These three institutions have provided the standards of behavior, circles of personal interaction, and a variety of social activities that collectively shape community ethos and identity. . . . So powerful is the interaction between community members and the school that rural residents often retain the feeling of belonging to the school, even into adulthood when they begin their own families. (Stern, 1994, p. 21)

The centrality of the school to the community is also discussed in the following:

> Ties to community, place, and family are often strong in rural communities, and it is in the local schoolhouse where many of these attachments are formed and solidified. At the the same time, the academic skills and values emphasized today often run counter to the values of place and community. This contradiction is particularly visible in places where personal relationships and attachments to place go back for generations. (DeYoung & Lawrence, 1995, p.108)

Consider also the importance of regional differences that form a rich tapestry, and thus provide both color and texture to issues that cease to be generic and become responsive to regional idiosyncrasies. Kincheloe and Pinar (1991) remind us of the qualities of "place" that set apart southern communities, and yes, even southern schools.

> Southerners have come to know their world through particularity and place. Such a way of knowing finds itself much more at home with philosophical, historical, and artistic modes of understanding human affairs than with the analytical modes of the behavioral and social sciences. . . . The modern era with its ever-spreading industrialization of the South and its conquest of more and more southern schools with its technocratic education is attempting to correct this "anachronistic" southernism. (p. 12)

Furthermore,

> A southern sense of place implies an historical awareness that expresses itself in an attachment to the extended family—a localism of the Gemeinshaft variety. This southern localism involves a tendency to think of communities as distinct from one another and to prefer one's own. . . . Such sensitivities often translate into a preference for the concrete over the abstract that places concern with personal, family, and community relations on a higher level of priority than legal, contractual, and formal bureaucratic conventions. (Kincheloe & Pinar, 1991, pp. 12–13)

While "place" impacts the schools in important ways, it is the intersection of rural poverty with geography that completes the picture of southern schools and communities. Rural poverty and the troubled schools that accompany limited resources do not occur equally across the United States. Books (1997) argues that "contrary to the idea that poverty 'concentrates' itself in the inner-city ghettos of the North, more of the poor live in the South than in any other region of the United States . . . The South contains all but eighteen of the 206 'persistently low-wage counties' in the nation, along with almost 54 percent of the rural poor" (Williams & Dill, 1995, p. 345, cited in Books, p. 76). Stern (1994) documents the existence of rural poverty in every region, but indicates that "it is most severe in the southern United States" (p. 9), where she found, "two-thirds of the nation's rural blacks and 95 percent of rural black children, as well as most of its growing rural Hispanic population, are concentrated there. The prevalence in rural areas of low incomes and poverty, as well as less educational attainment, is even greater among these population groups" (U.S. Department of Commerce, Bureau of the Census, 1991, cited in Stern, 1994, p. 9). Qualities associated with a lack of economic wealth set rural schools apart from their urban and suburban counterparts. DeYoung and Lawrence (1995) describe these schools in the following:

> It is still true that most chronically poor counties in the nation are located in rural areas, particularly in Appalachia and in the South. In 1986 the nonmetropolitan poverty rate was 50% higher than the metropolitan rate. In fact, general poverty rates in the late 1980s for all nonmetropolitan counties nearly equaled those of our central cities. The rate of rural poverty in the 1980s remained higher, rose more rapidly, and fell more slowly than the metropolitan rate. (p. 106)

However, Books (1997) directs our attention to the fact that most discussions of poverty ignore the realities of rural poverty, "rural poverty contrasts sharply with urban poverty, made hypervisible through a sensationalized focus on the sex, drugs, and violence to which the media has reduced the lives of the inner-city poor" (p. 74). Instead, the reality of rural poverty manifests itself as "unemployment and underemployment," which leads to "increased poverty, emigration, and changing family patterns" (Stern, 1994, p. 11). These conditions affect all aspects of life in rural communities, but most notably, they impact the availability of resources for those institutions charged with serving the civic, educational, and social needs of the community. Even in the South, where the funding of school programs has never been a high priority, schools were, nevertheless, important institutions central to the life of the community. Recently, however, economic woes have threatened the cohesiveness and vitality of these communities and their schools. "Local communities rely heavily on the use of property taxes to fund education . . . the result for much of Rural America is under-funded schools, declining enrollments, limited curricula, aging facilities, and persistent pockets of functional illiteracy" (Stephens, 1988; Bailey et al., 1992, cited in Stern, 1994, p. 21).

These figures may not be surprising but they contribute to stereotypical notions of rural Appalachia as "educationally and culturally deprived," and if one sees "education as the road to economic well-being for the nation" (Seal & Harmon, 1995, p. 119), the educational agenda of rural schools and communities beomes an important issue. And yet, Ogbu (1990) warns social scientists that "in their eagerness to bring about change, they often design their studies not so much to understand the total situation as to discover what *is wrong* and how the situation should be changed." His final caution is worthy of consideration: "this approach leads to the wrong kinds of questions, the wrong kinds of answers and the wrong kinds of solutions" (p. 398). He is telling us that the questions we ask often determine the answers. If we talk about the poor rural schools and communities in the South as a problem then the lack of advantages associated with economic wealth becomes the focus of our solutions. DeYoung and Lawrence (1995) also question notions about the "problems" in rural schools:

> The problem of rural schools in America is indeed a function of the problem of rural life, but we contend that the rural life problem is really to convince those who live in the city that their success is to no small extent built upon the backs and minds of those who still live (often, by choice) in the country. It may be difficult, if not impossible, to convince the American elite and the private sector that metropolitan living is not the ultimate human experince. (p. 112)

It seems important to redefine the national educational agenda within a context that recognizes the uniqueness of the issues affecting rural schools. While most of these issues are part of broader educational problems, they can only be effectively addressed if we recognize the strengths (and weaknesses) of rural schools and communities in the South and build our solutions upon that foundation.

"MAKING THE FAMILIAR STRANGE AND THE STRANGE FAMILIAR": TEACHING AND LEADING IN RURAL SCHOOLS

For most people, the hardest part about studying schools and questioning "taken-for-granted assumptions" about how we "do" schools is the fact that we are all so familiar with schools. We have lived, breathed, and often thrived in these institutions that have become a major instrument for the socialization of children in America. Thus, it is difficult to question the integrity of these institutions or the motives of those who work within the confines of public education (e.g., to make the familiar strange). And yet, central to any effort to reinvent school in a new image requires a consideration of the role of leadership in these schools and a visualization of leadership as a broader based, yet essential quality in most educators. Administrators have typically been seen as the key source of leadership in individual schools; however, recent efforts to empower teachers and consider their relationship to authoritarian leaders as well as efforts to initiate successful reform efforts at individual schools require a redefining of these relationships. The utilization of teachers as leaders will be especially important in rural communities where resources are limited and teachers provide important links between the community's values, beliefs, and attitudes and those reflected by the public schools. Additionally, teachers are often the first individuals parents establish a relationship with in the schools. Administrators, by virtue of their tasks and administrative responsibilities, are often perceived as inaccessible figures of authority. Once again, teachers represent the most likely candidates to lead schools toward a renewed vision of effective schools that articulate and work to achieve aims and purposes that are connected to and serving real communities.

Most of the decisions that guide the daily lives of teachers are made by individuals removed from the tasks and responsibilities that characterize teaching. A lack of control over their work environment diminishes the attempts of teachers to practice as autonomous professionals committed to providing both pedagogical and administrative leadership. Consider their sense of powerlessness in specific areas of their work. As a group, teachers are often powerless to implement meaningful change in their own classrooms. The talents of individual teachers are "chained" to "teacher-proof" curricula that limit independent and creative action (Giroux, 1988). This orientation has further contributed to the "deskilling" of teachers; a process whereby the level of skill required to teach is diminished (Pinar, 1989).

Teacher education does little to prepare teachers to become leaders in institutions where they have little power, status or decision-making ability. A failure to recognize the lack of congruity between teacher training and practice means that potential teachers receive training that provides little preparation for placement in teaching assignments where the "realities" of teaching force new teachers to exchange their ideals for educational practices that do not meet the educational challenges of a new decade or recognize the special skills, training, and expertise of some of the most highly educated individuals in the community. Teachers as leaders in their schools and communities are the key to good schools, yet we won't see these kinds of teachers emerge in environments that are authoritarian and do little to liberate the talents of individual teachers.

Teachers as leaders becomes a metaphor that should guide our thinking about how schools are structured and run on a daily basis; a metaphor that redefines roles and relationships while addressing issues of power and authority. And yet, a metaphor that disregards issues of gender, race or ethnicity unless one examines the statistics associated with gender and the delineation of roles and responsibilites in the schools. Ironically, while women teachers outnumber men seven to one in rural communities (Stern, 1994, p. 33) 83 percent of rural administrators are male (Stern, p. 36). While large numbers of rural teachers indicate that they exercise "considerable control over the instructional process in their classroom," a much smaller proportion report that they have " 'a great deal of influence' over various aspects of school policy that included discipline, in-service training, ability grouping, and curriculum" (Stern, 1994, p. 35). In contrast, "large proportions of rural school principals exercise considerable control over key administrative areas" (Stern, 1994, p. 37). Is it simply a coincidence that the vast majority of individuals in leadership positions in the schools are male? In Weiler's (1988) study of women teachers and administrators she found that "They inherit positions in already existing, highly complex institutions . . . Feminist and antiracist teachers and administrators who seek to redefine curriculum and social relationships inside and outside the classroom find themselves in conflict with existing patriarchal ideology and hierarchical relationships" (p. 101).

Teachers as leaders is by necessity a gender issue that forces us to confront institutional forces that limit the choices available to women teachers or that refuse to affirm and reward styles of leadership that vary from the traditional. This conflict is most evident in struggles surrounding power and authority. Teachers have traditionally played subordinate roles in the schools, and attempts to empower teachers and give them more decision-making responsibilities frequently meet with resistence in schools that are situated in tradition-bound, conservative communities. While there are many exceptions to any generalization, rural communities in the South have typically seen males in the most powerful, public positions, and women exerting their power within the domain of the church, family, and various civic organizations. These prescribed roles and responsibilities impact the ease with which teachers, who are for the most part women, can begin to challenge their subordinate roles and to demand a larger role in the leadership of these schools.

The qualities of rural communities that set them apart from suburban or urban communities are the qualities that "set the stage" for understanding the significance of the notion of teachers operating as leaders in the classroom and in schools and communities. Several years ago when I had the luxury of teaching about leadership in my preservice teacher education classes, I would begin the class by showing the film classic *Twelve Angry Men*. I encouraged students to begin to understand the power and agency of individual action, in particular, the power of individual action guided by a strong sense of ethics and the importance of equity. Students were often moved by a consideration of how powerful their roles could potentially be in classrooms, schools, and communities. Also in these classes, I had students follow up with a desert survival exercise where the mutual survival of the participants depended on thoughtful, collective (and collaborative) action. While these exercises were fun and interesting, they never failed to impress students with the importance of listening, really listening, to all perspectives. At some point our mutual success (and survival) depends upon individuals in the group working together toward a common goal and vision. Why should schools be guided by the vision or efforts of a single individual? Is it not more powerful to envision schools that provide multiple roles and levels of responsibilities for leaders working collectively toward a renewed vision of successful schools? A vision that honors the importance of schools and communities working together and setting an agenda that reflects the values, beliefs and attitudes of the people within that community. A vision that places the responsbility of "leading" on those people most likely to understand the community and its educational priorities; the teachers.

TEACHERS AS LEADERS

Teachers as leaders have several qualities, but perhaps the most important is one's willingness to treat leadership as both a managerial and intellectual process. The process must be emphasized, not the outcomes. A focus on outcomes obstructs a consideration of the proper role of the classroom teacher as an intellectual (Giroux, 1988). Good leaders are intellectuals first and critical decision-makers second. It is the ability of leaders to be constantly reviewing their actions and evaluating outcomes that sets them apart from machines. At a minimum, good leaders must constantly question the unstated or "taken-for-granted" assumptions and beliefs that guide the operation of schools. There is an absence of research on the ways in which teachers understand and think about school leadership or even the manner in which one experiences a mutual sharing of leadership responsibilities and roles outside the traditional definitions of how schools operate.

Seeing teachers in this manner requires that we have multiple models of teachers as leaders. Teachers, both good and bad, bring to teaching a culmination of experiences both personal and professional. They come to teaching with a set of beliefs about the world generally, and about school leadership specifically. Leadership styles are idiosyncratic and take different forms. It is a process that is defined and mediated by the experiences of particular teachers working in specific schools and communities. It is paradoxical that efforts to improve the schools have excluded teachers from the dialogue when ultimately they are the individuals who will fail or succeed at reforming American education. They will choose to assume important leadership roles in the schools or they will be faced with the dilemma of following or defeating the efforts of those who take these roles.

> Rural communities and their schools have unique needs—it is important for rural teachers to begin to articulate those social and cultural phenomena that impact their schools and classrooms and for us as educators to begin to train teachers to be leaders in rural schools—to empower teachers, students, and parents to articulate a vision of culturally relevant pedagogy that recognizes the unique social and cultural identities of southern schools and communities.

Teachers are accustomed to viewing the teaching process as both art and skill. So it is perhaps easier for them to recognize that leadership is also a creative endeavor. Good leaders facilitate the establishment of learning communities that produce teachers, students, and parents who are independent, self-motivated thinkers and actors. Good schools are characterized by an environment of mutual respect, collaboration, and connection. These schools recognize the cultural diversity that exists even in relatively homogenous rural populations. That diversity is both a part of the process and a product of "making do" in poor isolated communities that are nonetheless characterized by a "rich" awareness of a heritage that both binds and separates one group from another; a heritage that is both political, social, geographic and psychological. Good leaders take the time to recognize and affirm these differences. They create an atmosphere for dialogue, reflection, and debate, while simultaneously encouraging the development of intellectual skills that lead to critical, reflective thinking. Good leaders share the responsibility for learning with all members of that community. And not surprisingly, good leaders are also good learners. They are exemplary models of a lifetime commitment to thinking, questioning, and continuous learning. An appreciation of the many styles of good leaders would liberate teachers who see themselves to develop a style of leadership that reflects their understanding of teaching, leading, and learning.

LEADING "AGAINST THE GRAIN"

Seeing teachers as leaders in schools requires one to begin to confront the obstacles that have prevented them from assuming these roles in the past. Some of these obstacles are related to gender bias, but others are more personal, related to narrow definitions of leadership roles and responsibilities within schools and communities. It seems imperative that teachers be prepared to work as leaders in rural schools that are characterized by poverty and high levels of failure or underachievement. However, one cannot assume that these problems are characteristic of all rural schools; the research documents the following:

> Inequities in the availability of courses at the secondary level, though most small schools offered a basic curriculum and not all large schools offered an enriched one. Nevertheless, student achievement in small schools equaled or exceeded that of students in large schools, suggesting that the climate in small schools may propel students to excel in spite of certain material disadvantages. (Stern, 1994, p. 57)

And yet, once again it is important to consider that schools in the South continue to have high dropout rates and one still sees "the persistence of low average incomes, high rates of poverty, and low educational achievement " (Stern, 1994, p. 66). These schools may soon outnumber their more successful counterpart in the suburbs. New teachers often "shy away" from these environments out of fear and ignorance. And, who can blame them? Which one of us would seek out an opportunity to greet "failure," marginalization, and the effects of poverty on a daily basis? If demographic projections are accurate, we must acquaint large numbers of new teachers with the cognitive and pedagogical strategies that will enable them to be successful in these schools. Successful role models who are enthusiastic and excited by this challenge are a good beginning. Cochran-Smith (1991) conceptualized the notion of "teaching against the grain." I would like to propose that in rural schools, teachers who assume leadership roles must also embrace this concept. Cochran-Smith described this skill in the following:

> Teaching against the grain stems from, but also generates, critical perspectives on the macro-level relationships of power, labor, and ideology-relationships that are

perhaps best examined at the university, where sustained and systematic study is possible. But teaching against the grain is also deeply embedded in the culture and history of teaching at individual schools and in the biographies of particular teachers and their individual or collaborative efforts to alter curricula, raise question about common practices, and resist inappropriate decisions. These relationships can only be explored in schools in the company of experienced teachers who are themselves engaged in complex, situation-specific, and sometimes losing struggles to work against the grain. (p. 280)

It seems intuitively obvious that teachers acting as leaders must begin to "lead against the grain" in schools where poverty and school failure are pervasive, and the aims and purposes of the schools are not congruent with those of the community. "Leading against the grain" is critical in schools where teachers acting in leadership roles is implicitly expected, but not facilitated by a bureaucratic structure that govern the organization and structure of the schools. Teachers must become more involved in the day-to-day decision-making and planning that govern their lives. In collaboration with other teachers, they must create a "place" in schools for the dialogue and sharing that is a prerequisite for a critical examination of teaching and learning communities, and the creation of better teachers, better schools, and better students.

In rural communities, teachers need to provide leadership by respecting the consciousness and culture of their students and creating communities where students and parents can express the relationship of educational institutions to their needs and aspirations. The concept of "scaffolding" has often been used to describe the social relations and reciprocity inherent in the teaching and learning process (Erickson, 1984; Ladson-Billings, 1994; Wood, Bruner, & Ross, 1976). The value of this metaphor lies in its emphasis upon the interconnectedness of the teaching/learning process. I would like to propose that this metaphor is equally descriptive of the work of teachers acting as leaders in schools, classrooms, and communities. Borrowing from the ideas of Ladson-Billings (1994), I can see teachers as leaders providing "scaffolding" for other teachers. In this way, they are helping teachers "move from what they know to what they need to know" as both teachers and learners (p. 124). They are allowed "to build upon their own experiences, knowledge, and skills to move into more difficult knowledge and skills. Rather than chastise them for what they do not know, these teachers find ways to use the knowledge and skills" that others bring to the schools "as a foundation for learning" and leading (p. 124).

REFORM AND ITS RELATIONSHIP TO RURAL SCHOOLS: REDEFINING LEADERSHIP

The educational landscape is littered with the remains of failed school reforms, many of which failed because of the social conditions surrounding the schools.

> Only those reforms that recognize these conditions and actively engage them are likely to make a lasting difference in the lives of the children, educators, and communities served by the schools. . . . Democratic educators seek not simply to lessen the harshness of social inequities in school, but to change the conditions that create them. (Beane & Apple, 1995, p. 11)

Democratic schools need educators dedicated to both equity and excellence. The ideas encompassed by these ideals, however, must be modeled and "lived" by the individuals given primary responsibility for making our schools "work." We cannot ask teachers to create democratic classrooms if they do not work in schools and communities that give them a voice in the decisions that guide both their personal and professional lives. This voice in the affairs that guide their roles and responsibilities as teachers requires that they be utilized in meaningful positions as leaders in the school; roles that are inherently political and involve the granting of legitimate power and authority. Teachers in leadership roles not defined as simply control or management responsibilities, will, perhaps, redefine leadership as guidance and facilitation in areas vitally important; however, these may not be areas typically defined as key administrative areas. For example, areas where the contributions and leadership of teachers is vital include addressing working condition issues, instructional issues, issues related to licensure, evaluation, entry into the profession, mentoring, and so on. Additionally, teachers need to be central participants in a reexamination of staff development issues, school-community partnerships, and the creation of collaborative, collective responses to issues that have a negative impact on the profession. An important element of this process is the opportunity to tap a valuable resource in our schools, and, perhaps address some of the issues that cause teachers to feel most dissatisfied with their work environments (e.g., lack of autonomy, self-esteem, and extrinsice rewards). Using teachers' expertise to guide, judge, and direct the progress of their profession gives teachers opportunities to invest in the future of their profession to explore the sources of inequities and oppression both in the profession and in our relationships with students and parents. If we are to uphold the democratic ideal of equality of opportunity, the voices of good (and successful) teachers acting as leaders in their schools and communities must be included in our efforts to create democratic schools where teachers are purposefully working to provide quality of educational opportunity and excellence for all children in all communities.

Rural communities and their schools have unique needs—it is important for rural teachers to begin to articulate those social and cultural phenomena that impact their schools and classrooms and for us as educators to begin to train teachers to be leaders in rural schools—to empower teachers, students, and parents to articulate a vision of culturally relevant pedagogy that recognizes the unique social and cultural identities of southern schools and communities. Ladson-Billings (1994) describes this process as teaching (leading) that "uses student culture in order to maintain it and to transcend the negative effects of the dominant culture" (p. 17). While Ladson-Billings uses this concept to talk about successful teachers of African-American children, it seems equally relevant to discussions of the work being done by individuals in rural communities where they daily confront the biases of politicians representing the interests of a dominant culture that does not value the contributions (or needs) of rural schools and communities. And certainly, while bias does exist about the aims and purposes of education in rural regions of the country, this bias is exacerbated by preconceived notions about the inferiority of southern schools and southern culture.

Southern schools in rural communities can serve as sites for both the amelioration of social problems and institutions that support teachers as change agents charged with challenging the status quo. It is important that teachers question assumptions about the best policies for reforming rural schools in the South, particularly with regard to the social purposes of education. Bondy and Ross (1992) suggest that "Changing the status quo in schools requires the collective efforts of teachers. Teachers need to learn how to gain power and influence . . . [a need to] help teachers develop the micro-policical awareness and competence needs to foster collaborative action among teachers and improve the school experiences of students" (p. 13).

"Changing the status quo" is not easy, and those of us who make these recommendations must be cognizant that "teachers are more rewarded when [they] do not teach against the grain. The choice to work against the grain, to challenge the status quo, often has negative consequences" (Hooks, 1994, p. 203). And thus, teachers as leaders requires a restructuring, or perhaps a reinvention of the school environment.

Proposals for the reform of schools have emphasized the top-down control of the profession (Bennett & LeCompte, 1990; Hill, 1989). More recent legislative mandates have emphasized the establishment of site-based management in the schools. It is difficult, however, to not be suspicious of top-down mandates for bottom-up control of the schools. What if the people at the "bottom" refuse to cooperate with plans that do not support the implicit agenda of these legislators? Teachers acting as leaders in schools will help their colleagues (and students) better understand the purpose of a vision guided by the democratic principles that have shaped our society while simultaneously questioning practices that lead to the inequitable distribution of knowledge, power and resources (Giroux, 1989; Greene, 1985). Good teachers will become good leaders in their schools when they decide to do so, and they will only decide to do so when they receive from other leaders respect and affirmation of the special skills and knowledge they bring to the leadership process. First, however, these teachers must be pedagogical leaders who attempt to transform and empower students, parents, and even other teachers through experiences that foster critical and reflective inquiry. Teachers must work in environments that allow them to model theses skills. Administrators should work for these teachers, or at the very least, act as colleagues who share equally the responsibility for designing successful schools. Many people would find this latter proposition laughable, since it is a radical departure from the situation in most schools. However, it is the unequal distribution of power in most schools that has consistently led to the mediocre performance of both teachers and students. I argue that we will not see teachers as leaders become the norm in our schools until new teachers enter the schools with the knowledge and skills to confidently demand the right to work in an environment that recognizes them as competent professionals and allows them to freely and optimally do what they have been trained to do, teach and lead.

REFERENCES

Bailey, G., P. Daisey, S. M. Maes, & J. D. Spears. 1992. *Literacy in Rural America: A Study of Current Needs and Practices.* Manhattan, KS: Rural Clearinghouse on Lifelong Education and Development.

Beane, J. A., & M. W. Apple. 1995. "The Case for Democratic Schools," In M. W. Apple, & J. A. Beane (eds.). *Democratic Schools*, 1–25. Alexandria, VA: Association for Supervision and Curriculum Development.

Bennett, K. P., & M. D. LeCompte. 1990. *How Schools Work: A Sociological Analysis of Education.* White Plains, NY: Longman.

Bondy, E., & D. Ross. 1992. "Micro-Political Competence: How Teachers Can Change the Status Quo," *The Clearing House*, September/October, 10–14.

Books, S. 1997. "The Other Poor: Rural Poverty and Education," *Educational Foundations, 11*(1), 73–85.

Cochran-Smith, M. 1991. "Learning to Teach Against the Grain," *Harvard Educational Review, 61*(3), 279–307.

DeYoung, A. & B. K. Lawrence. 1995. "On Hoosiers, Yankees, and Mountaineers," *Phi Delta Kappan, 77*(2), 104–112.

Erickson, F. E. 1984. "School Literacy, Reasoning, and Civility: An Anthropoligists's Perspective," *Review of Educational Research, 54*(4), 525–546.

Giroux, H. 1988. *Teachers as Intellectuals: Toward a Critical Pedagogy of Learning.* South Hadley, MA: Bergin & Garvey.

Giroux, H. 1989. "Rethinking Education Reform in the Age of George Bush," *Phi Delta Kappan, 71*(8), 728–730.

Greene, M. 1985. "The Role of Education in a Democracy," *Educational Horizons, 63*, 3–9.

Hill, D. 1989. "Fixing the System from the Top Down," *Teacher Magazine*, September/October, 50–55.

Kincheloe, J. L. & W. F. Pinar (eds.). 1991. *Curriculum as Social Psychonanlysis: The Significance of Place.* New York: State University of New York Press.

Ladson-Billings, G. 1994. *The Dreamkeepers: Successful Teachers of African American Children.* San Francisco: Jossey-Bass Publishers.

Newman, J. 1994. *America's Teachers: An Introduction to Education* (Second Edition). New York: Longman Publishing Group.

Seal, K. R., & H. L. Harmon. 1995. "Realities of Rural School Reform," *Phi Delta Kappan, 77*(2), 119–124.

Stephens, E. R. 1988. "The Changing Context of Education in a Rural Setting," Occasional Paper 26. Charleston, WV: Appalachia Educational Laboratory.

Stern, Joyce D. (ed.). 1994. *The Condition of Education in Rural Schools*. Washington, DC: U.S. Department of Education.

U.S. Department of Commerce. 1991. Bureau of the Census. *Poverty in the United States: 1990*. Current Population Reports, Series P-60, No. 175. Washington, DC: Author.

Weiler, K. 1988. *Women Teaching for Change: Gender, Class & Power*. South Hadley, MA: Bergin & Garvey Publishers, Inc.

Williams, B., & B. Dill. 1995. "African-American in the Rural South: The Persistence of Racism and Poverty," In *The Changing American Countryside: Rural People and Places*, ed. by Emery Castle. Lawrence, KS: University Press of Kansas.

Wood, B., J. Bruner, & G. Ross. 1976. "The Role of Tutoring in Problem Solving," *Journal of Child Psychology and Psychiatry, 17*, 89–100.

CHAPTER 10

Students Are People, Too

You can BS a BS'er, but you can't BS the kids.—John Black and Fenwick English, 1986

This chapter presents a rationale for active involvement of students in rural school leadership, a review of the literature suggesting the advantages of rural schools and their relationship to student-focused reform, reasons for listening to students, an explanation of democratic schools, research on extracurricular activities and leadership opportunities, student participation in solving discipline problems, and student voices in the curriculum content and its delivery. The chapter also features exemplary programs.

INTRODUCTION

R ESEARCH and best practice, while providing valuable information for school improvement, are often based on the performance of students and the opinions of adults. Sometimes lost in the many recommendations for education are the fresh, insightful voices of students. Rural schools are in an ideal position to listen to these voices and many are responding through student participation in school governance, peer leadership opportunities, and provisions for choice in content and curriculum. Indeed, forward-thinking adults in rural schools are realizing that students are people too.

Anna Hicks, Department of Educational Leadership and Foundations, Western Carolina University.

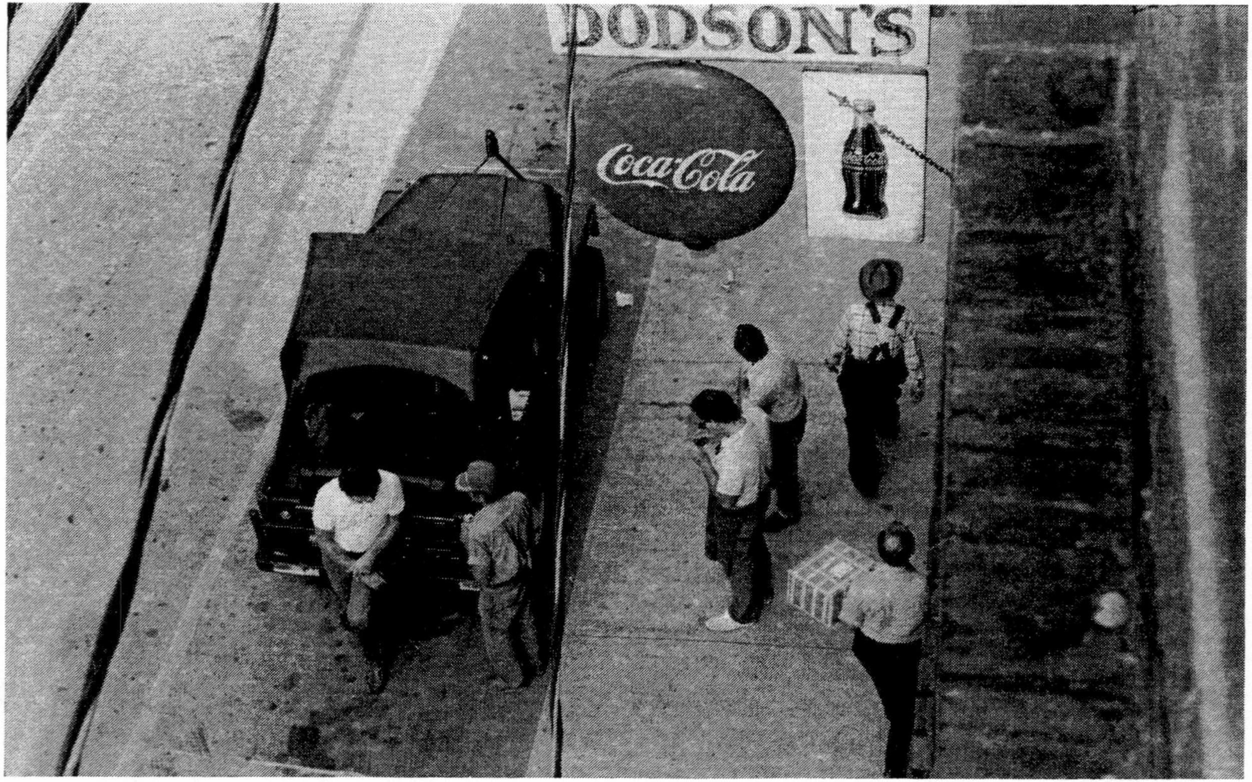

© Photo by Rob Amberg.

THE RURAL ADVANTAGE

LITERATURE REVIEW

A review of the literature suggests that rural schools enjoy advantages that place them in unique positions to embrace student-focused school reform. For example, Stern (1994) noted that seven million students, 17 percent of the K–12 population in the United States attend rural schools and that 20 percent of public schools enroll fewer than 100 students. Size is one of the rural school's greatest advantages. AASA Executive Director Paul Houston (1996) reminded the membership that a recent Northwest Regional Laboratory study in Portland, Oregon, by Kathleen Cotton showed that small schools are superior to large ones in almost every respect. He cited more positive student attitudes, higher attendance rates, lower dropout rates, and a greater sense of belonging. He also noted a higher level of participation in extracurricular activities and fewer incidents of negative social behavior.

CLASS SIZE, RELATIONSHIPS, SENSE OF COMMUNITY

Research on rural schools supports these findings and suggests that rural schools enjoy opportunities for peer tutoring, small class size, and whole grade sharing (1992, NREA Proceedings). Kearney (1994) observed more community involvement in rural schools with close personal relationships among the various stakeholders. Similarly Miller and Hull (1991) noted that class size in rural schools allows for more informal social climate and fewer discipline problems. Stern (1994) also found lower pupil-teacher ratios in rural schools. Nachtigal (1992) and Sher (1981) observed strong positive leadership, high expectations of student and teacher achievement, respectful relationships, emphasis on academic basics, a sense of community, lively interactions, mainstreaming, and a healthy balance of activities. Informal communication systems, integrated teacher roles, and greater community influence in rural schools were findings in Capper's 1991 work.

POSITIVE MESSAGES, GOVERNANCE, AND INTERDEPENDENCE

Other rural advantages are evident in Nachitgal (1992), who found rural schools to be well-cared for centers of the community where students receive positive messages about the importance of the school. Nachitgal's earlier 1982 work comparing urban to rural schools found that rural school leadership is more nonbureaucratic and focuses on teaching students to be entrepreneurs. Lewis (1992) observed that in rural schools, students receive extra attention, opportunities for active participation and for experiencing the presence of a significant adult, as well as the opportunity for cooperative and experiential settings for study. Dodendorf (1983) found in rural schools positive interdependence among students.

Such advantages suggest that rural schools perhaps offer answers to the problems created by the factory model of education that often results in large, unmanageable, impersonal settings for students. Often the result of consolidation in the name of efficiency, such schools often lose the opportunity to create communities of learners, where the voices of students could indeed be heard and valued.

ADVANTAGES AND REFORM

SCHOOL SIZE

Ted Sizer (1992), founder of the Coalition of Essential Schools, in his recommendations for redesigning the American high school, reminds us that, "Good schools differ" (p. 62). Augenblick and Nachtigal (1985), Sher (1981), and Stern (1994) observed much diversity in rural schools. In other words, there is no model; instead, good schools are reflections of the communities they serve. Sizer (1996) also advocates small school as places where relationships are possible. He observes, "Good large middle schools are an oxymoron" (p. 30). He adds, "It is that the school itself has to be of human scale—a place where everyone can know everyone else" (p. 91). Deborah Meier (1995) offers several reasons why small schools are essential to reform and meeting the needs of students:

(1) Democracy is possible.

(2) Faculty can be held accountable for their work collectively.

(3) Teachers can get to know a student's work.

(4) Small schools offer safety.

(5) Accountability to parents and public is a matter of access.

(6) Students can be immersed into a culture the faculty in the school worked to shape.

With the advantage of smallness, rural schools can position themselves to truly discover the most significant reform of all—the inclusion of students in school governance, leadership, and curriculum decisions of the school.

WHY LISTEN TO STUDENTS?

As educators make the move from top-down school management to a more flattened approach to school governance, it becomes clear that schools are not just about buildings, budgets, teachers, and curriculum. Schools are about relationships—relationships among all the stakeholders in the school—administrators, parents, teachers, support staff, community members, and students. And good schools realize that the core of all relationships and all decisions in a school is students. Such a focus changes the way educators play out their roles in schools.

NEW ROLES FOR EDUCATORS

John Black and Fenwick English (1986), in *What They Don't Tell You in Schools of Education about School Administration*, suggest that the role of the building principal is to ensure that, whenever possible, every situation in the building becomes a learning situation. Such a role is reminiscent of the early days of the principalship when the principal taught and was truly "the principal teacher." They also remind us of a special gift students bring to school relationships, "You can BS a BS'er, but you can't BS the kids" (p. 106). "BS-ing" is an unfortunate skill that comes with age and interferes with real communication. Students are fresh reminders of this reality.

HELPING RELATIONSHIPS

Pellicer and Anderson (1995) emphasize the importance of creating helping relationships in schools, suggesting that leadership is not about control, but about helping. Gibb (1964) observes that a truly helpful act results in something being done better than before the help was received and that the person receiving the help must become more independent. If we are truly helping students, it must follow that we must listen to determine the help they need and put them in situations where they can practice and become independent. The reality is that by listening, teachers and administrators have much to learn from students. The creation of opportunities for listening and fostering independence demands a democratic climate that must pervade a school.

DEMOCRACY IN ACTION

SELLING A PHILOSOPHY

John Dewey (1916) in his classic *Democracy and Education* advocated schools that promote shared interest and freedom in interaction, social relationships, and participation. Many educators can buy into such a philosophy for the adults in the school. But a truly democratic school provides students with learning experiences that promote a democratic way of life (Apple & Beane, 1995). Such experiences exist not only in the classroom but also in all the activities and experiences that represent the "hidden" curriculum of the school—"by which people learn significant lessons about justice, power, dignity, and self-worth" (p. 13). Such an emphasis recognizes the social construction of knowledge and the value of helping students to become informed skeptics about society.

TRUST AND DECENCY

The adults who can create such democracy in a school must be informed, confident individuals who seek to create an atmosphere defined by Sizer (1992) as a tone that stresses "trust (unless it is abused), and of decency (the values of fairness, generosity, and tolerance)" (p. 208). Roland Barth (1990) reminds us, "In all my work with students I have never known one to 'blow it' when the chips are down . . . children rise to the occasion.

Such a trust and belief in students is finding its way into rural classrooms where student voices are being heard in the areas of extracurricular activities, discipline, leadership opportunities, and choosing the content in a classroom.

EXTRACURRICULAR ACTIVITIES AND LEADERSHIP OPPORTUNITIES

In rural schools, extracurricular participation is an integral part of the school and provides opportunities to develop leadership, character building, and social skills (Nachtigal, 1982). Coladarci and Cobb's 1996 national study of extracurricular participation, school size, and achievement and self-esteem among high school students found extracurricular participation higher among students attending smaller schools. Participation was higher in all areas—academic clubs, sports, and performing arts.

While there was a negligible effect on academic achievement, there was a positive effect on self-esteem. The researchers recommend that such positive effects on self-esteem not be taken lightly by policymakers.

Chapin High School in School District Five of Lexington and Richland Counties outside of Columbia, South Carolina, was a well-kept rural secret for many years. And the community liked it that way. When rezoning occurred to build a third high school in the district, the powerful Chapin lobby succeeded in keeping their small high school untouched by the rezoning plan. But good secrets are hard to keep and word of Chapin High School's reputation for individual opportunities for students began to reach the ears of parents looking for a small, safe high school for their children. Of particular interest to parents and students were the strong extracurricular program and Principal John Anderson's persistent insistence that students be involved.

In a school of 720 students, Chapin High School has the largest student council in the state of South Carolina (75 members) and the only elected officers are members of the executive board. Membership is voluntary with a desire to serve as the only requirement. The council works by committee and is far more than just an activity to list by one's name in the yearbook or on one's college application. One of the group's most successful efforts was a Golden Eagle Dinner for 260 senior citizens in the Chapin area. Council members raised $1,600 to fund the event with audience participation in freethrow shots at basketball games. Two bus loads of senior citizens from the nearby Lowman Home retirement center enjoyed dinner, dancing, and fellowship to the sounds of the school's strings ensemble and jazz band. The event was an intergenerational celebration of community.

The Chapin High School student council has been recognized as the most outstanding in the state. The principal recognizes this valuable resource and frequently consults with student council representatives and class officers on such issues as whether or not seniors who do not qualify at the beginning of their senior year should march at graduation and the issue of zero tolerance policies on drugs, alcohol, and weapons. Students originated the idea of a one-class lockdown with the drug dog. Assistant Principal Paul Shealy (1997) notes, "Student leaders welcome those measures that discourage the appearance of illegal substances on school grounds. They indicate that someone who appears to be under the influence of drugs causes fear and apprehension in the classroom."

Athletic participation is also strong at Chapin High School with 370 of the 720 students playing two or more sports. So many students stay after school for such participation that assistant principal Linda Baldwin (1997) observes, "We doze but we never close." She credits the strong program to athletic director, Eddie Muldrow, who with a faculty committee was instrumental in helping design Chapin High's alternating-day block schedule and an enrichment period at the end of the day. Every teacher in the school is available for thirty minutes after school. This time is optional for students except for those involved in any interscholastic activity and who are making a "D" or "F" in any subject. Teams cannot start practices until enrichment ends. The rule also applies to band, orchestra, and choral students. Administrators have discovered, however, that many "A" and "B" students attend the sessions too. The enrichment period serves to enhance relationships in the school. Athletic Director Eddie Muldrow (1997) says, "We have always been a caring school for kids. However, the students now understand how much teachers truly want them to succeed in both the classroom and the athletic domain."

Student-adult relationships in the school seem to be the result of a commitment to that quality. As Assistant Principal Linda Baldwin (1997) observes, "We know every student; we know their names." This commitment is enhanced by genuine respect for what students can accomplish in schools.

The adult commitment to these beliefs is evident. Students at Chapin High School, with the assistance of the media specialist and the art teacher, designed the school's national award-winning web page. Many coaches coach as many as three sports. Ninety percent of the faculty sponsor some type of extracurricular activities. Band instructors work with one fifth of the total student body and have developed a program that has resulted in performances in London, England, and in Canada.

Tied closely to Chapin High School's success is a strong sense of tradition best exemplified by the school's Class Day celebration where the whole student body, parents, and grandparents gather for a three-hour ceremony. On this occasion, seniors dress in white dresses and coats and ties for a transitional ceremony as each graduating senior remembers his or her parents, grandparents, teachers, brothers and sisters, and friends in some way. Participants see this event as more significant than graduation.

Ted Sizer (1992) notes, "the essence of a school that is at once compassionate, respectful and efficient" (p. 45). The way such schools come to be, he contends, is "through the leadership of their adults . . . people who stay around a school long enough to give it a heart as well as a program" (p. 45). Chapin High School's three administrators bring years of stable, solid leadership to the school. Principal John Anderson has held that position for fourteen years. Linda Baldwin, assistant principal, brings fourteen years to her position and, Assistant Principal Paul Shealy taught and coached at the school for fifteen years before returning to serve as an administrator, a position he has held for three years.

In commenting on the success and reputation of his Blue Ribbon School, Principal John Anderson (1997) observes, "It is the active participation of all the stakeholders (faculty, support staff, students, parents and the community) that enables a small school to work together in developing a bond of trust and respect. When one generation consciously tries to influence another—and in turn is influenced—both adults and students see themselves as members of an institutional family working for the common good of all."

BEYOND STUDENT GOVERNMENT

There are many opportunities for students to be leaders outside the classroom. Barth (1990) suggests that student councils often become too preoccupied with proms or homecoming and function only to serve educator's goals. He recommends a forum where students "make what they believe in happen" (p. 125). He cites his elementary principalship experience when his school was frequented by visitors and no one had time to give tours. He turned this responsibility over to fifth- and sixth-grade students who had expressed an interest. Teachers developed a training program that included responses to hypothetical questions. At the end of the training, students knew the building, faculty, philosophy, and current problems and actually knew more than many adults. Tours began for student teachers and then expanded to school board members, the mayor, prospective parents, and even teachers within the school. Barth suggests, "All children can lead" (p. 126).

The office of student council president has often been a coveted one in the American high school; unfortunately, it usually becomes the school's "lip service" to student involvement in school governance. One North Carolina High School that serves both rural and city students changed the traditional role of students when then eighth-grade student body president Jason Summey heard about the dropout problems at the high school he would enter the next year, Clyde A. Erwin High School in Buncombe County near Asheville, North Carolina. Jason, when preparing for his eighth-grade graduation speech, asked himself, "Wouldn't it be awesome if everyone was still here when we graduate from high school?" (Summey, 1997). And so Jason issued the challenge to his classmates, the future graduating Class of 2000 of Erwin High School, and a dropout prevention program that has received national attention was born. The "Be Cool . . . Stay in School" Program with its support group the Dropout Patrol won Jason a coveted Citizen of the Year award in his community.

Jason is now an energetic, engaging fourteen-year-old ninth grader at Erwin High. He said that he first approached his parents, brother, and a few close friends with the idea. Erwin High School Principal Malcolm Brown provided key behind-the-scenes work to secure faculty support and provide the administrative logistics to get the program off the ground. Erwin High School with 1,150 students serves the lowest socioeconomic population in the school district. Until Brown became principal, it had a dropout rate of 11.2 percent. After instituting such changes as a four-period day and the EXCEL Program, a recognition and awards program, seven years later Brown saw the dropout rate decrease to 7.3 percent. Brown's challenge was serving a diverse population ranging from Ukrainian students with intense ESL needs, Hispanic and African- American students from city housing projects, to the most rural of rural students in the mountains of Buncombe county. He saw Jason's idea as a way to lower the dropout rate even more.

Brown cleared the way with the message to the faculty that dropout prevention was a priority. He authorized meetings of the dropout patrol during the school day but alternated the periods to minimize the loss of instructional time. Letters were sent to ninth-grade parents and an informational meeting was held. Funding for the program came from donations from clubs and business and the sponsor list grew from thirty to over one-hundred. Brown also made certain that adults provided guidelines for the student-run program. His advice (1997) to Jason was, "Don't make commitments you need to check with me about." Dropout Patrol members received instruction on matters that might need to be referred to a guidance counselor or administrator and the school's dropout prevention coordinator served as a contact.

Brown (1997) notes that a premise of the program is "using peer pressure in a reverse manner." Students help students by providing tutoring and friendship. When asked what he feels makes a difference in whether or not students drop out, Jason's response was, "Friends" (Summey, 1997). He adds that he and his group are attempting to do what adults have tried to do for years, too often with failure. Though data will not be in until graduation in the year 2000, Jason feels that because students are often inclined to listen to other students rather than adults, such positive peer pressure has a chance to make a difference. The group celebrates with a party at the end of each six weeks if no one has dropped out.

Jason's first year with the program has taught him that keeping everyone in school may not be possible. However, his program may make a difference in other ways. Jason recalls a seventeen-year-old freshman who declared his intention to drop out. Jason made contact attempting to change the young man's mind. In one telephone call, the student revealed to Jason that he had taken forty pills and was waiting to die. Jason and a friend went to the student's house and saw to it that he was rushed to the hospital and his life was saved. Though the student is no longer in school, Jason takes comfort in the role he played in averting a suicide.

Has the effort been worth it so far? Principal Malcolm Brown awaits the data to comment, but he notes that the biggest difference he has seen in the school is a heightened awareness of the dropout problem. The dropout problem is something students talk about and the over one-hundred community and business sponsors have committed themselves to. The program is an example of adults being willing to listen to students, to support them, and to sit back and let them take the credit for their efforts.[1]

DISCIPLINE

WHO'S IN CONTROL?

For many educators, discipline is about control: "We the administrators make the rules and you the students follow them." Such inflexibility often comes to a head in the middle and high school years when hormones rage and students begin the normal developmental search for identity and answers to tough questions. What many adults in schools fail to recognize is that the adolescent who questions and challenges is asking the significant adults in his or her life two important questions: "Do I have permission to be different from you?" and "If I am different, will you still love and accept me?" Many adults are too busy being in control to listen.

William Glasser, M.D. (1990), advocates noncoercive lead management and control theory. According to Glasser, students, as well as adults, have four needs in addition to survival: love, freedom, fun, and power. The adults in a school must see that their own needs for these four are being met personally and professionally. Then they must turn their attention to ensuring that these needs

---

[1]Erwin High School's "Be Cool . . . Stay in School" Program and "Dropout Patrol" are registered trademarks.

are being met for students. Educators who balk at the notion of freedom and power for students fail to see the possibilities of students, faculty, and administrators coming together in a cooperative venture to run a school.

CREATING A COMMUNITY

Kohn (1996) agrees and offers several suggestions for creating a school that moves beyond compliance to community. A prerequisite is a caring relationship with students. With such a relationship established, a teacher may need to teach certain skills to students such as listening carefully, calming themselves, generating suggestions, or imagining a problem from someone else's point of view. The importance of an adult diagnosing the problem is critical. This involves standing back to ask, for instance, if two children are fighting, "What is this really about?" Kohn also stresses the need for teachers to examine their own practices. Only a confident professional engages in the "line of inquiry that takes us beyond the reach of classroom management—which is exactly the point" (p. 125).

Teachers are then encouraged to talk less, and ask more, involving students in the solving of problems. Kohn describes an elementary school where the student solution to poor behavior in the cafeteria was to turn the cafeteria into a restaurant for which students picked the theme, designed the plan, and made a budget. The principal reported an end to the discipline problem. An authentic solution was the answer.

Kohn also advocates restitution—replace, clean up, repair, or apologize for a destructive act. She recommends class meetings for brainstorming, discussion, and follow-up. Flexibility and minimizing the punitive impact on students are also important as well as using control as a last resort strategy. She says, "We can create classrooms where students are members of democratic communities. We can move beyond discipline" (p. 137).

Are elementary students capable of such involvement in handling classroom problems? The Council of Peers in third grade at Cherokee Elementary School on the Cherokee Indian Reservation in rural western North Carolina is an example of such an endeavor. The council, known as the Peacekeepers, is the result of an action research project funded by a Mountain Connections Grant provided by the Special Education Program at Western Carolina University to develop model programs for at-risk children. Graduate student Lorraine Scalone assisted with the development and implementation of Peacekeepers and worked with the third-grade teachers and the school counselor.

Weekly council meetings are facilitated by a counselor and teacher. Students write and discuss compliments for each other. They then discuss concerns that have been placed in a suggestion box and develop solutions and restitutions. Working in a circle, the children use and preserve their Cherokee themes and traditions. Children elect their chief, vice-chief, and recorder each six weeks and sit with members of their Cherokee community based on the location of their home. The child speaking holds a blessed and beaded eagle feather used only for meetings and considered sacred to the children and the Cherokee people. To symbolize their sense of community, the children maintain a Basket of Acceptance containing something special each child has brought to school. The basket is placed in the center of the circle for each council meeting. The Peacekeepers' Pledge is "I promise to be respectful, truthful, and caring to all." School counselor Roseanna Belt (1997) observes, "I believe Peacekeepers could work at any school but one thing that makes it work here is that it is culturally based and relates to Cherokee Tribal Government."

Has Peacekeepers made a difference? The adults involved enthusiastically believe so. Jonnie Walkingstick (1997), a third-grade teacher, notes, "The bullies and the bossy children are now more gentle and nurturing leaders." She believes Peacekeepers has taught the children that there are options in life, positive ways to deal with feelings such as anger and disappointment. Resource teacher Kathy Norris (1997) brings a unique perspective to the program: "We work with different grade levels. We haven't had to deal with discipline as much in third grade because of the Peacekeepers. BEH kids feel cared about because the other students have offered help and suggestions dealing with their problems." She sees a strength in such a process and in the fact that it is not teacher-directed.

How do the teachers feel about the children taking on more responsibility for their behavior? Linda Thoresen's third graders came up with their own monitoring system for problems concerning their lines in the hallways. The students solved the problem and Linda (1997) adds, "It's nice not to have to walk backwards all the time." Teacher Debbie Harris (1997) feels, "Kids are better at doing the right thing even when the teacher isn't looking." She describes observing her children playing kickball on the playground and working to help a child who was struggling with the game. When one student heard another make a disparaging remark to a little girl, he said, "You shouldn't have said that. What if it was you?" The teacher wrote a compliment and put it in the box to be shared.

The teachers have also observed growth and maturity in their third graders. Mollie Robinson (1997) suggests that concerns that come before the group have changed: "They've gone from 'He looked at me or touched my chair;' to more indepth community-oriented concerns. Expectations are higher and compliments are harder to get. How did we do without Peacekeepers? It takes the worry off of us of always having to solve all the problems that occur in a classroom."

Peacekeepers is also unique in that it is central to the theme of community in the third grade curriculum. Teacher Linda Thoresen (1997) believes it cannot work as merely a packaged program. Principal Doyce Cannon (1997) is committed to seeing class councils move through the grades: "It's letting kids feel they are a part and the most important part of the classroom."

STUDENT VOICES IN CURRICULUM AND CONTENT

WHO MAKES THE DECISIONS?

Democratic schools take the most meaningful leap when they involve students in increasing their active participation in classroom learning experiences. Apple and Beane (1995) suggest that the curriculum in democratic schools "is based on the belief that knowledge comes to life for students and teachers only when it is connected to something that is serious" (p. 102). The researchers suggest that thematic curriculum is prevalent in such schools because it links knowledge to real-life problems. Students come to an awareness that knowledge is a powerful tool in making a difference in their lives.

Passe (1996) concurs and calls for "decentralized curricular decision making." He defends his position based on three reasons: "(1) A single broad curriculum cannot meet the different needs of students; (2) Those closest to students are in the best position to understand their needs; (3) Teachers already make many important curricular decisions each day" (p.vii).

A MODEL FOR STUDENT INVOLVEMENT

Passe advocates a model that includes students in the curricular decision-making process. This model was tested in his middle school classroom and is consistent with many of the principles of Rousseau, Dewey, constructivism, brain research, and quality schools. A central premise is that the students' ownership of the curriculum is a powerful motivator because the curriculum reflects their needs and interest. Parental support exists as long as parents perceive the teacher's decisions as responsible.

Passe maintains that other benefits include autonomy, student learning, and improved classroom behavior. Through discussion with their teacher students choose topics while the teacher retains veto power if necessary. Passe demonstrates how he met North Carolina's knowledge and skills goals for ninth-grade social studies while allowing students to choose the content. For instance, to meet the goal related to knowledge of responsibilities associated with citizenship, students chose such topics as civil disobedience, community social services, the judicial system, the legislative process, and the Bill of Rights.

STUDENTS IN ACTION

Custer High School, a rural school in Custer, South Dakota, was the site for a learning experience that involved students in creating the curriculum and in understanding the connection of knowledge to problem-solving. Students in Dave Versteeg's economics class took on a project to research and file the forms for a FmHA Loan for low-cost housing for senior citizens in their community. They also conducted a survey of student purchasing power and product/service needs and worked with local business owners to bring in those dollars. The students even ran a vending operation and invested their profits in the stock market.

Versteeg (1993) and his students participated in the Rural School and Community Development Project. The basic belief of this project is the interdependency of rural schools and their communities and the fact that in many rural communities the school is the largest economic enterprise. Versteeg cites other rural schools in South Dakota with similar projects. At Belle Fouche High School, for example, a language arts class used writing and interview skills to collect the personal memories of the elderly, and to publish and sell them as local histories. Students at Lyman High School in Presho, South Dakota, provide market research for area businesses. Such learning experiences connect students to their communities, provide opportunities for the social construction of knowledge, and enable practical application of problem-solving skills.

STUDENTS AS INSTRUCTIONAL OBSERVERS

Student voices are meaningful not only in the choice of curriculum and content but delivery as well. Lorien Belton (1996) was a senior at Sheridan High School in rural Sheridan, Wyoming, when she wrote for *Educational Leadership*, "What Our Teachers Should Know and Be Able to Do: A Student's View." Her contention is that students are in the best position to know how teachers really perform in the classroom and can help teachers perform better. Her definition of a good teacher is as follows: "Essentially a good teacher tells us what is out there to learn, shows an enthusiasm for acquiring knowledge for the purpose of learning, and then turns us loose to learn at our own pace, all the while looking over our shoulders" (p. 66).

Belton proposes a student evaluation system composed of student volunteers chosen by a group of teachers. These students would observe teachers, record teaching techniques, try to get a feel for the enthusiasm level of the class, subject matter, control, and students' respect for the teacher. She maintains that students notice details adults do not. Student observers would attempt, if time allowed, to interview students about the class and to speak with the teacher as soon as possible to clarify any confusion. The report would be read by master teachers who would then offer suggestions for improvement. She suggests that such observations be formative only and not evaluative. Belton is now a student at Stanford University.

CONCLUSION

The message is clear—relationships with students matter and school renewal begins at the school site with the thoughtful acceptance and involvement of the young whose minds and hearts are not weary of the frustrations, political motives, and all-to-often self-serving actions of adults.

Will the adults in rural schools and other schools around the nation follow the lead of these exemplary programs and listen to the all-too-often silent voices of students? There is hope that even at a national level, forward-thinking educators recognize the wisdom of student involvement in design for schooling.

Breaking Ranks: Changing an American Institution is a report of the National Association of Secondary School Principals (NASSP) on the high school of the twenty-first century. The work, completed in conjunction with the Carnegie Foundation for the Advancement of Teaching, was unique in its approach of putting together a national commission of practitioners—eight principals, an assistant principal, two teachers, a central office administrator, two professors, a senior fellow of the Carnegie Foundation for the Advancement of Teaching, senior staff members of NASSP, and—significantly—two students. The result was more than eighty recommendations for the high school of the next millennium.

One area of recommendation concerns school environment and creating a climate conducive to teaching and learning: "The school will accord meaningful roles in the decision-making process to students, parents, and members of the staff to promote an atmosphere of participation, responsibility, and ownership" (NASSP, 1996, p. 18).

The report also emphasizes the importance of relationships in the reform process:

> A high school builds on its success on a series of strong and positive relationships with and among those both inside and outside the building. These relationships start with the ways in which teachers, students, and others in the school relate to each other and continue through the links that the school forms with parents, public officials, business representative, neighboring schools, and others on the outside. (NASSP, 1996, p. 25)

The message is clear—relationships with students matter and school renewal begins at the school site with the thoughtful acceptance and involvement of the young whose minds and hearts are not weary of the frustrations, political motives, and all-too-often, self-serving actions as adults. Rural schools with the advantages of smaller size and opportunities for meaningful community are fertile ground for the positive growth and development of learner-centered schools and places where the voices of children can offer honest insights into the meaningful direction of school renewal.

REFERENCES

Anderson, J. 1997. Interview, April 24.

Apple, M.W., & J.A.Beane (eds.) 1995. *Democratic Schools*. Alexandria, VA: Association of Supervision and Curriculum Development.

Augenblick, J., & P.M. Nachtigal. 1985. *Equity in Rural School Finance*. Paper presented at the National Rural Education Forum, Kansas City, MO.

Baldwin, L. 1997. Interview, March 11.

Barth, R.S. 1990. *Improving Schools from Within*. San Francisco, CA: Josey- Bass Publishers.

Belt, R. 1997. Interview. April 29.

Belton, L. 1996. "What Our Teachers Need to Know and Be Able to Do: A Student's View," *Educational Leadership, 54*(1), 66–68.

Black, J.A., & F.W. English. 1986. *What They Don't Tell You in Schools of Education About School Administration*. Lancaster, PA: Technomic Publishing Co., Inc.

Breaking Ranks: Changing an American Institution, Executive Summary. 1996. Reston, VA: National Association of Secondary School Principals.

Brown, M. 1997. Interview, April 17.

Cannon, D. 1997. Interview. April 29.

Capper, C. 1991. "Rural Community Influences on Effective School Practice." A paper presented at the annual meeting of the American Educational Research Association, Chicago.

Coladarci, T., & C. Cobb. 1996. "Extracurricular Participation, School Size, Achievement and Self-Esteem Among High School Students: A National Look," *Journal of Research in Rural Education*, Fall, *12*(2),92–103.

Dewey, J. 1916. Democracy and Education. New York: Macmillan.

Dodendorf, D.M. 1983. "A Unique Rural School Environment," *Psychology in the Schools, 20*, 99–103.

Gibb, J.R. 1964. "Is Help Helpful?" *Forum and Section Journals, 45*(2), 289–293.

Glasser, W.G. 1990. *The Quality School: Managing Students Without Coercion*. New York: Harper Perennial.

Harris, D. 1997. Interview. April 29.

Helge, D.I. 1991. Rural, Exceptional, At-Risk. Reston, VA: The Council for Exceptional Children.

Houston, P. 1996. "Thinking Small Makes a Big Difference," in *Education Outlook. Leadership News, 173*, 2.

Kearney, J.M. 1994. *The Advantages of Small Rural Schools. Final Report to the Idaho Rural School Association* (ERIC Document Reproduction Service NO. ED 373934).

Kohn, A. 1996. *Beyond Discipline: From Compliance to Community*. Alexandria, VA: Association of Supervision and Curriculum Development.

Lewis, A.C. 1992. *Rural Schools: On the Road to Reform*. Portland, OR: Northwest Regional Educational Lab.

Meier, D. 1995. *The Power of Their Ideas: Lessons for American from a Small School in Harlem*. Boston, MA: Beacon Press.

Miller, B.A., & J.A.Hull. 1991. *Overcoming Professional Isolation in Small Rural Schools*. Portland, OR: Northwest Regional Educational Lab.

Muldrow, E. 1997. Interview, April 24.

Nachtigal, P.M. (ed.) 1982. Rural Education: In Search of a Better Way. Boulder, CO: Westview Press.

Nachtigal, P.M. 1992. "Rural Schooling: Obsolete or Harbinger of the Future?" *Educational Horizons, 70*(2), 66–70.

Norris, K. 1997. Interview. April 29.

Parker, W.C. 1997. "The Art of Deliberation," *Educational Leadership, 54*(5), 18–21.

Passe, J. 1996. *When Students Choose Content: A Guide to Increasing Motivation, Autonomy, and Achievement.* Thousand Oaks, CA: Corwin Press.

Pellicer, L.O., & L.W. Anderson. 1995. *A Handbook for Teacher Leaders.* Thousand Oaks, CA: Corwin Press.

Proceedings: National Congress on Rural Education. Traverse City, Missouri, Rural Education in Urbanized Nations: 1992, October 11. Oak Brook, IL: North Central Regional Educational Lab.

Robinson, M. 1997. Interview. April 29.

Schneider, E. 1996. "Giving Students a Voice in the Classroom," *Educational Leadership, 54*(1), 22–26.

Shealy, P. 1997. Interview. March 11.

Sher, J. (ed.) 1981. *Issues and Innovations.* Boulder CO: Westview Press.

Sizer, T.R. 1996. *Horace's Hope. What Works for the American High School.* Boston, MA: Houghton, Mifflin Co.

Sizer, T.R. 1992. *Horace's School. Redesigning the American High School.* Boston, MA: Houghton, Mifflin, Co.

Stern, J.D. 1994. *The Condition of Education in Rural Schools.* Washington, DC: U.S. Department of Education.

Summey, J. 1997. Interview. April 17.

Thoresen, L. 1997. Interview, April 29.

Versteeg, D. 1993. "The Rural High School as Community Resource," *Educational Leadership,* 54–55.

Walkingstick, J. 1997. Interview. April 29.

LEADERSHIP AND ORGANIZATIONAL SKILLS FOR RURAL SCHOOL LEADERS

Rural Education: Leadership and Technology

Last year, I challenged America to connect every classroom and library to the Internet by the year 2000, so that, for the first time in our history, children in the most isolated rural towns, the most comfortable suburbs, the poorest inner city schools, will have the same access to the same universe of knowledge.—William Clinton, 1997

By the end of the decade, 60 percent of our nation's jobs will require skills that only 20 percent of the existing U.S. population has—and many of these will be technology-based.—Larry Irving, Assistant Secretary for Communications and Information, U.S. Department of Commerce, 1996

- Why does technology evoke déjà vu?
- What further conceptual and technological knowledge must educational leaders add to what they already have to make the proper strategic and tactical decisions for the information age?
- What funding and knowledge-base support exists for integrating technology into educational practice?
- What potential does the information-age wave have for innovation and transformation in the rural school system and its relationship with their surrounding community?

Chapter 11 provides the answers to these questions and provides the link between technology and the rural school.

Robert Houghton, Director of Technology, Department of Elementary and Middle Grades Education, Western Carolina University.

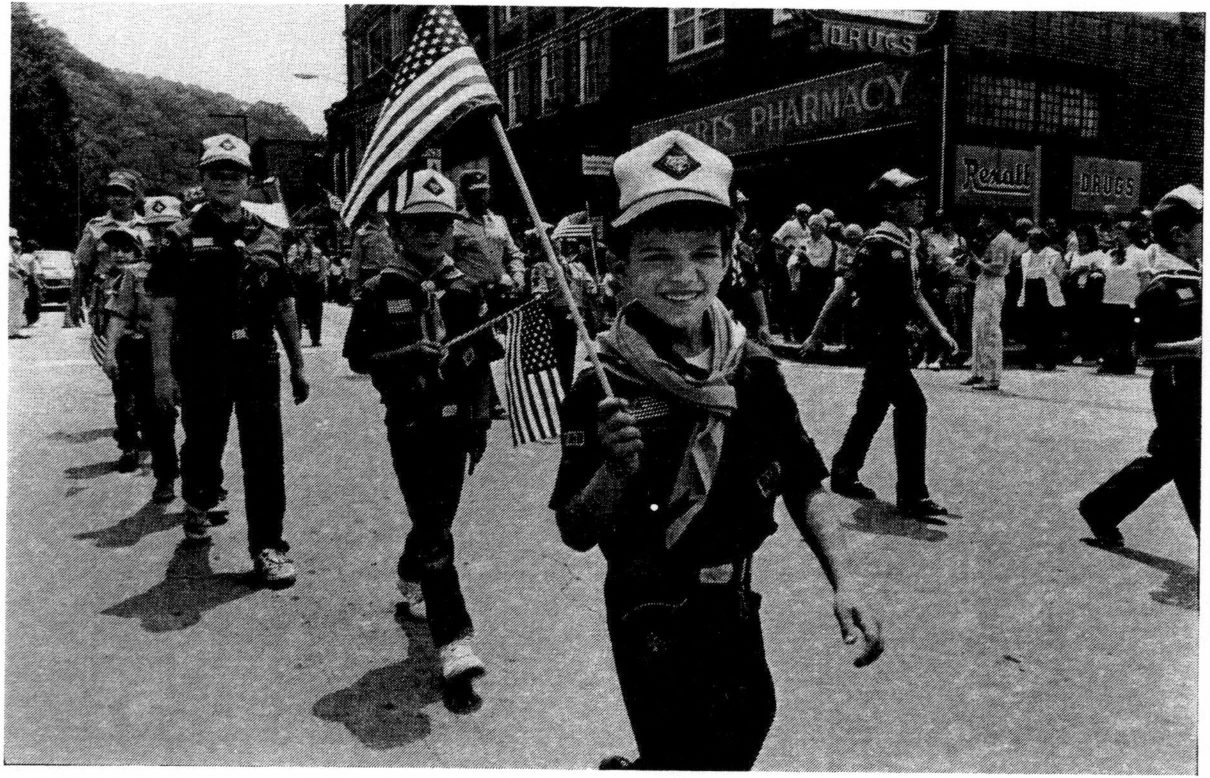

© Photo by Rob Amberg.

INTRODUCTION

IN visiting a rural school district and its schools one cannot fail to observe that rural life long ago left behind any association with the myth of a more bucolic life style. Rural education leaders are just as busy and pressured as any of their more urban counterparts. Adding to their crowded schedule is the need to grapple with a complex and significant topic, computer technology. These rural education leaders are often well aware of the educational, business, and political rhetoric about technology and fear a growing distance between their schools and schools that have "taken off" in their use of this technology. The dramatic growth in the cultural importance of computer technology has left many anxious and a bit bewildered and among those veterans of rural life, a sense that they have been here before. This chapter addresses many of the questions the author heard within the rural educational community.

Why the déjà vu? What further conceptual and technology knowledge must educational leaders add to what they already have to make the proper strategic and tactical decisions for the information age? Are there other sources of funding and knowledge to support this growing mission? What potential does this information-age wave have for innovation and transformation in the relationship between the rural school system and its surrounding community?

WHY DOES TECHNOLOGY EVOKE DÉJÀ VU?

Throughout the industrial era, innovation frequently worked its way out of urban population centers. Time and again rural communities and their educational systems followed movements set in motion by city brethren. Pressure to "wire up the schools" with computer networks is upon us. Is it déjà vu? The similarities are sufficient to disguise important differences.

One interesting similarity is with the era of rural electrification. Long after city dwellers gave up hand wringers for washing machines, rural inhabitants did their work manually. It took special legislative pressure and funding in the 1950s to complete the effort of extending the electrical grid into the farthest reaches of rural communities. In various guises, a movement is underway that some have labeled "rural datafication." This means that an effort is being made from national and state levels to provide special funding and leadership to extend computer networks into all parts of the country, especially rural areas. Such work will have similar transformational effects among the communities that accomplish this goal.

The differences are more subtle. Electrical networking was managed as a highly centralized affair over which individual communities had little control and electrical standards had decades to settle. Rates were subsidized by the government to keep them highly affordable. However, computer networking is still undergoing rapid transitions. The details are complex. Costs vary widely.

Long-term policies about networking implementation made at the state level need to be revisited with regularity. Urban and rural solutions may not always be the same amidst a rich array of alternatives. For example, one rural school district has received two competitive offers to provide a computer data line per building that will carry the traffic from the building computer network, one at four hundred per month and one at six hundred dollars per month. The data speed is 56KB or 56,000 bits of data per second. In a moderate-sized city, a fifty-minute drive away from the rural district, a business can obtain a computer data line for thirty dollars a month for a data speed of 128KB or 128, 000 bits of data per second. For at least ten times less than the rural cost, the urban dweller can receive more than twice the service.

How will rural implementors know that designs conceived by central planners living in dense population areas fit the rural scene? For example, rural areas might be better served by wireless networking solutions over long distances while keeping the wiring runs just within buildings. Towers and soon satellite delivery are also possible alternatives to expensive monthly charges that pay for the long wire runs between cities and towns.

Rural educators need to ascertain that they have adequate advocates for rural solutions. Collaborations of rural educators may be needed to hire consultants to determine that the most efficient solution for rural areas is being found. Further, simple checks on proposed systems are possible but you must at least have the knowledge that there are alternatives. For example, have rural educators banded together with community leaders in your area to ask cellular developers if they can offer competitive solutions to land lines? Power companies sometimes string fiber optic cable across their electrical towers for internal communication. Light waves are not bothered by electromagnetic interference. Do they have some spare bandwidth that your school could use? Do you have a competitive local or county government that is considering making data services a basic utility along with water, sewage, and electricity for luring new businesses to the area? Can you extend their thinking to include the public schools? This is not to argue that others will have a cheaper and better solution, but rather to point out that you can work the competitive system to determine whether the solution being advocated is the best available. Things are not always what they seem, especially with educational technology.

What further conceptual and technological knowledge must educational leaders add to what they already have to make the proper strategic and tactical decisions for the information age?

INFORMATION AGE AND COMPUTER DEFINITIONS

In short, the information age is defined not by its crops or manufacturing goods, but by its knowledge products. "Knowledge itself . . . turns out to be not only the source of the highest-quality power, but also the most important ingredient of force and wealth" (Toffler, 1990, p. 18). Toffler (1970, 1981, 1990) and Peters (1987) are but two who have written classic works on this concept and deserve closer study that cannot be detailed here. The perceived impact of the information age is enormous. Dr. Michael Hooker, chancellor of a major research university, University of North Carolina-Chapel Hill, noted that "the rules are going to be rewritten and every deck in society is going to be reshuffled. . . . The only thing that will confer economic advantage on this region is the extent to which it has developed, fostered and nurtured its brain power" (Blake, 1996, p.1). This is an age that educators ought to love.

In sometimes counterpoint to this positive swell for educational systems is a complex technology that undergirds this age. This technology has generated its own special category of concern, computer anxiety, a sort of subspecies of the educational literature on math anxiety. The rhetoric of the age and teacher uncertainties have contributed to computer literacy agendas that appear as long lists of basic and advanced skills to be mastered (North Carolina Computer Competencies for Educators, 1995). The state committees that form them disband only to discover that the essential computer skills target metamorphosizes into something else.

"Computer literacy" is also an abused phrase, in disrepute as not really a form of literacy; but the term persists. To be computer literate is to be capable of using the current range of computer software in ways that integrate with your daily needs. These daily needs also include working with items that contain computer chips and code but do not look at all like computers. Even more significant, however, is a tension with the very term "computer" itself. The term has lost its relevance, its power in conceptualizing our use of the tool. Prior to the invention of electronic devices the term "computer" meant a human being who carried out calculations. Before and during World War II, tens of thousands of people carried out the activities of today's simple and multifunction calculators. At first, the primary function of computers was to run calculations and this emphasis carried through to the dawn of what was then termed the "microcomputer." The major impetus for the spread of the personal computer was the invention of the electronic spreadsheet Visicalc.

But use has changed radically in the last ten years. A current direction of computer technology development is to integrate all prior forms of communication, including telephone, television, radio, mail, and print publishing. The calculation function is not dead or even less important than it was in any absolute sense, but it has been buried under an avalanche of competing activities. This activity centers around organizing and communication. Even word-processing and database work are being merged with Internet features. The term "telecomputer" is then a much more descriptive word. It may come to pass that the PC of personal computer will evolve to mean personal communicator. Plugged into 1997 vintage Internet software, your telecomputer is as much a typewriter as it is a miniature radio and television station and tele-video phone booth. Consequently, in this writing the term telecomputer (TC) will be used.

These changing definitions point toward a new level of language arts skills as yet unnamed and, therefore, difficult to define. Out of this information age is emerging a new level of curriculum that is every bit as important as the process of reading and writing. "Linking" (as in web page links) has become the more modern term that resonates with a deep well of curriculum on organizing skills. One definition of adult illiteracy is 8th grade or below reading skills with the older technology of reading. How long will it be before grade level distinctions are drawn with these newer technologies for communication and composition? Where will this line be drawn? On this shift into the twenty-first century, your teaching staff must discover and invent the new educational system that is emerging. You will build this system on a foundation of telecomputers and with a collection of refocused content skills. Your community will build its business stragtegies for the next century on these same resources.

ADMINISTRATIVE PERSPECTIVES

Essential knowledge continues to evolve rapidly. There is no short list of five stable key facts or skills. A deep knowledge of evolving information age skills and concepts needs to play a role in major school district decisions. School boards and superintendents need to decide whether they have sufficient knowledge in-house to lead the information-age charge. If they do not, they must weigh the options for and against hiring district leadership in information-age development, that is, hiring second-tier leadership under the superintendent that places an information-age voice in a position to influence critical decisions.

> A deep knowledge of evolving information age skills and concepts needs to play a role in major school district decisions.

Whatever they call this position, educational leaders should not constrain its role with the title of director of technology. The very presence of such a title as technology or computer director or coordinator may indicate that district leadership has missed the higher-level transformative role that information-age resources can have. A better label might be information director or the business label of chief information officer (CIO). This position must be at least as much concerned with educating the district administrative leadership as with influencing classroom practice. This administrative education must merge the strong critical thinking skills of successful administrators with the power tools of the information age. The age requires leadership sufficiently immersed in the technology to begin to see it as another form of paint with which they can transform their community's educational canvas.

The opportunities of the information age also imply that this information director position could go beyond the routine boundaries districts set for themselves. Rural schools districts do have advantages over their urban cousins that may be unexploited. To take advantage of the closer relationships of rural communities, the board has the potential to create a position with responsibilities that reach beyond the current school district, to not only raise the strategic skills of district leadership, but to address those of surrounding community leaders as well.

Many districts believe that they have already addressed the need to increase their information-age expertise. They have created computer specialist positions. Such positions can and have played an important role in developing teacher capacity. Too often, however, they are too many layers away from the inner council that makes the critical strategic budget and other decisions, or such a role is given to a capable but extremely busy person hired to meet prior commitments and whose information-age knowledge does not keep up with developments.

The role of the change agent that has emerged from the innovation-diffusion literature is relatively clear and unchanged (Rogers, 1962, 1971, 1983, 1995). To best effect change, change agents must be perceived by those they would change to be not be too distant in social status and general ability. The change agents hired have often done their jobs well. Computer coordinators are often teachers taken from front-line positions or front-line teachers who have gone back to complete a master's degree in educational technology. They have played an important and capable role in working with front-line teachers to effect change and have built a growing pool of information-age-ready teachers. But has this level of change agent moved the central office perspective and empowered administrators to feel comfortable in leading their front-line teachers who are ready to move in new directions? Or has this level of change agent allowed key administrators to keep computer technology at arm's length and thereby miss the influence of new levels of understanding in their strategic decisions?

It has been the author's experience that those charged with strategic and tactical (long- and short-term) planning (school boards, central office and building administrators) are too often further removed from the necessary and current knowledge base than the front-line teachers they would direct. This administrative team must also absorb the culture of the information age to be able to reinvent it for educational use. It is one thing to read about French or to observe the practice of French culture around you. It is quite another to claim to be able to influence and direct the French culture without being fluent in its practice and being part of the culture itself. To best reach the administrative team, a leader must be added whose mission includes training and guiding teammates into fluency within this new culture. But further, this team leader must carry out a similar mission with regard to the larger community, reaching into the base of political and economic leadership and working with university leadership to put key leaders at the same level in discussions of strategic information-age planning for their rural community. In turn, this team leader must reach into his or her school district team and include the lead teachers and administrators with this community group and build a planning team with a sharp eye on future possibilities.

Whoever wears the information director hat, the superintendent or someone else, has a number of models in each state to turn to as a source of professional example. Higher education institutions have significantly beefed up their computer centers in recent years, especially staff devoted to academic needs. Some computer center leaders have moved out of a major role in academic integration while others play a central role. But whatever their current arrangement, all can share their experience of the last few years with regard to the rapid planning, development, and rising costs of membership in the information age. School districts might work with their state legislature to create special liaison officers within these computer centers who can take school districts under their wing during critical growth periods. State educational leadership has a rich source of data from which to extrapolate long-term trends and costs. Rural educators must lobby hard to address the higher costs of rural areas and find ways to enlarge the size of their negotiating group to bring down costs. While university campuses have had decades to grow their computer centers, school districts will only have years.

Information-age developments will have serious implications for rural community life. It has been many decades since the youth of our culture could play a significant role in the political and economic advancement of our communities. As the 1800s came to a close, the dominance of the agricultural age was ending and the industrial age was reaching full throttle. Youth who had worked side by side with adults and parents in the economic life within their agricultural communities were increasingly separated as parents went to factories and children went to school. Those in the middle years (junior high) have been too long locked out of substantive work and high school students too long relegated to the most menial chores of the industrial age system of our communities, making deliveries, flipping burgers and stocking shelves. If generation X'ers are disaffected it is not hard to see why. But as the twentieth century closes and the twenty-first century begins, the cycle appears to have come full circle. Many of the latest generation have not waited for public schools to provide current culturally relevant education for the information age. Outside of public schools they have gained a level of understanding that surpasses that of peers, adults and even the adult community leadership. Bit by bit, the business community is recognizing this development and hiring them as soon as they turn sixteen or sooner to assist with their business's information development and company education. It is time that the educational system recognize this more fully as well and better integrate school, business, and community development and ways that empower all parties to the strategy. The information age is not about muscle power or financial power, it is about brain power, change, and creativity.

As will be shown in some detail later, there is much about the information age that those confined during business hours to public school grounds can do on school time and still meet curriculum requirements. This will require that our educational leadership see to it that the public schools and our communities have the telecomputer-based resources that are at hand. It is this networking development that forms a major current challenge to this leadership. Rural schools with their closer communities ties may be in a better position than any others to move in this direction. However, rural schools must find new sources of funding to address their relatively weaker economic base.

ANALYSIS—BREAKING DOWN THE PROBLEM

What should administrators, teachers, and students know? There is a danger that by defining minimums we actually set an upper boundary that can become difficult to cross later as conditions change. But somehow a starting point must be created and this warning taken into consideration. Different perceptions are being employed in identifying what a computer or technologically literate educator should know. It should not be seen as unusual that the breakdown generally depends on the analyzer's area of training. Educators, however, must integrate technology within their own schemata.

Those with significant computing backgrounds prefer to break down the problem by software applications. Educators counter with major divisions of teaching activity. A third route would be to consider the specific needs of the information age and integrate all three. In turn, rural educators need to pick from these strategies the elements that best fit their communities. These strategies need to be considered in further detail to flesh out current thinking on computer literacy.

The North Carolina approach will be described further, in part because it includes both the computer perspective (basic competencies) and the teaching perspective (advanced competencies). Analysis of this state's approach provides a counterpoint for later development.

The North Carolina computer competencies were defined by a team of K–12 and teacher education faculty in meetings over several months. Fourteen major areas were defined by the School Technology Users Task Force (1995):

I. Basic Technology Competencies
  1. Computer Operations
  2. Setup, Maintenance, and Troubleshooting
  3. Word Processing/Introductory Desktop Publishing

   4. Spreadsheet/Graphing
   5. Database
   6. Networking
   7. Telecommunications
   8. Media Communications (including Image and Audio Processing)
   9. Multimedia Integration
II. Advanced Technology Competencies
   1. Curriculum
   2. Subject-Specific Knowledge
   3. Design and Management of Learning Environments/Resources
   4. Child Development, Learning, and Diversity
   5. Social, Legal, and Ethical Issues

Some of these areas require further definition. Networking (6) refers to local area networking (LAN) and activities such as using a file server to share files and selecting and deselecting network zones. These features appear as soon as you network a cluster of computers. Telecommunications (7) refers to a global network, that is, the Internet and features such as electronic mail, the World Wide Web, the file transfer process, distance education features, and much more. Media communications (8) is an extension of the audiovisual (AV) or media literacy agenda, including shooting and editing video, making electronic slides, using videodisc and videotape players, and more. Finally, multimedia integration merges the older audiovisual skills with digitizing and editing audio and video. This information becomes an important part of linear presentations of information (electronic slide shows) and nonlinear (web pages and sites).

The basic computer competencies component creates some interesting issues in balance for rural schools, which may be developing their facilities later than other districts. There are also some unexplained absences in these general groupings of applications.

This basic inventory clearly takes a computer-centered paradigm. It is useful to look at the school setting from the perspective of this world view, but rural districts may want to have their own technology planning teams improve on it. That is, this inventory is confused about whether it is a taxonomy of major areas or a list of applications. It lists four applications separately, but puts other applications in four large sets of applications. It also promotes computer setup and maintenance, a subfunction of managing the computer operating system, to the equal of word processing. The four specific application types are operating system, word processor, database, and spreadsheet. In fact, these four are the more common computing applications across school districts, with operating systems as fundamental and word processing widely accepted. Databases and spreadsheets still require some political effort to incorporate into classroom activity. Planning teams ought to weigh the functional use of databases and spreadsheets against the growing importance of other applications from the telecommunications and multimedia sets.

In comparison, the four sets of applications are really advanced technical competencies that could be divided into two groups, telecommunications and multimedia. These areas should be important targets for planning team development. With regard to telecommunications, many districts do not have their building computers networked. If some computers are networked, it is usually just within a computer lab classroom, not with the rest of the building or the larger Internet. Further, these labs often do not have many of the peripherals that are required for multimedia, such as videotape players, or they do not have the software and hardware to use them if the equipment was moved to the computer labs, such as digitizing hardware and software for camcorders. Putting these needs on the table in planning for future growth in district technology will give rural districts an edge if they meet them.

This particular arrangement of nine basic topics gives clear bias on four applications but little or no application guidance in other areas. For multimedia integration, districts need programs that draw, paint, digitize, and edit video and audio, convert different file formats, and create special effects. Telecommunications will require applications such as web browsers, chat, file transfer, and e-mail. The web browser, in turn, would give access to other applications found at various Internet sites. Web sites are becoming as interactive as desktop applications and can become a kind of application in themselves requiring training to use effectively, further taking market share away from current basic applications such as spreadsheets.

Other application topics are noticeably absent from the basics set, but the planning team must consider them as well. For example, instructional software (computer-assisted instruction) represents an enormous category of applications including the subcategories of simulation, tutorial, drill, games, and more. The North Carolina competencies place the integration of instructional software under the advanced competencies. Further, many schools have large instructional software collections. The more significant the collection, the greater the need for evaluation guidelines to be in place.

A new important category, sometimes called groupware, is also missing. Such software is used to facilitate the work of teams and committees, helping with organization, management, and communication within the group. This category has important pedagogical implications and also provides many useful administrative functions.

In summary of this analysis of basic competencies, any attempt to designate areas to be covered for teacher education by software category is open to the application de jour criticism. That is, every day a different application or its upgrade has its moment in the sun of critical importance, only to replaced by another the next day. Promoting such a computer-based perspective leaves educators both looking and feeling perpetually behind. It also leaves the computer industry to set the educational agenda. "Those who set the agenda control the meeting."

Over two decades ago, another computer-based perspective was popular, which makes a more memorable approach to planning and development than the North Carolina taxonomy of computer competencies. This was Taylor's (1980) model: tutor, tool, and tutee. That is, all educational computer activity could be categorized as teaching the student (tutor), providing leverage for a student's daily work (tool), or giving the student the opportunity to teach the computer (tutee or programming). It too, however, is weakened as an educational perspective in that it describes computer technology use instead of prescribing educational and intellectual goals. In many ways, the North Carolina prescription for computer competencies for educators is just a more complex view of the Taylor model. Our ongoing metamorphosis in teacher education for computer use needs new models to guide its growth. Fortunately, there are other frames of reference besides the various categories of applications.

The five "advanced competencies" of this list clearly target educational missions. Unfortunately, nearly every application can be applied to each of the five educational categories. That is, a word processor might have as much relevance to curriculum as to the topics of subject-specific knowledge, design and management of learning environments/resources, child development, learning, and diversity or social, legal and ethical issues. Consequently, the titles of these headings put the emphasis properly on educational themes but lack even heuristic guidance in the integration of different software applications or in the approach to the use of the application within the educational category. This list would be better titled "basic educational competencies." Nevertheless, this "advanced" list does serve a useful reminder that technology has relevance to all areas of education.

Ask a different question and receive a different answer. Instead of asking what teachers need, cast the question differently. What features of our educational agenda touch critical information-age characteristics and how can educators address these connections?

Strong if not steadily increasing rates of change are one characteristic of the age. The implication is that memorized knowledge must play a secondary role to the process of life-long learning. This process is viewed by many as requiring various higher-order thinking or problem-solving skills such as critical thinking, creative thinking, comparison, analysis, inference, and evaluation (Houghton, 1995).

High rates of interaction, including international communication, are another characteristic of the age, and the Internet and features such as electronic mail represent the cheapest and fastest way yet invented to carry out this knowledge trade. This interaction has a focus: problem-solving. Though problem-solving has received long-standing recognition in the rhetoric about academic classroom activities, rapidly changing environments also have a strong need for problem recognition, both in the recognition of something being wrong with a setting and the ability to invent that which is not yet visible, to create something new. This form of problem recognition could also be re-conceived of as opportunity recognition.

Once recognized, the problem may further require the ethical motivation to act on one's conclusions. Though one capable person can do much in rapidly changing environments, capable problem-solving teams can do more in less time. Those that lead in the twenty-first century will be accomplished collaborators. Expected continual major adjustments will require significant teamwork, which in turn requires significant communication skills. Strong communities, that is, those with good communication and cooperation should have a significant advantage in the information age. That aspect of the age, in turn, should provide advantages to exploit for the inherent strengths of rural schools and rural communities. Technology alone is not being promoted here as some panacea to rural concerns, but allied with rural assets, the potential appears significant. This topic will be explored in some depth in the concluding section of this chapter.

For now, having criticized standard views of approaching technology integration, it is only fair to offer a different model, a model based on the theme of problem-solving. A simple four-stage problem-solving model can be used to address these critical information-age features and lead the integration of new technologies. Systems for managing problems can be found in all the major content areas and have been well discussed. The need is to bridge these different models and bring them round to support each other in a manner that gives direction to the application of computer tools. The LEAP model presented below represents part of a unified model for problem management.

LEAP[1]

LEAP is a problem-solving centered model for the integration of computer applications based on the aforementioned conclusions about the information age (Houghton, 1994a). LEAP stands for Look, Evoke, Assess and Publish (also Perform). Each represents a different stage of the problem-solving cycle (see Figure 11.1).

LEAP seeks a tighter integration between broad content area goals and computer technologies and also seeks to widen the view of the computer-mediated tools that should be in use. In doing so the model connects a wide range of crosscurricular thinking processes, involving discovery learning and critical, reflective, and evaluative thinking. It further complements prior work across many content areas (e.g., science, Germann, 1991; critical thinking and social

---

[1]An earlier version of the ideas in this section on LEAP were published in the *Proceedings of the 8th International Conference of the Society for Information Technology and Teacher Education*, Orlando, FL: Association for the Advancement of Computing in Education, 1997.

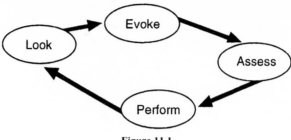

Figure 11.1

studies, Peters, 1987 and Clarke, 1990; reflective thinking, Gipe & Richards, 1992). The model has application for the learners/students, preservice and inservice teachers and administrators, a group that will hereafter be called "the thinkers."

AN OVERVIEW OF THE SIMPLE MODEL

In this model, the learner first *looks* for and collects data, constantly cycling through decisions based on relevance and interest. The quantity of data streaming through our computer networks has been likened to a firehose operating at capacity, but a firehose surrounded by the needy who are holding out small and specialized cups. To throttle this deluge and move just the needed information to the problem at hand makes management a critical skill for the learner at this stage of the thinking cycle. Further, the tremendous range of "information highway" options through our computer networks (e.g., the Internet) along with the numerous high-capacity local workstation tools (e.g., the full Compton's encyclopedia with multimedia on CD-ROM) make for both complex and sometimes costly decisions, costly in terms of time and access charges.

The thinker uses the found information of the previous stage to *evoke* a response. That is, the composer must create with sufficient skills to stimulate a response from others. Without a response, the effectiveness of the communication cannot be known. The greater the communication skill, the greater the ability to put the newly found information of the Look phase in a context readily understood by the creator or by the listener(s). To date, primarily just one computer tool has been heavily promoted for composing thought, the word processor. However, not only is the text manipulated by the the word processor, just one of many means of computer-mediated expression (e.g., paint, digital video editing, music), but it is no stronger than other equally available tools for efficiently and playfully mapping and guiding developing thought (e.g., outliners, draw programs or spreadsheets).

The learner must next pause to *assess* progress. Assessment runs from low-level spelling and grammar checking to reflective discussions among members of online work groups of projects underway. This stage requires emphasis on value judgment. Evaluation skills must cover the wide range of potential means of expression noted in the previous stage, from word processor programs to spreadsheet programs to multimedia. This assessment is formative in nature. That is, the goal of assessment at this stage is to have an impact on a creation still in development.

Last in this cycle, the thinkers *publish* their creations. Publishing implies far more than submission for a grade in a classroom. It calls for targeting an audience most similar to the focus of the author or creator. Publishing is sharing among peers, among those with genuine interest in a topic. Further, I use the term synonymously with "perform." I intend for this stage to appeal equally to those whose means of sharing do not necessarily involve the simple frame of a page or a video screen, such as a choreographer, a conductor or a gymnast. The emerging information highway gives thinkers an instantaneous neighborhood and global reach for their effort. Yet, publishing is not really last in the cycle. Publishing often serves as the incentive to begin the cycle again, a recycling stimulated by feedback on the performance or publication. Inherent to the publishing stage is a more summative assessment of achievement. Critics (e.g., a movie critic) provide comparison with similar work and give some indication of overall quality.

A DEEPER VIEW OF THE MODEL

The concept of a cycle facilitates description within the linear nature of an essay on paper and aids initial instruction for students. However, it disguises the nonlinear nature of the process in the real world. Further, it works against the author's intention of the model as supporting nonsequential interaction between any two or more stages of the model. In a more realistic model (Figure 11.2), the arrows go both ways and to all stages, not just the "next" stage.

AN OVERVIEW OF THE COMPLEX MODEL

The implication for the more experienced thinker is simple. There is no cor-

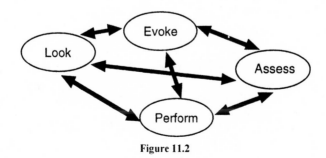

Figure 11.2

rect place to start; there is no mandated next stage. The time spent at any one stage varies with the experience of the thinker and the needs of the project at hand. Yet it is my experience that when the student's project is finished and the communication has been "published," thinkers will find that the better the balance among the time spent at each stage, the higher the quality of their work.

APPLICATION

A simple introduction to many aspects of the model can be created with an electronic bulletin board (a software program that shares electronic mail with remote users) and a word processor, expressing ideas in units of but a few paragraphs. At the Look stage the thinker might look through ideas expressed on the bulletin board. A stimulating thread (a connected set of e-mail messages from multiple authors) can be cut and pasted into a word processor. In the Evoke stage, the e-mail collection is assembled and reordered in the word processor. This e-mail text provides not only a target audience for the author, but provides the equivalent of a story starter and perhaps structure for the thinker's more complete essay to follow. In the Assess stage, the collected e-mail contains the electronic addresses of those interested in this thread. These addresses provide a ready audience for feedback during this formative stage. A spelling checker might be used. In the Publish stage, the thinker might copy the developed essay and paste it into an e-mail message to be sent back to the original electronic bulletin board so that all could read or just send it back to the original set of e-mail authors discussing the particular idea.

2-D: THE TOOLS DIMENSION

Using the above two applications (a word processor and a bulletin board e-mail system) pales in comparison with the real possibilities for designing vehicles of thought. The wider range of tools available for such design do not abandon e-mail and word processors as a means of assembling and expressing our thoughts, but take the learner far beyond them. Each stage of the LEAP model leads to a wide array of tools for that level. For example, the Publish level leads to desktop publishing tools, resources for web authoring, digital audio digitizing for radio clips, and so forth. LEAP, then, provides a second dimension, the tools dimension.

3-D: THE CURRICULUM DIMENSION

A third and more complex dimension to the LEAP model also beckons. In the same way that one can move from a pair of computer tools (word processor and electronic mail) to a rich panoply of electronic tools, so one can expand the simplest model of learning provided by LEAP to a chart rich with the concepts for

TABLE 11.1. Curriculum Integration and the LEAP Model.

| Process | Curriculum | | Technology | |
	Information Literacy	Science	Local Actions	Global Actions
Look	1. Task Definition —Define task or info. problem —Identify info. needed to solve it 2. Info. Seeking Strategies —Brainstorm all possible sources —Select the best sources 3. Location and Access —Locate the sources —Find info. within the source 4. Use of Information —Read, hear, view, touch —Extract relevant information	Problem Posing observe	find, read, cut, copy, paste, renumber, outline (humans, not computers, choose problems and purposes)	search online databases know online contact & reference systems
Evoke	5. Synthesis —Organize information from multiple sources	Problem-Solving develop hypotheses conduct experiments draw conclusion	type, record (humans, not tools, generate and elaborate)	computer conferencing (Netnews, LISTSERVs) collaborative screen use of any program collaborative writing, talk, chat, e-mail

(continued)

209

TABLE 11.1. (continued).

Process	Curriculum		Technology	
	Information Literacy	Science	Local Actions	Global Actions
Assess		Persuasion	check, lookup, read, listen (tools have nothing to say about the substance of the teacher's and learner's work)	e-mail, groupware, netphone, video conferencing (CU-SeeMe, private networks)
Publish/Perform	5. Synthesis —present the information 6. Evaluation —judge the process (efficiency) —judge the product (effectiveness)	Share Findings	table of contents, index, format, print, broadcast, narrowcast (humans, not tools, have value systems through which to appreciate or take comparative measurement of the works of others)	Net tools: FTP, gopher, World Wide Web Legacy systems: TV, radio stations, publishing houses

Note: The Information Literacy column is summarized from Eisenberg, M.B. & Berkowitz, D.J. (1988).

thinking in many content areas. (See Table 11.1 for a portion of this chart.) LEAP creates links that cut across the work of those developing thinking process skills in many curriculum areas (e.g., writing, Kelvin & Leonard, 1992 and Pelletier, 1992; critical/creative thinking, Manzo et al., 1992. p. 25; science, O'Loughlin, 1992; math, Pruett, 1993; problem-solving, Reschke, 1991).

The curriculum columns on the left of this table provide an example of the language used by those writing about information literacy and science. Similar columns use the terminology for language arts, social studies, and other content areaas. Each column expands the definition of each stage of the LEAP model. Through these curriculum-specific terms, the LEAP model can more tightly wire computer tools to specific content areas. From another angle, however, LEAP provides a crosscurricular structure, taking a generic thinking model and its associated computer tools and applying them to solving problems across a number of content domains.

LOCAL VS. GLOBAL COMPUTER

The curriculum goals on the left of this curriculum integration chart connect with the two computer tools columns on the far right. (See Table 11.1.) These far-right columns separate computer tools into local and global functions. If you can operate only on your immediate computer workstation, then you use the local computer. Instead of repeating the names of specific applications used at the local computer (e.g., word processor), I have converted the applications from Figure 11.1 to sets of actions that are universal to the wide range of local tools. These action terms are more generic for their insertion into curriculum plans, which cover a continually changing array of applications.

If you can operate from and on computer systems that are remote from your immediate workstation, then you can also use the global computer. Global computing requires computer networks. They are advancing at an accelerated pace with much to offer those educators who acquire this power to extend their reach (e.g., Anderson, 1993; Hunter, 1992). The right-most column points to many applications that require connection to computer networks in order to function usefully. The extensive nature of this global list reemphasizes the importance of thinkers having access to the Internet and other computer telecommunication utilities.

NOT!

A balanced discussion of new technologies must also consider actions not performed by the computers of today or of the foreseeable future. (See Table 11.1.) These processes are highlighted by boldfacing text in the column on local computer tools (e.g., "humans not computers choose problems and purposes"). That is, at the look stage, somehow a selection must be made among all the vast things at which one might look. Our selections are based on human intentions, on problems and purposes as thinkers see them. Only when these decisions are made can computers amplify human intelligence. At each LEAP stage, the most substantive actions are not taken by computer technologies, but by the value-laden actions of human beings. Consequently, these actions taken at the local computer highlight aspects of thought that are unique to humankind. I pass for now a more extended discussion of the question of whether technology can ever fulfill them or whether it should. It is my bias that the computer cannot perform these value-laden roles, but if it could, it should not. However, connecting our value systems with these wide-reaching computer capabilities is essential in allowing the technology to provide the greatest possible magnification for the role of human intelligence, for the ethical direction of technology, and for the even more critical role of intelligent teaching. The importance of this issue requires educators to consider carefully the degree to which our system of education emphasizes instruction in ethics. Without a significant ethical base, increasing human power to think (through the enhanced ability to deal with information) merely empowers a two-edged sword to also cut in both random and negative directions.

COMPLEXITY

There are other dimensions within the LEAP model that will be briefly discussed in closing, both the dimensions of multicultural and multisensory expression. The new reach of our computer networks into the global dimension creates new situations in which to discuss manners and demeanor. The possibility of miscommunication across languages and culture has been expanded greatly. For it is now as quick and easy for a child to type a letter to a next-door neighbor as to "share" with a child in Hong Kong through the magic of computer telecommunications. Further, the nature of communication for the youngest of our school-age children is being transformed from the textual to what is now sometimes referred to as multimedia. It is nearly as easy to create and edit sound/music, video, and images as it is to create and edit word-processing text. The excitement brought by the newness of these phenomena provides a window of opportunity to change the status of education as well, to be perceived as a cultural leader in forging the twenty-first century.

The perspectives found in North Carolina's Taylor-type (1980) model still guide educational planning for computer technology at the highest level of our states. Such an approach inherently lags behind developments in computer technology. However, from LEAP's perspective, our educational concepts are in the lead, awaiting computer technology to catch up with our goals. To change our status as educators, we must move to lead developments, not follow those set by corporation products (such as computers and multimedia) and by national economic planning (the national information infrastructure agenda). While attention is drawn to education to see how we are doing with these new technologies, it is a good time to change the perspective to our educational concerns.

Those with responsibility for curriculum development and integration of technical innovations can already see that teaching the use and mastery of these concepts and tools will require a deep scope-and-sequence chart spread across the K–12 spectrum and beyond. But it is a challenge that educators have faced and managed before. The challenge will be better met if we improve the framing of the problem. The challenge of teaching these concepts and tools matches the complexity, the time, and the importance of teaching the reading process. But if the accent is to be placed anywhere in the LEAP model, it falls not on the Look stage with its inherent emphasis on reading skills for a wide range of media (e.g., Look), but on the creative skills of the Evoke stage. LEAP provides an educational framework for integrating new technologies with the critical and creative processes of finding, inventing, and sharing solutions to real-world problems.

If you have set in motion the training and the technology acquisition that enables your school to LEAP into the information age, you should also reach out to include your community. A simple "transition technology" that is readily available is paper. Using paper, your school can start a "Question Ambassador" program. This program would begin by challenging a select number of students to take home a community question form. The form asks a community member for a question that a school or class team can research on the Internet. As Question Ambassador, the child presents the community question to the teacher and later presents the answer or contribution to the answer to the community member. Scaling up such work over time could play an important role in receiving community funding for additional technology resources.

In the nonlinear and tumultuous environment in which we live, our inventiveness and our ethics, not just our forecasting skills, may yet keep the human race alive. In the meantime, how do we find the funding and support to find and keep the tools of the age available?

WHAT FUNDING AND KNOWLEDGE-BASE SUPPORT EXISTS FOR INTEGRATING TECHNOLOGY INTO EDUCATIONAL PRACTICE?

The bullish federal leadership towards the information age creates an atmosphere supportive of initiatives from state legislatures as well. Superintendents should not overlook that opportunity for lobbying. Many states are answering the call for information-age infrastructure and development. Administrative leadership will have to stay alert to funding opportunities as they emerge. But there are two developments of some duration at the national level that can and should be influencing district planning, the Department of Commerce's National Telecommunications and Information Administration and the NetDay movement.

Through the White House Office of Science and Technology Policy, the administration formed the Information Infrastructure Task Force (IITF), which communicates the administration's goals for the National Information Infrastructure (NII). The Department of Commerce is home to the National Telecommunications and Information Administration (NTIA). Through NTIA, the federal government is distributing millions of dollars to construct and support the national information infrastructure. Their funds place special emphasis on factors that are supportive of rural schools and communities. Unfortunately, schools have been less active than public service groups in organizing for these grants. Further, the rhetoric about information-highway need has been stronger than the funding. The $21.5 million available for 1997 is barely a half million per state. However, the organizational meetings and contacts developed by those working on NTIA grants can provide effective leverage for other funding approaches to rural telecommunication needs. Through such awareness-building operations, schools receive further opportunity to share their computer technology needs with their communities.

Rural educators should actively support NTIA's lobbying of the FCC, in which NTIA argues that schools should receive free service or at least special telecommunications discounts. NTIA further encourages state regulators to set low prices for school and library access, including long distance Internet access from rural areas. New initiatives from the federal level are also expected. It is reasonable to expect that news about such developments will appear most quickly in the web site for the national NetDay 2000 (1996) movement.

State legislatures are also sympathetic to telecommunication needs, but again the rhetoric is generally stronger than the funding. North Carolina, for example, has invented the ConnectNC program in which the governor's office helps to organize a state region for business and general public access to the Internet. These organizations, in turn, can compete for small planning grants.

Districts should also consider their own grant program internally. There is so much to do and such a need for information-age direction that regional cooperatives that pool resources and expertise should be encouraged. Special grants should be offered to administrators and teachers who will tackle ways to use information systems that are in place and thereby increase the knowledge sharing among themselves across district and across regions. Released time may be equally as effective as funding.

Given that tax dollar support has been constrained, volunteer organizations are very valuable. NetDay began in California in March of 1996 and spread quickly across the country becoming known as NetDay96. Their stated goal was to train community volunteers to wire all the schools in California to the Internet on the same day and to fund the effort with voluntary community contributions. Other states have picked up on the idea and it has become a national movement. Widely supported by business, industry, and civic leaders, NetDay has created important organizations in nearly every state that have answered the call to build infrastructure and to organize people networks that can carry the movement further. This is one of the lowest cost alternatives that the schools will find and needs to be supported by schools through whatever means are possible. Now relabeled NetDay 2000 (1996), the movement furthers the next critical step, which turns the computers of the 1980's into the telecomputers of the next century upon which the next generation of curriculum depends. The Net-Day 2000 web page address in the references provides numerous contacts for organizational, funding, and technology assistance.

Spin-offs of NetDay developments can have a direct impact on two rural school needs, ongoing planning and technical support. Participants in NetDay are frequently asked to contribute to or to help form technology plan teams for the school. Another spin-off of the NetDay people networking is the formation of Tech Corp, which states that "(w)e are passionate about giving America's students a chance to have the most technologically advanced education possible. By working together we can make this happen through volunteerism" (Tech Corps, 1997, p. 1). Over thirty-seven states had chapters by July of 1997 with every indication that the rapid growth will continue.

What potential does this information age wave have for innovation and transformation in the rural school system and their relationship with their surrounding community?

Howley notes a powerful claim made against small and rural schools, "that small high schools cannot provide a curriculum with adequate breadth and depth to meet students' diverse needs" (Howley, 1994, p. 4). This perception is challenged by Haller, Monk, and Tien (1993), who report that tightly focused curricula can provide an excellent education and that this is best done in the context of the smaller schools. "If restructuring truly is an aim of school reform, then the scale of schooling is a major structural issue" (Howley, 1994, p. 4). Telecommunication capacity, especially through the Internet, dramatically changes the nature of this debate. The real issue becomes one of technical development and community access, not size and depth of the school. The LEAP model changes the perspective on how curriculum and technology can be merged within the classroom community. Sergiovanni (1994) notes that carrying the metaphor of community to the heart of district organization also changes the theory of how schools should operate and places everything in a larger context. This thinking in turn lays the groundwork for another model, CROP (Communities Resolving Our Problems), which lays a foundation for more effective integration of community and educational missions.

CROP

CROP's basic idea (Houghton, 1996), its Question Ambassador (Houghton, 1997) program and other variations, incorporates the LEAP model for problem-solving into its design and then adds two other key elements. CROP takes Sergiovanni's perspective on community to a new scale, to direct interaction between community activity and school curriculum. Further, the CROP model emphasizes an intellectual steering system for travel on the information-age highway, thinking skills.

LINKING SCHOOL AND COMMUNITY

In our homes from time to time we use the device of a job jar. Things that need to be done are placed in it awaiting a special someone to come along and deal with the job. Imagine that instead of a job jar you had a problem jar. Further, this "jar" would allow any one in your community to drop a problem into it at any time, day or night. Next, imagine a school district of trained problem solvers surrounded by a community of problem identifiers and problem reporters. There would be great overlap in roles between the school and community team members. That is, either might provide a problem or work to solve one. A community computer network provides the tools to make make such concepts a reality today.

CROP proposes extensions to variations on such service today. Not only do web sites and individuals on the network advertise they are willing to receive questions, they collate the answers and place sets of questions back on the community network (the Internet) for others to use in similar situations. These files are labeled FAQ files. FAQ files represent basic answers to "easy" questions, questions for which answers have been well formulated.

The CROP model adds the concept of SUP (Still Unsolved Problems). Communities would be able to hold on to their deeper and more long-standing questions through publicly accessible databases of community questions. Volunteer or paid individuals or classroom teams could filter the incoming questions and pass them on to appropriate teachers who would incorporate the hunt for their solution into course activities. The smaller and more coherent the communities, the greater the likelihood that such activity will occur. To the degree such civic engagement occurs, the community grows a social capital that can be reinvested to its profit over and over again. Through the process everyone takes a turn at being both a teacher and a learner. School-based and work-based communities can use these models to build the bridge to the integrated learning community of the twenty-first century.

THINKING AND LINKING

In Britain there is an extensive area of old canals that were once major thoroughfares across the country before the "infernal" combustion engine became the rage for travel. A collection of volunteers began sailing down these canals to points where the canals had fallen into decay and began refurbishing and rebuilding. The idea caught on and large "navies" of helpers gathered periodically to continue the resurrection of the canal system. They build the waterway while they use it. The World Wide Web component of the Internet is very similar. Net surfers run up against problems. They build web pages to address those problems and then invite others to create links to the page to construct even more to tackle the problem. They build the highway as they use it. They are guided in their activity by an underlying ethic to build, restore, and rebuild. To the degree that such underlying thinking skills are evoked, the fabric that is woven on the web will be more reliable and more valuable.

Already web weavers have created a new virtual space that addresses many rural problems. By definition, rural areas exist in some isolation from more active cultural centers. Yet television, public libraries and their lending services, and radio have played an important role in bringing ideas from other more rapidly changing environments. Those remaining in conceptual isolation remain so out of the will not to look and not to listen to different voices. But such mass media has not enabled rural citizens to equitably carry on two critical aspects of the knowledge trade, the ability to return fire with equal power and the ability to provide remote control. The author means this quite literally as the ability to move, change, and control distant events. Telephone voice lines provide only marginal support as long distance rates throttle down extensive communication beyond the isolated rural area. Fortunately, the web can equalize the potential flow of information if rural regions acquire the knowledge to use the tools.

Web technologies have bypassed the long distance system. The telecomputer makes a local call to a local computer acting as a telecommunications hub. The hub is part of a cloud of networks that trade knowledge and data through flat fees, not per-minute long distance charges. This has enabled online research from the home or the office desk, a simple extension of the local library carried to global extremes, peering into electronic card catalogs everywhere. Shopping is equally as close as your keyboard fingertips. This is true for both durable goods and for media and information products such as software. But this is still a kind of receiver-mode application.

There is a much more significant development. If you add server software to your web Internet connection that distributes computer files, that desktop computer has the equalizing return fire power of the Old West six shooter. Through server software providing a variety of web features, your computer simultaneously becomes a radio tower delivering audio files, a television broadcast center delivering video clips, a publishing house, a postal service, and a party chat line.

Beyond that, remote control is emerging as a major opportunity. This is in part conceptual control, the power of a controlling idea. Rural leaders now have low-cost access to other thinkers and decision-makers through electronic mail, and audio and videoconferencing. Beyond the power of interaction, there is the power to manipulate the physical environment. A wide variety of sensors and robots can be tapped and controlled from the same researcher's desktop. It is almost as feasible to use the Internet to manage your garden water system at your own home as it is to manage a garden water system in Australia. NASA's Mars expedition, like control of remote robots and sensors, can be done as well from downtown New York as from a farmer's front porch. The marketing and related economic implications of this are only beginning to be explored.

A great power needs great concepts to guide its use. This potential must be invented. Rural educators must grow the talent to discover these opportunities. Education has already developed many approaches to teaching underlying critical, creative, ethical, and other higher-order cognitive activities. The CROP model is but one that reinforces their use through highly visible links to problem-solving activity. Since Benjamin Bloom and his colleagues highlighted the issue of higher-order thinking skills in the 1950s, they have attracted attention on the educational agenda. Such attention continually invites others to use these ideas to guide and frame their question formats and their problem solutions.

Schools cannot dictate ethical behavior to communities but they can and do create standards by which their educational community will function and by which they allow interaction with the larger community. They can and do regulate the nature of the interaction among their members. Creative, ethical, and critical thinking skills can be encouraged and insisted on in the information age in the context of education. To the degree that rural communities predictably have safer environments and healthier lifestyles, rural communities will predictably use such standards to build sounder communication systems that better resolve their problems as they discover them.

SUMMARY

Through the concepts outlined in this chapter rural educators can lay the groundwork for not only active participation in the information highway of the twenty-first century, but for actively leading the world in the creation of high-technology-based jobs and careers. Along the way they can point out that the high-touch communities for which the rest of the world so intensely searches can easily be found in the same place.

REFERENCES

Anderson, P. 1993. "Connecting with the 'Real World,'" *Momentum, 24* (1), 26–27.
Blake, B. 1996, September 13. UNC Chancellor Hooker: "Knowledge Will Drive the U.S. Economy in the Future," *Asheville Citizen Times*, 1.

Clarke, M. 1990. "A Critically Reflective Social Studies," *History and Social Science Teacher, 25* (4), 214–20.

Clinton, W. J. 1997, February 7. *State of the Union Address.* [Online]. Available: http://www.whitehouse.gov/WH/SOU97/.

Eisenberg, M. B., & D. J. Berkowitz. 1988. *The Big Six Skills Approach to Information Problem Solving in Computer Skills for Information Problem Solving.* ERIC Accession No. ED 392 463.

Germann, P. J. 1991. "Developing Science Process Skills Through Directed Inquiry," *American Biology Teacher, 53* (4), 243–47.

Gipe, J. P., & J. C. Richards. 1992. "Reflective Thinking and Growth in Novices' Teaching Abilities," *Journal of Educational Research, 86* (1), 52–57.

Haller, E., D. Monk, & L. Tien. 1993. "Small Schools and Higher-Order Thinking Skills," *Journal of Research in Rural Education, 9* (2), 66–73.

Houghton, R. 1994a. *Curriculum Integration and the LEAP Model* [Online]. Available: http://www.ceap.wcu.edu/Houghton/LEAP/LEAPtable.html [1997, March 10].

Houghton, R. 1994b. *LEAP.* [Online]. Available: http://www.ceap.wcu.edu/Houghton/Learner/learnerhomeeasy2.html (1997, March 10).

Houghton, R. 1995. *THINK.* [Online]. Available: http://www.ceap.wcu.edu/Houghton/Learner/think/thinkhome.html (1997, March 10).

Houghton, R. 1996. *CROP's Basic Idea.* [Online]. Available: http://www.ceap.wcu.edu/ Houghton/Learner/basicidea.html [1997, February 20].

Houghton, R. 1997. *Question Ambassadors.* [Online]. Available: http://www.ceap.wcu.edu/Houghton/Learner/Publish/Review/QA/homeQA.html [1997, February 20].

Howley, C. 1994. *The Academic Effectiveness of Small-Scale Schooling: An Update.* ERIC Accession No. ED372897.

Hunter, B. 1992. "Linking for Learning: Computer-and-Communications Network Support for Nationwide Innovation in Education," *Journal of Science Education and Technology, 1* (1), 23–34.

Irving, L. 1996, October 28. *Equipping Our Children with the Tools to Compete Successfully in the New Economy.* Speech at Conference on Technology & the Schools: Preparing the New Workforce for the 21st Century. Randolph Center, Vermont. [Online]. Available: http://www.ntia.doc.gov/ntiahome/speeches/102896li_vermont.htm [1997, July 1].

Kelvin, P. R., & S. A. Leonard. 1992. "Computer-Assisted Writing Classes: Problems Among the Promises," *Bulletin of the Association for Business Communication, 55* (4), 21–25.

Manzo, A. V. et al. 1992. *Dialectical Thinking: A Generative Approach to Critical/Creative Thinking.* ERIC Accession: ED352632.

NetDay 2000. 1996. [Online]. Available: http://www.netday.org/ [1997, July 10].

North Carolina Computer Competencies for Educators. 1995. Raleigh, NC: North Carolina State Department of Public Instruction.

O'Loughlin, M. 1992. "Rethinking Science Education: Beyond Piagetian Constructivism Toward a Sociocultural Model of Teaching and Learning," *Journal of Research in Science Teaching, 29* (8), 791–799.

Pelletier, P. 1992. "Word Processing as a Support to the Writing Process," *International Journal of Instructional Media, 19* (3), 249–57.

Peters, R. 1987. "Modeling to Enhance Critical Thinking and Decision Making Skills Development in the Instructional Process: The Social Studies," ERIC Accession: ED287781, 26.

Peters, T. J. 1987. *Thriving on Chaos: Handbook for a Management Revolution.* New York: Knopf.

Pruett, P. L. et al. 1993. "Utilization of the Microcomputer in the Mathematics Classroom," *Computers in Human Behavior, 9* (1), 17–26.

Reschke, R. 1991. "The Future Problem Solving Program: How and Why It Works," *Gifted Child Today (GCT), 14* (2), 30–31.

Rogers, E. M. 1995. *Diffusion of Innovations* (4th ed.). New York: Free Press.

School Technology Users Task Force Report. 1995, October. *North Carolina Technology Competencies for Educators.* Raleigh, NC: Public Schools of North Carolina. [Online]. Available: http://www.ofps.dpi.state.nc.us/OFPS/hm/te/techcomp.htm [1997, June 10].

Sergiovanni, T. 1994. "Organizations or Communities? Changing the Metaphor Changes the Theory," *Educational Administration Quarterly, 30* (2), 214–230.

Taylor, R. 1980. *The Computer in the School: Tutor, Tool, Tutee.* New York: Teachers College Press.

Tech Corps. 1997. [Online]. Available: http://www.ustc.org/ [1997, June 20].

Toffler, A. 1970. *Future Shock.* New York: Bantam.

Toffler, A. 1981. *The Third Wave.* New York: Bantam.

Toffler, A. 1990. *Powershift: Knowledge, Wealth, and Violence at the Edge of the 21st Century.* New York: Bantam.

CHAPTER 12

Nobody Is as Smart as All of Us: Collaboration in Rural Schools

Nobody Is as Smart as All of Us.—William Clauss

The 1990s gave rebirth to an old idea: collaboration. On the surface, collaboration seems simple and straightforward "working together." Almost every staff development program encourages the audience to network, communicate, empower one another, develop team skills, develop quality circles, and cooperatively set goals. The audience nods their approval and offers testimonials as to how they are doing all this at their school or agency. Everyone also agrees that "two heads are smarter than one," but with few exceptions, collaborative efforts end when the trainer goes home. The title of this chapter is an invitation to the reader to reexamine the potential power of the collaborative process.

INTRODUCTION

COMMUNITIES across our country are seeking ways to reclaim the one child in four who is at-risk of failing or dropping out of school. They are pondering the highly interrelated problems that place kids at-risk, such as poverty, substance abuse, child abuse, teen parenthood, untreated or undiagnosed health problems, delinquency, gang activity, and even homelessness. It is not surprising that kids who face these kinds of problems are difficult to reach and teach. Responding to the complex problems presented by todays families is not the sole responsibility of one agency, organization, or institution. The schools already have full plates, but if schools want to increase the learning potential of children, then they must be one of the key players in resolving some of the social and health-related problems that

William Clauss, Director, Office of Rural Education, Western Carolina University.

221

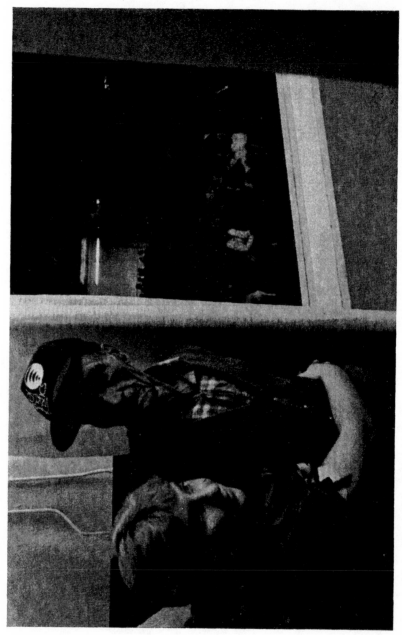

Man and his granddaughter at the Democratic Party fish fry, Marshall, North Carolina. © Photo by Rob Amberg.

interfere with or disrupt the learning process. But how can schools or community agencies help solve these problems when resources are declining? No single educational, health or social service institution has the finances, knowledge or capacity to do the job alone. Collaboration may not be a silver bullet, but it does provide a process for beginning to address community problems as a community instead of single agencies working in isolation.

Joy Dryfoos (1994) acknowledges the difficulty of interagency collaboration when she defines collaboration as "an unnatural act between non-consenting adults" (p. 149). She also mentions that in *theory*, the directors and staff of various community agencies (Education, Health and Human Services) simply gather together and create a safety net of programs to meet the interrelated needs noted earlier. In *practice*, however, this process becomes difficult because agencies have their own unique missions, goals, and budget authorities. It is also difficult to convince "entrenched bureaucrats to change their ways and share authority and decision making" (p. 149). Even though the process is neither easy nor simple, collaboration can be accomplished. The chances of long-range success are more likely, however, if each of the participants is aware of the barriers, can identify goals that are common to each agency, and continues to work together even when the going gets tough.

> Collaboration may not be a silver bullet, but it does provide for beginning to address community problems as a community instead of single agencies working in isolation.

MODELS/LEVELS OF COLLABORATION

The most common collaborative efforts take place between people not agencies. Individuals develop personal or professional friendships that continue to expand as mutual trust levels are established. They begin to share successful and unsuccessful ideas, professional secrets and visions. Such exchanges often culminate in informal networks in which the shared expertise produces better results with a smaller expenditure of energy. These efforts will continue to grow and expand as long as both parties benefit and each individual does not violate the basic rules of friendship and trust. These same efforts can be applied to broader levels of collaboration.

Calvin Stone (1995) conducted research on various school and community collaboration efforts and identified three types or levels of collaboration. At one level, collaboration can involve chief executive officers of various agencies, such as the superintendent of schools and the directors of various county health or social service agencies. Meetings or exchanges between these officials could result in modification or streamlining of policies and practices of each of the agencies so as to facilitate better service delivery and fewer bureaucratic barriers and gaps in service provision.

Stone also identified a second stage of collaboration between mid-level professionals (principals, deans, etc.). The professionals at this level are closer to the day-to-day contact with the clients such as students and teachers, and information exchanges between them are the rule instead of the exception. This kind of collaboration can result in shared knowledge, responsibility, and professional support.

The third level is the opportunity for on-site professionals (teachers, agency case workers, etc.) to collaborate with youth, parents, and families. This model provides a forum for each of the parties to have a voice and vote in decision-making. The philosophy that guides the process assumes that the clients (students, parents, and families) are active participants and can contribute to solving the problems rather than being passive consumers of services.

The unifying thread between each of these models is that people or agencies can work together to increase efficiency of service delivery. Reducing duplication can stretch diminishing resources and build a continuum of efforts instead of a collection of fragmented individual attempts. In the best of all worlds, the best collaborative effort would be a combination of each of the models described. The ultimate objective of any cooperative venture is not to do anything *for* or *to* anyone—but rather *with* someone.

HOW TO GET STARTED

Collaboration is the process of working jointly with others, including those with whom one is not normally or immediately connected, to more efficiently develop and achieve common goals. Characteristics of this process include the following. The partners establish or identify common goals and agree to share, pool, or exchange resources to implement, monitor, and evaluate the new services and/or procedures associated with these goals. In a collaborative agreement, input from each partner is continually solicited to develop more comprehensive services or to change or modify existing systems (Calfee & Wittwer, 1995).

Interagency collaboration can take place at a variety of levels. A simple form may be for a school to open its classrooms to a college or university that offers a teacher preparation program. The university would now have a site for field placements or student teacher experiences and the school would benefit from the new ideas and energy that the beginning teachers would bring.

A more complicated collaboration may be between a school and the county health office. In this initiative, the school may provide office and clinic space for a health worker to be co-located. Health screening and diagnosis is more efficient when services are brought to a concentration of clients instead of the clients traveling long distances to the county health facility. Several schools in Florida have more than twenty separate interagency collaboration efforts working together at the school site (Calfee & Wittwer, 1995). These include health, social service, and law enforcement agencies.

Interagency coordination and collaboration can take place at a variety of levels, from simple to complex, from family-based teams at a local level to state-level, policy-making councils. All, however, share a common belief: that coordination of services across agencies can yield increased efficiency, improved products, increased client satisfaction and even financial savings.

An interagency initiative does take leadership and extra work. Most educators already face heavy workloads and responsibilities and the thought of working and coordinating with other agency staff can be overwhelming. It is a fact that in the beginning extra duty is inevitable, but in the longer view, schools will be able to do their job of teaching better, because the children will have fewer health and social problems and can now focus their minds on the academics.

There are a number of ways to begin an interagency collaborative arrangement, but nothing will happen until someone assumes the leadership for making the first contact. It should also be noted that there is no single "best" collaborative model because each community is unique in its needs and political structure. But every community has some characteristics in common with every other community. The following guidelines for building an interagency cooperative agreement are based on these commonalities.

Step 1: The process of collaboration begins when a small group of committed leaders decides to act together to address a common problem that their own organization cannot solve independently. In this first stage, a community problem is tentatively identified from an informal needs assessment. The identified problem area dictates the agencies and representatives who are to be involved in the next stage of development.

Step 2: The identified stakeholders meet to define shared visions and goals. A formal community needs assessment may be conducted in this step to confirm or redefine the problem area for cooperative resolution. These interagency meetings provide a forum for establishing a baseline of common knowledge about each other's agency as well as the problems each faces. At each step of the process, the partners will need to reinforce their individual and collective commitment to overcome previous layers of resistance to change—in attitudes, policies and relationships. It is in this step that trust will begin to be built and a new way of doing business will be forged. New partners are added on an as-needed basis. It may also be helpful to identify a neutral partner, to keep the records and to maintain the initiatives that have begun. A university or community college provost, dean, or other appropriate public official can be this neutral partner. Involving a nearby university or community college also holds the potential for free database searches, research designs, and evaluation as well as problem-specific expertise.

Step 3: During this developmental period, the various stakeholders need to formulate very specific plans regarding the targeted population, the geographic area to be served, and the kinds of services that are to be provided. It is during this step that interagency agreements need to be put in writing. This is also a good time to involve the general public via town meetings, press conferences, and general media releases. It is important that the targeted populations and neighborhoods also have a representation as stakeholders. It is often the clients who best know what services and services delivery system will be successful. Your consortium is now ready for a small pilot study to determine if the plans written on paper can survive a field test. The pilot study will yield valuable data on the strengths and weaknesses of your plan. It is important for the stakeholders to realize that new ventures often crash. It is even more important that the team holds together and tries again if a crash should occur.

Step 4: When the field tests begin to indicate that your collaborative plan is working, it is time to make the final adjustments and to design a short- and long-term documentation and evaluation plan. The data obtained from the evaluation should provide information to continually adjust and fine tune your plan.

Step 5: Once the project is up and running, take about twenty minutes to celebrate and then continue to meet and strengthen the trust levels that brought the partners to this level. Projects may need to be expanded and continually refined. Local leadership from the targeted service recipients must also be developed so that the clients can help keep the program going.

There are many reasons why diverse agencies should seek out and form interagency linkages. One of the most obvious is to reduce unnecessary duplication and waste. The resulting savings can be applied to the provision of new or expanded services. Such voluntary sharing also provides a positive public relations image to community citizens who appreciate reduced bureaucracies and taxes. In fact, the sharing of cost and clients may help each of the agencies to survive in an uncertain economy. The effectiveness of agencies working together is also increased by the joint delivery of services. Most clients, for example, have more than one problem or need. In these multi-problem instances, working effectively on only one problem while ignoring or neglecting the others is inefficient for an agency as well as ineffective for the client. If resources are pooled, then limited and mutually exclusive skills, equipment, or specialized space (such as medical facilities) can provide seamless and comprehensive services that would not otherwise be possible. This kind of networking also builds a sense of solidarity in a community. This solidarity is the keystone for replacing competition and politics with common sense.

There are barriers, however, that inhibit the establishment of interagency consortia. One of these barriers is fear that there will be loss of control when several agencies agree to work together. For example, a smaller agency may fear being gobbled up by a larger agency.

Many agencies are also constrained by boards of directors or funding limitations that prohibit their involvement with clients who are not directly defined as their targeted clients. Another barrier to the formation of linking relationships is the perception of incompatible goals or philosophies. Sometimes agencies may share a common funding source that has limited resources to allocate. In these situations, the incentives may be to compete rather than cooperate. The final barrier may be that no one wants to take the first step in forming a consortium. Indeed, many agencies are funded through long-standing legislative support in the form of taxes. These agencies may feel little or no pressure to form inter-agency agreements.

GRANT WRITING IN RURAL SCHOOLS: HIGHER EDUCATION/LEA COLLABORATION

Many ideas, programs, or innovations can be achieved through interagency initiatives by refocusing or redirecting existing resources. However, sometimes you need to obtain grant funds in order to accomplish new or expanded services. To obtain a grant, a proposal will need to be written. Again, a collaborative effort may increase the likelihood that your proposal will be successful in obtaining funding. A regional university or community college has a wealth of resources that can facilitate proposal writing and most of these resources are available without cost. Faculty and staff have research knowledge and skills for conducting or preparing literature revisions, needs assessments, evaluation designs, and even potential funding sources. Colleges and universities also have access to demographic data that can be used to prepare a description or documentation of the need stated in your proposal. Of course, you can write a grant proposal without involving a university or any other partner; however, a proposal is usually stronger if it is prepared by a team. But before the writing begins, there are some questions that, when answered, may serve as guidelines for developing the proposals.

(1) Have you clearly identified a significant problem that will capture the imagination and matches the funding priorities of the funding sources?

(2) Does your proposal offer a sensible, do-able and unique approach to solving the problem?

(3) Is your proposal cost effective? Can you show that the anticipated benefits will outweigh the costs?

(4) If your plan is successful, can it be replicated in other communities? Grant funding is short term, what will happen to your project when the grant funds are no longer available?

If you are satisfied with your answers to the above questions, then you are ready to begin writing. If you decide to use a team-writing approach, select members who have the knowledge, skills, and abilities to match your program objectives. If you can identify one of the members who has experience in writing grants, you are off to a good beginning. A good starting place is to do a search of the research literature to determine if there have been similar previous and successful efforts. Computer searches of databases make this job rather easy. Provide your team members with printouts, journals, and other sources of relevant information. Each team member should be assigned a role with clear guides as to their task and time frame. One task will be to develop a list of funding sources and to request proposal guidelines. Every university has references listing the names, addresses, and funding priorities of major foundations, corporations, and government/agencies. If your request is small, you may want to check with the businesses and service organizations in your local community.

Almost every funding agency will have specific proposal guidelines that must be followed. It is important to follow these guidelines to the letter. Be certain to provide every document or piece of information that is requested. A typical proposal requires the following:

(1) Cover letter
(2) Abstract
(3) Narrative, including an introduction, needs assessment, statement of the problem, goals, objectives, evaluation and budget (including future funding)
(4) Appendices

The *cover letter* should be clearly written. It will be the first impression you make on a potential funder. This letter must contain the name, address, and phone number of the individual who will be the contact person, and the organization submitting the proposal, as well as the subject and title of this proposal. A description of the targeted population is helpful along with a short discussion of the objectives and proposed solutions your program presents.

The *abstract* is a summary of your proposal's significant points. Limit it to about one well-written page. The *proposal narrative* should answer the questions *why* you are asking for money and *what* you seek to accomplish and *how* you will accomplish your goals.

Specifically, *the narrative* will include the statement of the problem, the purpose, the programs goals and measurable objectives, and a compelling logical reason why it should be supported. It should include the approach or method and process of accomplishing the goals and objectives, as well as the implementation plan and timeline for accomplishing each step. It is important to write the objectives so that there is a logical flow from the goals. The objectives should state *what* will be done, and *to* whom and *by* whom and *when* it will be done. If the objectives are clearly written, it will be simple to determine when an objective is accomplished. The accomplishment of the objective is, of course, the intent of the program *evaluation*—which sometimes calls for very technical measurement results. Additionally, credentials should be included providing information about the applicants, certifying their ability to successfully undertake the project.

A proposal budget should be realistic and defensible and be directly related to the needs, objectives, and activities described in the narrative section. The funding agencies' proposal guidelines usually state the format of the budget and list items or categories that are not excluded by that agency. They also like to look at questions such as, is the budget adequate, are costs reasonable, is it consistent with the proposed activities, and is there sufficient detail and explanation?

If your proposal is accepted by the funding agency, you will be notified of your award. If you accept the award, your proposal has become a legal and binding contract and you are obligated to do the promised work. It is important to track all funds carefully and to always be prepared for an accountability audit.

CONCLUSION

The role and public expectation of education continues to expand at a time of reduced funding. The demand to do more with less is a common expectation. Since these problems will not go away, educators must assume the leadership to explore the options offered by collaborative initiatives. This notion of collaboration is easy to say but difficult to do because it is a significant change in the way we are used to doing business . . . but it may be the only game in town.

REFERENCES

Calfee, C., & F. Wittwer. 1995. *Building a Full Service School: Florida's Model of Collaboration for School-Based and School-Linked Services.* Edited by Mimi Meredith. Tallahassee, FL: The Florida Department of Education.

Dryfoos, J. D. 1994. *Full-Service Schools.* San Francisco, CA: Josey-Bass Publishers.

Melaville, A. I., & M. J. Blank, with G. Asayesh. 1993. *Together We Can. A Guide for Crafting a Profamily System of Education and Human Services.* U.S. Department of Education Office of Educational Research and Improvement. Washington, DC: U.S. Government Printing Office.

Skiba, R., L. Polsgrove, & K. Nasstrom. *Developing a System of Care: Interagency Collaboration for Students with Emotional/Behavioral Disorders.* Bloomington, IN: The Council for Children with Behavioral Disorders.

Stone, C. R. 1995. "School/Community Collaboration: Comparing Three Initiatives." *Phi Delta Kappan,* June: pp.794–800.

CHAPTER 13

School-Community Collaborative Vision Building: A Study of Two Rural Districts

Vision when developed collaboratively between the rural school and rural community creates a powerful force that cultivates the development of the greater sense of community.—Ed Chance, 1997

This chapter discusses one method that has proven successful in creating a sense of greater community in several rural school districts and communities throughout the country. The process centers on the development of a shared educational vision for the rural school for the twenty-first century. The concept of vision is not new but the development of a vision is often focused within an organization, not shared with separate entities such as the community and school. This chapter discusses the process and shares the stories of two school districts in the southwestern part of the United States.

RURAL schools and rural communities exist in a unique symbiotic relationship. The rural school is often the center of the rural community's activities and focus. The rural school provides entertainment, jobs, and intellectual strength to the community by educating its youth. In turn, the rural community provides an infrastructure that includes economic support, raw materials (i.e., students), and strong community encouragement for school activities. The level of mutual collaboration, and the degree of intensity, found between the school and community directly reflects on the success of both.

In truth, a collaborative school and community represent a "greater" community. This greater community epitomizes people who share a common core of values regarding the young people of that community and their potential future. The concept of a greater community is not just a reflection of geography or membership or affiliation, although these may be important elements, but rather represents a shared sense of belonging, caring, and community focus. In

Edward W. Chance, Department of Education, University of Nevada-Las Vegas.

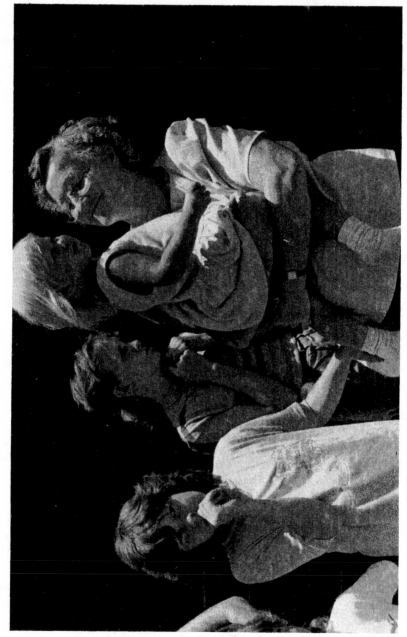

Family at the Fourth of July parade, Marshall, NC. © Photo by Rob Amberg.

this greater community, people are partners in the educational process of their most precious commodity—their children. Teachers and parents do not exist in separate worlds but are united with others in the community into a milieu of common purpose and direction.

This is not meant to imply or suggest that all rural schools or all rural communities have a sense of this greater community or recognize the interactive symbiotic relationship that exists. Some rural schools and communities never realize the importance of nurturing and supporting such a relationship. Too often rural schools and rural communities only discover the need for such a relationship when it is too late because the school is being closed, the community is losing one of its primary businesses, or the community has declined to a level of ineffectiveness. It may simply be impossible to develop a collaborative, entwined interdependence at that stage of the game.

But many rural schools and communities do recognize each other's importance and do seek to create a web of collaboration as part of this greater community. This realization of the need to collaborate is often the result of leadership exhibited by an individual or individuals in the school or community. Such leadership effort usually builds on shared school and community values.

The importance of values and shared belief systems has been supported by numerous studies. Blumberg and Greenfield (1980) discuss the creation of a culture and environment based on values. Their views are supported by the work of Cunningham and Gresso (1993) and Whitaker and Moses (1994). But the question remains as to how one creates this sense of greater community and how one determines those shared values and beliefs that exist between and within rural schools and communities.

> A strong school-community vision provides a sense of direction. It allows for a school-community partnership to exist not just in words but in action.

This chapter will discuss one method that has proven successful in creating this sense of greater community in several rural school districts and communities throughout the country. The process centers on the development of a shared educational vision for the rural school for the twenty-first century. The concept of vision is not new but the development of a vision is often focused within an organization, not shared separate entities such as the community and school. This chapter will discuss the process and share the stories of two school districts in the southwestern part of the United States.

A vision has been variously described, ranging from "the development, transmission, and implementation of a desirable future" (Manasse, 1985, p. 150) to "a blueprint of a desired state" (Shieve & Shoenheit, 1987, p. 94) to a "journey from the known to the unknown . . . creating the future from a montage of facts, hopes, dreams . . . and opportunities" (Hickman & Silva, 1984, p. 151). The core of all vision research and a multitude of vision definitions is that a vision shapes an organization or an institution as it moves toward a better future

(Chance, 1992; Rutherford, 1985; Shieve & Shoenheit, 1987). That vision, when developed collaboratively between the rural school and rural community, creates a powerful force that cultivates the development of the greater sense of community previously discussed.

How does one go about building this collaborative school-community vision in order to create this greater community? It doesn't just happen. Chance (1992) has developed a process by which this shared collaborative vision is developed. This school-community vision process is predicated on a five-step procedure. Step One is the development and clarification of a personal vision by school district leaders. These leaders include, but are not limited to, the superintendent, central office personnel, building administrators, board members, and lead teachers. Step Two is the development of an overall organizational vision through the involvement of community leaders, parents and nonparents, teachers, staff members, board members, administrators, students, and even those in the community who are educational critics.

The development of this organizational vision is the result of a multitiered effort that gradually moves from numerous small groups to one large group. Figure 13.1 provides an overview of the process. Members of the small groups consisting of community-school members answer a series of questions related to school district strengths, weaknesses, community support, community concerns, and district focus. They utilize a consensus-building process that allows them to agree upon their answers. Representatives then move to the next level where consensus is again reached. The process continues until consensus answers are agreed upon by all members or their representatives. Participants at the lowest level create their individual personal and organizational vision and the procedure repeats itself.

Subsequently, in Step Three, they determine how to communicate the vision;

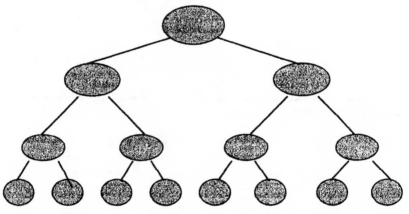

Figure 13.1 A multi-tiered effort to develop organization vision.

how to actualize the vision in Step Four) and, in Step Five) how to sustain the vision process. The result or outcome of this vision activity, an overall collaborative school-community vision, is important but not as important as the process that takes place. Members from a variety of viewpoints are allowed to discuss the future and direction of the school district. This sharing of ideas and concerns allows for a common belief and value system to be identified. It also provides everyone an opportunity to discuss their viewpoints. The focus of the school district and the community become unified as they move towards a greater community sense of collaboration and cooperation. The process represented by extensive discussion and debate is as important as the eventual outcome, which is a vision statement.

After the development of a school-community vision, individual school sites embark upon a similar process to build a school site-specific vision. These site-driven visions exist under the umbrella of the overall school-community vision. They are just as important as the overall vision because they determine building-specific focus and goals. This individualization of the vision process by school site provides an opportunity for all faculty and staff with the parents within the district to be involved in determining the direction of the school.

As important as the vision is the heightened level of school-community collaboration. It is this collaboration that ensures the success of the process and creates the greater community feeling. The following case studies provide an overview of the collaborative vision building process and is the result of the community-school partnership.

THE DISTRICT AND THE COMMUNITY: DISTRICT ONE

The DeKalb, Texas, school district was established in 1831 in far northeastern Texas. The district is bounded on the north by the Red River and the Oklahoma state line. The district encompasses 255 square miles. The school has been at its present site since 1900. The district has a property wealth valued at 77 million. The current school population is 1,000 students equally distributed between the elementary, the middle school, and the high school. The student population is 63 percent Caucasian and 37 percent African-American. The average daily attendance for students is 97 percent.

The community is a typical rural farming/ranching community of approximately 2,000 people. The largest employer in the community is the school district with approximately 150 staff members, 96 who are certified. Over half of the teachers have a master's degree. The second largest employer is the Red River Army Depot, a nearby military installation. The community also has a considerable number of retirees. Politically, the community is strongly Democratic. Economically, most citizens are middle class to lower class. The strongest religious affiliations are Southern Baptists and Methodists.

LEADERSHIP IN THE SCHOOL

The superintendent and the curriculum director were the two primary forces behind the vision-building activity. Both are female with strong convictions. They are viewed by the school staff and the community as being crucial to any school improvement. It is through their leadership that the district has received the Texas Successful Schools Award for both the elementary and the middle school. The elementary school has also been selected as a Texas Partnership School and a Texas Mentor School. This recognition has led to visits to the school by the Texas commissioner of education and then governor of Texas, Ann Richards.

The other administrators are the building principals, who are all male. They are enthusiastic and student-oriented. Their staffs, especially at the elementary and middle level, protect and assist the principals whenever possible. The high school has the greatest number of problems, many of which are related to staff inconsistency and intransigence. The high school principal is the only minority administrator but is supported by both white and nonwhite community members. In fact, he helped create the atmosphere allowing all the disparate community groups to begin to work together.

The seven-member school board consists primarily of professionals and businessmen. Board members are extremely supportive of the school superintendent and her activities, and the board is stable and willingly works with administrators in setting goals for the district.

THE VISION PROCESS

The process of building a school-community vision began with a two-day retreat with central office administrators, district principals, board members, the athletic director, and Region VIII Education Service Center representatives. This two-day intensive training focused on team building; leadership and management styles; shifting education paradigms; the Reform Movement; assessment of school, community, and personal strengths and weaknesses; personal visions; and strategies for communicating a vision. The intent of the retreat was to create an atmosphere of support and confidence in those present so that they were comfortable with the next stage of the process.

One month later, an initial meeting was held in the district to begin the formal process of creating an overall organizational vision. This meeting, and the next two, were conducted by the superintendent. Forty-two people from the community and school were invited to participate in the process. These individuals were carefully selected so they represented all community interests. Six teams, consisting of seven people each, were utilized for this initial stage. Each team consisted of a board member, a professional staff member, a parent, a community member, a paraprofessional staff member, a support staff member (bus driver, maintenance, or cafeteria), and an administrator. Each group answered a series of questions individually and then through consensus developed a vision statement, motto, and symbol. Three members from each group were selected by the group to move to the next level of the vision process.

Two weeks later a second meeting was held with the representatives from the original six groups. The eighteen people in attendance were divided into three teams of six people. Each team was to reformulate and refine the results from the first meeting of forty-two. Their work included examining the strengths and weaknesses of the school district as well as determining which vision statement or combination of statements they preferred from the first session. Three people from each team were selected to attend the final organizational vision meeting.

One week later, nine individuals met to finalize and articulate the organizational vision statement, the vision motto, and symbol. At this final meeting, the superintendent moved from the role of observer to that of facilitator/leader. Her focus was to guide the nine people into developing an overall vision that was representative of all previous meetings and which represented a futuristic view and direction for the school district.

The result of this effort was the following vision statement:

> DeKalb Independent School District, through continuous improvements and growth, will provide a caring, motivated, and supportive administration, faculty, and staff. This educational network will recognize the value of fairness and equality for all while working cooperatively with parents and community to produce confident students. With pride, character, and life skills in hand, our students will be equipped to assume their meaningful place in society.

The motto selected for the DeKalb vision is "DeKalb Schools... Where Tomorrow Begins Today." The symbol is a five pronged starfish with students in the middle and each of the five prongs representing fairness, character, equality, confidence, and pride.

After the development of the overall organizational vision, it was time to develop the separate site-specific visions. Vision-building sessions were conducted on each campus by university personnel and a format similar to that which had been utilized districtwide was followed. Each site also developed a procedure to communicate its vision and identified goals that were to be achieved within the calendar year as well as within the next five years.

The school district is currently at a crucial juncture. Too often administrators and teachers lose sight of the school's vision once it is developed because of daily demands of the profession. To counteract this possibility, the superintendent constantly asks building administrators for status reports and expects the principals to do the same to their faculty. The superintendent provided a lapel pin that represented the vision to all teachers, support staff, administrators, and selected community members. This activity, done with all the participants in a circle, was a way to reemphasize the district's and community's commitment to the vision process. This activity took place after the district's administrators had cooked breakfast as a means to express their appreciation for all the collaborative efforts.

Various community and school district members were randomly interviewed regarding the vision building process. One parent stated, "I'm excited to be a part of the vision process because this can only make the school better with all the people pulling together." Another parent indicated, "it is wonderful to see the school system become a progressive system." A board member in discussing the vision activity asserted, "it gave me a chance to be involved in a more personal nature with the people in our community and school system." A teacher stated, "the entire community knows what is going on in our system and we are all working together for change. We can set our goals high and their is no limit to what we can achieve." DeKalb schools and its greater community have continued its collaborative efforts. A recent passage of an important bond issue by 70 percent is a reflection of this collaboration.

THE DISTRICT AND THE COMMUNITY: DISTRICT TWO

The Altus School District is located in far southwestern Oklahoma near the Texas border. When the town of Frazier, Oklahoma, located on the banks of Bitter Creek, was destroyed by flood waters in 1891, the residents moved their community to higher ground and changed its name to Altus. Shortly after selecting a new location, these pioneers established the first school, which doubled as a church.

Currently, the Altus schools are housed in fifty buildings on 121 acres. The district encompasses 196 square miles and attracts students from many adjacent rural areas. Composed of six elementaries, a middle school, junior high, high school and learning center, the system is attended by 4,676 students with a 94 percent average daily attendance. The average Altus teacher has been in the classroom for over fourteen years and has earned at least twenty hours of graduate-level training. Over 45 percent possess a master's degree.

The student body represents a rich diversity. Approximately one-fourth are dependents of active duty personnel of Altus Air Force Base. The majority of the students are of English, German or Irish descent, but 11.4 percent are Hispanic and 9.2 percent are African-American. Nearly 3 percent are either American Indian or Asian.

The Altus community is composed of three major facets including business, farming/ranching and the Altus Air Force Base. The base employs over 3,000 active duty personnel and 600 civilians. The next largest employer is the Altus Schools with 484 employees, followed by Jackson County Memorial Hospital with 475 employees and Bar-S Food with 400. Altus Athletic Manufacturing and the City of Altus employ over 200 people each.

Just over 74 percent of the community population has completed high school with nearly 25 percent having earned at least an associate's degree. The median community income is $21,175. Fifty-three percent of the household incomes are middle class, and slightly over 40 percent are lower class. Registered voters are mostly Democrats, with Republicans making up slightly over 22 percent. The three primary religious affiliations are Southern Baptist, Church of Christ, and Methodist.

LEADERSHIP IN THE SCHOOL

The superintendent represents the primary leadership force in the district with a strong desire to bring about positive change. With the assistance of central office personnel, he has provided the necessary guidance in the vision-building process. The other administrators are building principals, all of whom are male except one. Five of the six elementary principals have been at the current assignments for six or more years. The sixth elementary principal and middle school, junior high and high school principals have had four or fewer years at their current positions.

While all are student-oriented, leadership styles vary. Six adhere to a traditional administrative style, strive to maintain discipline and see their roles as managers. The other three are making great strides towards becoming instructional leaders. Of these three, the high school principal makes the greatest efforts at instructional leadership but has been hampered by discord among the faculty. The dissension is due in part to his leadership style, in part to the fact that he became principal during the year the state mandated the greatest number of prescribed educational changes. A unified vision provides a common bond to overcome such past problems.

The five-member school board consists of one professional, three business persons, and a minority white-collar employee. While they represent distinct points of view, the board members are extremely supportive of the school district and teachers. The board is stable and willingly works with administrators and the community in setting goals for the district.

THE VISION PROCESS

The community vision process began with a similar format as that described for District One. A two-day retreat was held with university personnel meeting with central office administrators, principals, board members, and the migrant program director to train them to facilitate the collaborative vision process. Activities and objectives were the same as those described for District One with the exception that procedures and processes reflected school district needs and community expectations.

Six weeks later over 180 parents, teachers, support staff members, students, community leaders, and others representing the entire community, including those who had attended the retreat, met to begin the formulation of the collaborative school-community vision. With the superintendent conducting this meeting, the entire group was divided into twenty-four teams consisting of five to eight members each. Each team included an administrator, a certified staff member, a support staff member, a parent, a student, and at least one other person representing another facet of the community such as a minority group, Altus Air Force Base personnel, or business interests.

At that initial meeting, each of the teams listed the internal and external factors that affect the effectiveness of the district and the strengths and weaknesses of the district. Subsequently, members of each team described their ideal school and drafted a vision statement. Consensus building was extremely important during this part of the process, because it assists in creating the sense of a greater community.

Input from each of the first twenty-four teams was included as representatives from each moved to the next level where twelve new teams were formed. Ideas were pooled and vision statements consolidated. At the second level the teams also formulated mottos and symbols to correlate with their vision statements.

Representatives from the twelve teams moved on to form six new teams where the process was repeated and representatives moved on to form three new teams. From these three teams the final eleven-member group was formed. The superintendent became a member of the final team as the members assembled with three vision statements and three mottos and symbols to combine into one on which all could agree.

The following Greater Community Collaborative Vision emerged:

> Altus . . . Where all students are primed to become successful and productive citizens in a safe, positive environment by accountable stakeholders who develop high academic skills and inspire personal dreams.

When sharing the vision statement with the community, the vice commander of the 97th Air Mobility Wing of the Altus Air Force Base said that while the vision looks to the future it also goes back to the beginning for the students to their personal dreams. "In Altus Schools," he said, "those dreams will be nurtured and they will grow. The students will have a reason for being, and we hope to help them learn how to make their dreams a reality."

"Altus Schools—Where Dreams Grow" became the motto to complement the symbol, an apple with a large A in the center and a lamp of learning resting on the bar of the letter. In describing the symbol and motto to the community a parent said, " 'Where Dreams Grow' expresses that thing inside every child that wants to be something special when he or she grows up." He went on to say that the A expresses excellence and achievement and that the lamp signifies learning and knowledge, what schools are all about.

The greater community vision was shared with the total community at a special celebration event in the late spring. The superintendent opened the event by saying that the vision was designed in such a way as to challenge, to empower, and to determine the destination of the school district. "With this vision," he said, "we will get somewhere and know where we are headed. I believe that our schools and our community will become a lighthouse community as everyone joins in shaping what education is to be and everyone helps in making it happen." A board member said during the celebration, "The vision process has given the district the tools to reach district goals. We can really be proud of what we have accomplished here by including the community in determining the direction we will go."

Once the vision had been shared, lapel pins were presented to the more than 200 in attendance. The superintendent closed with, "The Greater Community Vision is just the beginning. We now must commit ourselves to seeing that we do not lose sight of that vision and to work diligently to see it actualized for every student in our schools." District Two developed school site-specific vision statements in the same manner described for District One.

Altus has also established community shared goals and objectives and has established leadership teams at both the school and community levels as well as the building level in order to maintain their focus on the greater community vision. A variety of activities are planned as Altus begins to implement and actualize its vision for the future.

CONCLUSION

The vision-building process has assisted these two school districts and their communities in focusing their energies. It has created a collaborative community atmosphere where everyone is excited about school improvement. That excitement exists because the school-community vision and goals are uniquely theirs and not someone else's. As one teacher in District One said, "it is exciting to be working in a school . . . that knows where it is going." A strong school-community vision provides a sense of direction. It allows for a school-community partnership to exist not just in words but in action. Whether these districts ever achieve their visions is problematic. But one thing is for sure and that is that the school-community vision journey will be an exciting one, beneficial to all involved. The school and community partnership is very real in these two districts, nurturing the sense of greater community so necessary for rural schools to survive and prosper.

REFERENCES

Blumberg, A., & W. Greenfield. 1980. *The Effective Principal: Perspectives on School Leadership.* Boston: Allyn and Bacon.

Chance, E. W. 1992. *Visionary Leadership in Schools: Successful Strategies for Devel-*

oping and Implementing an Educational Vision. Springfield, IL; Charles C. Thomas.

Cunningham,W. G., & D. W. Gresso. 1993. Cultural Leadership: The Culture of Excellence in Education. Boston: Allyn and Bacon.

Hickman, C. R., & M. Silva. 1984. Creating Excellence: Managing Corporate Culture, Strategy, and Change in a New Age. New York: New American Library.

Manasse, A. L. 1985. "Vision and Leadership: Paying Attention to Intention," Peabody Journal of Education, 63(1), 150–73.

Rutherford, W. L. 1985. "School Principals As Effective Leaders," Phi Delta Kappan, 67(1), 31–34.

Shieve, L. T., & M. B. Shoenheit. 1987. "Vision and the Work Life of Educational Leaders," In L. T. Shieve & M. B. Shoenheit (eds.), Leadership: Examining the Elusive (pp. 93–104). Washington, DC: Association for Supervision and Curriculum Development.

Whitaker, K. S., & M. C. Moses. 1994. The Restructuring Handbook: A Guide to School Revitalization. Boston: Allyn and Bacon.

CHAPTER 14

Politics and Decision-Making: The Rural Scene

We Must Leave Politics at the Schoolhouse Door.—Bill Clinton, 1997

Rural school leaders must understand the infusion or, as the case may be, the intrusion of politics into educational decisions. This chapter explores the political climate in small and rural schools and offers suggestions for how to cope with the frustrations of political action. The chapter begins with a view of political paradigms that have developed historically in the United States. The author then investigates politics originating at the federal, state, and local levels, and how each impacts the rural scene. Extra-legal political action in the form of rural pressure groups is also explored. A special feature of the chapter is the exploration of micro-politics or building politics. The author concludes with suggestions for rural school leaders who must daily cope with politics.

PEOPLE like to think that their local school is apolitical. After all, politics to most people conjures up images of "dirty tricks," graft, favors, or corruption. "Not our school," says the community. But, in the real world all schools act as miniature political systems. In recent decades, a surge of education legislation at the federal, state, and local level has brought politics boldly into the school setting. At the same time, individuals and groups have overwhelmed the schools with expectations about what teachers should teach and how administrators should allocate scarce resources. The success of a school now depends largely on how well educators deal with political issues, and deal with them they must, for politics is too important to be left to the will of politicians.

In many respects, political influence operates from a predictable base regardless of rural or urban location. The rural version, however, is unique, and one

Donald M. Chalker, Department of Educational Leadership and Foundations, Western Carolina University.

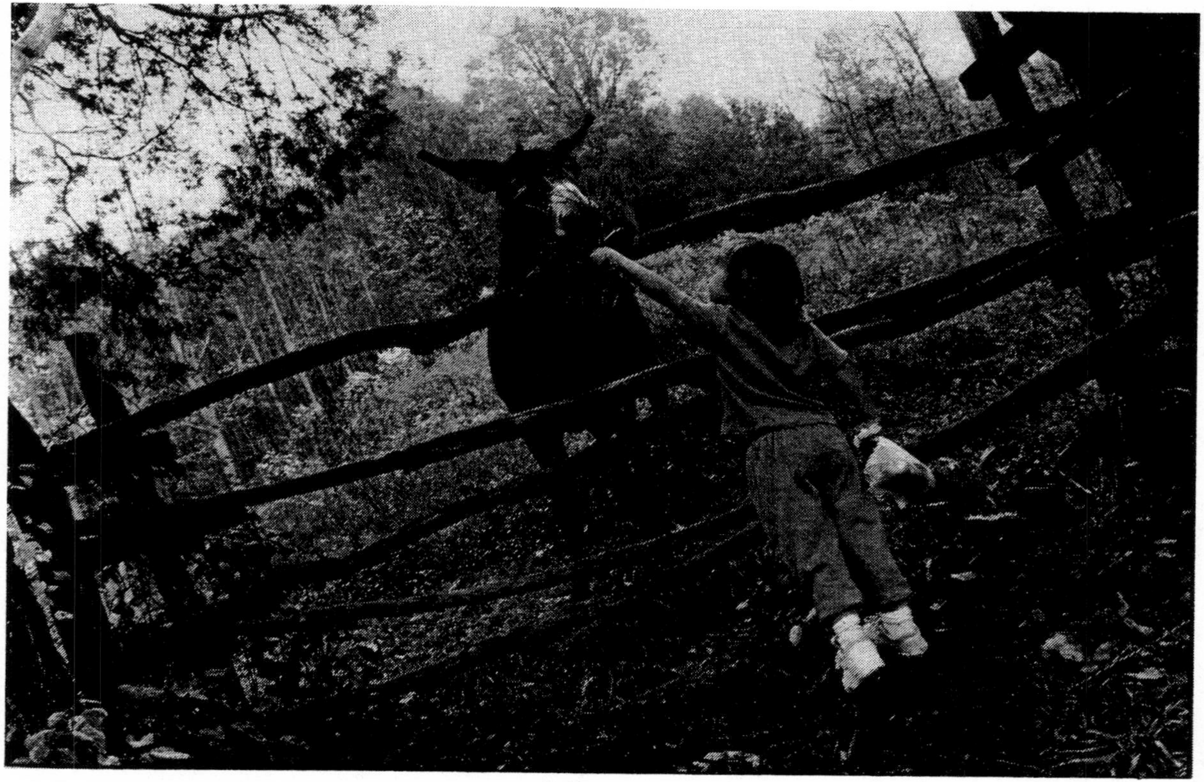

© Photo by Rob Amberg.

purpose of this chapter is to explore this uniqueness. Three differences come to mind. First, schools in rural areas or small towns have constituencies that are probably more open and more knowledgeable about local politics than their more cosmopolitan neighbors in suburban or urban America. Second, rural politics operate from a smaller population base where almost every political player is known in the community. And, third, rural politics focus more on local issues than state or national issues, for the state capital or Washington is often far away physically and mentally from rural schools. These differences call for a different approach by rural leaders.

THE HISTORICAL PARADIGMS OF EDUCATIONAL POLITICS

The political nature of American education, rural or urban, exists in paradigms that have deep historical roots. School leaders can better understand the complexity of education today if they understand these paradigms. The paradigms are numerous; they challenge the imagination. The author has chosen a brief look at paradigms with rural roots to provoke thought about the importance of the past to the understanding of the present.

The first paradigm, individualism, has strong ties to rural America. Colonists came to America to fulfill the dream of individual freedom, and citizens remain passionate about their legal, inalienable rights. The passion burns more brightly in small town/rural America. Educators who struggle with parents wishing to select their child's teacher, dictate the curriculum, and select books and other resources should remember that: "it's the paradigm, stupid." When home schooling proliferates, censorship of library books surfaces and headaches arise over sex education, the issue largely is heritage. In rural America, it is individualism that moves bright, talented youth to leave the small community and seek fame and fortune in the big city.

A second paradigm evolved from the representative, democratic government carefully crafted by the colonists. Today, educators find themselves in an atmosphere where elected politicians (usually without education credentials) determine educational policy. It is frustrating and often degrading, but it is the democracy paradigm and democracy is to be protected. At the local level, the school board reigns; at the state house, the legislature has become more involved since the damaging reports of the 1980s; and from Washington comes national education policy. The preponderance of political decision-making makes school administrators wizards attempting to make sense of it all, particularly in rural America where schools are often far from the big city.

Pragmatism encompasses a variety of related ideas bound together by the promise of observable, practical consequences. A few pragmatic educational ideas from the past are universal education, equality of opportunity, and a literate populace. During the thirty-five years preceding the Civil War, Horace

Mann, Henry Bernard, and others espoused the common school as a pragmatic approach to a civilized nation. The goal was free, universal education at the elementary level. Mann believed that the common school could solve all societal problems and even make law enforcement unnecessary. In spite of these early beliefs, the school administrator stares daily at a paradigm that guarantees free public education for all youth, but has not produced a model for securing the success of that goal. The rural model, featuring small schools and a more basic approach to learning, went out of favor during the rush to consolidate in the 1960s, but the rural model is returning as a viable way to reach the goal of universal education (see Smith, Chapter 3).

The business of socializing students to meet the needs of society has evolved into an established, yet controversial paradigm. During the colonial period and through the first quarter of the nineteenth century, education in America was class conscious. Schooling was for the rich, and the common man struggled to either gain an education at home or go without. The United States has not completely dispelled the early trend of a class-conscious education. The struggle to integrate classrooms in the second half of the present century clearly shows that on paper, people want students socialized equally, but in reality, many covet educational advantage for the privileged.

The political question that plagues school administrators today is, "Whose needs are to be met?" Selakovich (1984) reminds Americans that there is not always complete agreement on the function of the school. Community and religious groups have different expectations and, in recent times, have expressed them more vocally. Also, people have deluged the school with programs to improve social conditions, and educators daily make decisions about teaching the basics or social conditioning such as sex education or values education. Rural school leaders can identify with the War on Poverty initiated by President Lyndon Johnson in the 1960s as an attempt to reduce social tensions caused by economic inequalities. The poor cited by Johnson were the rural Appalachian poor. More than two decades later the ability of the schools to eradicate such complex conditions as poverty is questionable.

THE CURRENT POLITICAL PARADIGM: TURBULENCE

Wirt and Kirst (1989) define educational politics as "the struggle of schools to gain support for their values from the government." Any institution that must struggle for support from a bureaucratic government will indeed experience controversy. Almost every element of school governance could become embroiled in this current paradigm of political turbulence, and rural turbulence is again unique. Politics probably influences 80 percent of educational decisions, and 80 percent is a conservative estimate. Consider the following examples of political turbulence advocated by Wirt and Kirst (1989, pp. 1–27), and the rural implications of each.

(1) *Schools are subject to competing groups that require too much of schools.* Rural communities tend to be more isolated and population is often sparse and scattered. Competing groups exist but are fewer and better known to the school leader.

(2) *Schools lack focus on a common core.* Rural schools usually are smaller and poorer. The core might be all that the system can afford.

(3) *Parents do not enforce student learning at home.* The lack of motivation for learning in the home plagues rural schools as much as suburban or urban schools, but educators in rural areas have the advantage of knowing the parents, the home environment, and the student.

(4) *Expectations for graduation are not high.* Again citizens accuse the entire educational establishment of low expectations. Rural educational leaders, however, face the challenge of raising the expectations of children beyond those expectations of parents who grew up in the small town or farm served by the school, and who are content to have their off-spring follow in their footsteps.

(5) *Teacher quality is questionable.* People question the competency of teachers in every community, but teachers are well prepared in the United States, and hopefully the incompetent are a small minority. Rural school leaders could turn this turbulent issue into an advantage if they could overcome the propensity of school board members and administrators to give preference to applicants who live in the community or happen to know the right people. In fact, prospective teachers often wish to contract with rural schools where safety is less of an issue and simplicity and aesthetics are advantages.

(6) *States have usurped power from local units, and the federal government plays a vague role in educational development.* The state capitol is often a long way from small, rural schools and Washington is even further. The promise of the state government in the 1980s to reform education never reached fruition, and rural schools always seemed to be on the fringe of reform. The inequalities in funding are the best example of failed promises. The number of states where small systems have had to sue the state over inequalities is a statement of this fact. Seldom do national political leaders include the condition of rural schools in the national agenda.

(7) *Educators' promise to the public that universal education was possible has failed.* Surely universal education has been difficult to achieve in rural and urban areas, but the goal is admirable and virtually untried in any other country. Failure is not the best descriptor. Schools have made progress in an atmosphere laden with societal problems, and the reality is that education remains a hope for equal opportunity.

(8) *The move for equality has failed.* Schools, particularly rural schools, have

made great progress since the 1950s in promoting equality for all students regardless of race, nationality or gender. In matters of equality, however, statistics do not lie, and the figures tell us that many minority students face discrimination and higher failure rates. School leaders must deal with individual prejudices and groups who enjoy the privileges of a half century ago and hate to give them up.

The basic political problem faced by school administrators of rural schools, therefore, is the tension between the community's need for school leadership that can lead and be trusted, and the same community's desire to have its own will carried out by the leadership. After leading a study of four diverse school districts of varying size where educators attempted to lead school reform, Fargas (1993) concluded:

> The results of the study were discouraging. In each district, what started as a good-faith effort to work together on school reform became a tug-of-war over turf. We observed poor communication, widespread suspicion, and outright anger among the factions. Parochialism prevailed. Because this pattern of behavior was so consistent in all four of these diverse school districts (little or no difference was detected between large or small districts), we can only conclude that it was not the individuals but something about the system itself that encouraged conflict, not cooperation. (p. iv)

Armed with a knowledge of history and the paradigms that control educational decision-making, effective rural leaders must respond to the current political dimensions of educational decision-making. Political decisions are either legal, meaning that they originate from a political body empowered with legal authority, or they are "extra-legal," meaning that they originate with individuals or groups who wish to influence educational decisions without legal authority to do so. Legal political influence originates from the national, state, and/or local level, and for purposes of simplicity, each level of government is approached separately. The author then looks at extra-legal political influence. Both forms of politics have features relevant to the rural educator.

THE LEGAL POLITICS OF EDUCATION IN RURAL SCHOOLS

THE FEDERAL GOVERNMENT AND RURAL POLITICS

When President Clinton delivered his second State of the Union address in 1998, the national agenda for education bulged more than at any other period in history since the Kennedy-Johnson years. The Clinton agenda, in fact, bolstered Head Start and compensatory education, products of the 1960s. Clinton borrowed from President Bush the concept of national guidelines and national testing. He endorsed charter schools, increased loans for higher education, and repeated the goal to make the United States first in the world in science and mathematics achievement. If rural educators detected the absence of reference to small or rural schooling, they were accurate, but the breadth of the agenda could be advantageous to rural education, and rural school leaders would be wise to advocate its implementation.

Other than donating food for school lunches and providing funds for vocational programs and Indian education, the federal government did not affect schools much until after World War II. Unlike most other developed nations, the founding fathers left primary responsibility for education to the states. The first major federal legislation passed by congress was the National Defense Education Act (NDEA) of 1957. The impetus for the movement of the federal government into educational curriculum was the shock the country felt after the U.S.S.R. beat the United States into space. America worried about the state of its military readiness. NDEA provided funds to improve math and science education and practically launched the position of school counselor. It was Washington's most intimate brush with school curriculum (Sergiovanni, Burlingame, Coombs, & Thurston, 1992).

The civil rights grass-roots movement, however, caused the federal government to enter the arena of educational politics as the defender of equal educational opportunity. The Supreme Court's decision in *Brown vs. the Board of Education*, 1954, declared that racially segregated schools were unconstitutional, and that decision led to the 1964 Civil Rights Act. The federal government denied federal funds to schools that did not provide integrated classrooms and developed sanctions against school civil rights violators. Rural America seemed to adjust more quickly to the notion of desegregation, because minority populations were concentrated in urban areas, and rural schools were often too small to provide a dual system.

In 1974, again because of a Supreme Court decision *[Pennsylvania Association for Retarded Children (Parc) vs. Commonwealth of Pennsylvania]* that guaranteed an education for every handicapped child, the federal courts forced schools to accept handicapped students. In 1974, Congress passed the Education for All Handicapped Children Act (P.L. 94–142) declaring the rights of handicapped children to a free, adequate education in the "least restrictive environment." Ingenious political strategy now provides each potential handicapped student an individual educational plan (IEP) to be developed jointly by the local educational agency and the child's parents. P.L. 94–142 has mushroomed into a costly program for all schools because the special education enrollment has reached almost 12 percent of the school population. The federal government has not provided the funding for these children as promised because of the large numbers; consequently the state and local governments must pay the balance of the added cost for special education. The small, mandated classes are costly in two ways: (1) the teacher-pupil ratio is usually less that half that of regular classrooms, and (2) additional space is needed to house the preponderance of new special education programs. Rural administrators are especially burdened by both issues. Special education teachers are hard to find in rural areas, and smaller systems have limited classroom space.

The human rights agenda of President Kennedy and the attack on poverty by President Johnson during the 1960s led to the most comprehensive federal legislation of all in 1965. The Elementary and Secondary Education Act (ESEA) provided funding for a series of Title programs designed to improve educational opportunities for low-income and educationally disadvantaged students. President Johnson's vision for ESEA came from his knowledge of rural Appalachia and although the program has reached most every school district, its influence on rural schools continues to be significant. Title I, the largest of the programs, provided funds to local schools serving students from low-income families. The programs have changed over the years, but ESEA continues to be the flagship of Washington's contribution to quality education. President Reagan, in 1981, changed ESEA through passage of the Education Consolidation and Improvement Act. Title I changed little except that it was named Chapter I, but the provisions for teacher training and library resources were grouped into Chapter II, and funds were made available to all schools through "block grants." Rural schools, without the benefit of grant writers and the resources owned by larger systems, benefited from block grant funds that were relatively easy to access. The hidden result of Reagan's efforts, however, was a reduction in federal funds for education from about 9 percent of the education budget to about 7 percent of the education budget. The "Reagan Regression" not only reduced federal funding for education but also resulted in an attempt to desolve the Department of Education as a Cabinet-level department. The effort failed along with attempts to establish a "moral agenda" for schools that included school prayer and vouchers for parents to use if they wished to send their children to parochial or private schools.

The latest thrust by the federal government to improve education targets the perceived incompetence of public schools. President Reagan led the dual effort to improve the productivity of American students and to improve the productivity of the American economy. The president used the infamous report launched by the Commission on Excellence in 1983 called the "Nation at Risk." The report's powerful rhetoric described "a rising tide of mediocrity" in our schools and claimed that it would have been seen as "an act of war" if an unfriendly power had imposed our own educational system on us. The Reagan administration exacerbated the rhetoric through the "bully pulpit" occupied by William Bennett, Secretary of Education. The public began to echo the belief that the country had to improve our system of schooling in order to compete internationally and improve our economic system. President Reagan maintained that this was a problem for the state and local governments to solve, not the federal government.

Goals 2000 dominated the early 1990s and continues to impact the national education agenda. Started by President Bush and continued by President Clinton, Goals 2000 turns the school improvement rhetoric of the 1980s into an action plan for the 1990s. The goals speak little of the needs of rural schools and drip of platitudes that only remotely identify with the strengths of public schools. The goals are not guided by scientific theory, they are fragmented, sometimes contradictory, and conspicuous in their lacunae (Kamii, Clark, & Dominick, 1994). In fact, if the citizens of the United States put all of their energy into the one goal to improve parent involvement in schools, the other goals would not be needed.

Federal educational policies have not targeted rural education for special favor and are not likely to do so in the future. If the Department of Education is to target any entity, it will most likely be urban areas, where the problems are so vast that only federal intervention is likely to bring improvement. But, rural educational leaders must remain vigilant towards federal politics. Rural schools offer a model of education that most closely meets the descriptors of desirable public schools.

STATE POLITICS AND RURAL SCHOOLS

The legal responsibility for schooling in the United States rests with the fifty states. This authority is a reserved power arising from the Tenth Amendment, which reserves for the states those powers not expressly given to the national government. Strangely enough, however, the states did not exercise much legal authority until the last two decades. Previous to the 1980s, state governments considered education to be a state responsibility administered locally. The proliferation of state control resulted from two movements. First, state control increased with the entrance of the federal government into educational equity issues and the enforcement of civil rights. By the early 1980s, federal funds supported 50 percent of the staff in state education agencies (Spring, 1993). Second, the reports on the condition of education that dominated the early 1980s raised the concern level of the public about the effectiveness of education. President Reagan reaffirmed the role of the states as governing agencies for education. State politicians seized the opportunity to promise reform at the state level, specifically higher graduation requirements, improved retention rates, and school improvement. Many states developed curriculum standards and state testing became the yard stick for measuring competence. Governors led by Jim Hunt of North Carolina and Bill Clinton of Arkansas developed political strategies for improving education, and encouraged the legislature to increase support of education.

The authority in all fifty states is amazingly similar. In each state, educational policy comes from the legislature. Legislators depend on "educational experts" that sit on education committees and recommend to the legislature as a whole. Policy is carried out by a state board of education and a chief state school officer who presides over a state department of education. As mentioned earlier, the political strategist is the governor. This cadre of politicians has pulled back power from the local government, parlayed it with power delegated from the federal government, and created a layer of control for schools titled "legislative learning."

The success of legislative learning, however, is questionable. Wise (1990) looks back on a decade of increased state control and characterizes the results as follows:

> It was a world characterized by standardized testing . . . not educational standards; teacher-proof curriculum . . . not curriculum reform; standardized teaching . . . not professional teaching; and management-by-the-numbers . . . not instructional leadership. It was a world where policy dominated, schools were bureaucratic, and state and local boards of education became irrelevant; teachers were told what, when, and how to teach; and administrators, caught in the cross-fire, could not figure out whether to follow their educational instincts or the law. (p. 400)

One cannot stretch the imagination far enough to conclude that increased state regulation has improved student learning. Disenchanted with this fact, each state government began a process of downsizing during the mid–90s and began exalting the virtues of site-based management as if they had invented it. Rural schools wait in the wings ready to make public an educational organization that fits the site-based model to a tee.

Legislated learning is not the only state initiative that impacts rural schools. Two state political movements during the decades since World War II have had a tremendous effect on rural education in the United States: (1) the consolidation movement, and (2) school funding.

The consolidation movement that gained steam in the 1960s picked up momentum by painting small rural schools as inefficient models that produced an inferior student. State politicians talked of research that proved that bigger is better. Harry Wilson, a legal specialist for the North Carolina Department of Public Instruction, wrote in 1987, "It became clear that education often was better served by consolidating school districts than by expanding them and by more efficient use of school funds" (pp. 9–11). North Carolina reduced its 4,830 schools in 1934 to 1,963 schools in 1987. In 1997, North Carolina has 119 administrative units with plans to reduce the number to 100.

Rural educators such as Jonathon Sher have pointed out the inaccuracies of research used by state politicians to promote consolidation. Sher (1986) also gathered statistics to investigate school district size as it correlated to dropout rates, school retention, and reading and mathematics competency. Small districts correlated positively with desirable characteristics in each category. Monk and Haller (1990) claim that the small, rural school fits the organizational model proclaimed best by the school improvement movement. Hence, they propose that it would be unfortunate if state bureaucrats continue the further consolidation of rural schools, for those who have thought thoroughly about school size do not view large schools as a desirable goal. Haller, Nusser and Monk write about rural schools in Chapter 15. Rural school leaders must stand strong against consolidation movements for they are political rather than educational. At the same time, rural school leaders must extol the virtues of their smallness and ruralness.

The second political issue nurtured by state legislators in a majority of the states is funding inequalities. In over half of the states, rural and small school leaders have sought litigation against their own state legislature. The reason is that legislators chose to ignore funding inequities in their state formulas until forced to move by the courts.

Although major differences exist in the specific approaches taken, states finance public schools through local property taxes. There exists, however, a wide variation in the local property tax base, with rural areas generally generating a low per-pupil tax base (Odden & Picus, 1992). Kozul (1991) found privileged school districts with more than twice as much available per-pupil funding than poorer districts. A recent study of Ohio schools found the poorer schools to be rural; Ohio is the latest state to have its funding policy declared unconstitutional.

In state after state, rural and small school leaders have formed an alliance, hired an attorney, and sought litigation to equalize school funding formulas. In Kentucky, the court decided that not only the funding but also the governance, structure, and programmatic aspects of the system were unconstitutional. Kentucky created an outcome-based, reward- and sanction-oriented, site-managed education program and finance system (Odden & Picus, 1992). Rural schools have been the winners.

The issue of size and the issue of funding indicate the need for rural school leaders to remain vigilant against a state bureaucracy that seems to favor the suburban model.

LOCAL POLITICS IN RURAL SCHOOLS

Since colonial days, the local school board has determined significant educational policy. The school board is part of a local governance paradigm that has deep rural historical roots, and it is not likely to disappear. Should it disappear? The literature is divergent on the issue, so wise administrators must learn how to cope with board politics rather than hope (or pray) that they will become more functional or disappear.

Some political axioms of school boards are:

(1) Board members, both rural and urban, do not accurately reflect the social, educational, racial, economic, and demographic characteristics of the public they serve. Over 60 percent of school board members are male with

only 7 percent minority. The majority are between the ages of 41 and 60, have four-year or advanced college degrees and earn incomes above $40,000. Over half live in small towns or rural areas. Interestingly, 40 percent have no children in school during their tenure on the board (Saks, 1992). Therefore, if educational decision-making is to have input from all people, it behooves the professional staff to guarantee it.

(2) Board members and their constituents often do not agree on what the major educational problems are, although rural school boards usually have a better feel for less diverse community needs and values.

(3) Even if board members agree on the problems, there is no guarantee that they will agree on how to solve them.

(4) Board of education members must run for office or be appointed by another political body. Each member, therefore, is a political creature respectful of those who placed them in office. Small rural communities are often unforgiving of board members, well known in the small community, who do not promote local wishes.

(5) Board members are also beholden to their personal agenda. Too many serve to "get rid of a teacher or administrator" or secure favorable status for the marching band or the football team. In all small communities, the latter is predictable.

In rural communities, all administrators and teachers are probably closer to the public and to its elected board of education. This familiarity can promote consensus or breed contempt. The wise superintendent establishes a working relationship with the board that is comfortable and productive. This means rendering to the board policy issues and taking charge of administrative responsibilities. It also means, however, understanding that the board may occasionally cross the line into administration, and that the superintendent must occasionally cross the line into policy-making. Both parties should be comfortable when this happens. Being productive does not imply that the superintendent or professional staff can achieve everything desired for the district. There may be a number of things that the administrative team cannot accomplish because of the makeup of the board. What often results is a mechanism by which the board can control the behavior of the superintendent and staff without lifting a finger (Sergiovani et al., 1992). Superintendents last longer who wisely choose their battles and know not to go to the wall over every educational issue.

Wise superintendents know that the superintendent-board relationship is on display monthly at the board of education meeting. Two suggestions can make the experience less political and more positive. First, plan meetings that are short. The public interprets long meetings as indicators of disorganization and a politicized relationship between the board and the superintendent. Both the administration and the board benefit from short, directed meetings. Second, anticipate the presence of community representatives who can be disruptive and send the wrong message to the press and public in attendance. Superintendents should watch who attends the meetings and plan when disruption is evident. Black and English (1986) call these disrupters "board watchers." Board watchers must have a special reason for attending board meetings, for even the superintendent and board would probably not come if they had a choice. As one experienced superintendent once remarked about his board, "This is the only place I know of where the inmates are in control" (p. 55). Both suggestions will pay dividends when the media reports the board actions to the public. Reporters love controversy. Educators don't need it.

When voting for board of education members and when exercising their referenda right, the public directly controls educational decisions. In a majority of states, the voter can shut down the school by refusing to approve millage requests submitted by the board of education. Even in states where boards do not have taxing authority, the board must initiate local referendums for construction through the county commissioners. Often the refusal of the public to approve funding for education is a symbol of the community's displeasure over one or more local educational issues or the imposing specter of higher taxes. Again small or rural communities seem closer to the local school, and its issues become more glaring in the election spotlight.

Rural school leaders can learn from school election theory that has crystallized over the past few decades: Avoid alerting the opposition and ignore them if they do surface, mobilize the positive voters, play down problems and play up positive events (Sergiovani et al., 1992). In a way, the author believes that this is easier to do in rural communities where people focus more on the school as a community institution. One certainty is that a successful millage campaign becomes a feather in the cap of the district superintendent and, therefore, a feather in the cap of all district employees who support the superintendent.

> A small town school is like the whirlpool of a river. It engages everyone because, like the river's eddy, it irresistibly draws the community's residents into it. (Schmuck & Schmuck, 1990, p. 9)

The power structures of the school community involve themselves in local school politics. Spring (1993) cites the 1971 study by Donald McCarty and Charles Ramsey as the significant research study of community politics. The researchers classified community power structures as follows:

(1) Dominated

(2) Factional

(3) Pluralistic

(4) Inert

The classifications assume that the community power structure determines the nature of the school board and the superintendent's administrative style. An inert community system, claimed the research, occurred most often in *rural communities*. No visible power structure existed and, therefore, little interest existed in the school. The primary concern was with a solid general or vocational program for most students and a college preparatory curriculum for a select few. The inert community shows little interest in the school board and invests the majority of power in the superintendent.

While many rural schools still fit the inert classification, the complexity of schooling during the 1980s and 1990s has moved the rural school closer to the remaining three classifications. Too often, however, rural communities still select local superintendents who are comfortable with control but lacking in skills required by leaders in dominated, pluralistic, or factional systems. The characteristics of these models follow:

(1) *Dominated Communities:* In dominated communities, the majority of power is exercised by a few individuals or groups. These persons generally belong to the communities economic elite or their ethnic, political, or religious group dominates the community. The system often exists in small towns where a single industry prevails. Board members represent the elite, and the superintendent acts in their interest.

(2) *Pluralistic Communities:* Pluralistic communities have several competing interest groups and a high degree of community interest in education. McCarty and Ramsey found the structure in suburban America where citizens valued the pursuit of a college education. The board of education in these communities represented the interest groups, but were found to be open-minded and interested in facts. The superintendent served as advisor to the board and was very professional.

(3) *Factional Communities:* Factional communities usually have at least two factions that compete for influence. Religion is usually the dividing issue and often secondary to educational concerns. Control on the school board passes from one group to the other, and the superintendent becomes a political strategist balancing the competing groups.

It is arguable that other political influences steer local politics of education. Certainly the educational bureaucracy exerts its own brand of political influence. The bureaucracy makes it difficult to fix responsibility, the bureaucracy filters information that reaches the school staff and the community, and the bureaucracy tries to convince the board and the public that only administrators have the technical expertise to make educational decisions (Spring, 1993). While it is true that rural schools suffer from a lack of administrative help, the smaller administrative staff does prevent the politics associated with large bureaucratic organizations.

EXTRA-LEGAL POLITICS IN RURAL SCHOOLS

POLITICAL PRESSURE GROUPS

Extra-legal political pressures, pressures from interest groups and individuals with no legal authority, are often more of a nuisance than legal mandates. In rural America, extra-legal pressure comes from small town groups usually well known to the educational establishment and tuned to the needs of small-town, rural America. Such groups can support the schools or they can seriously interfere with the educational process.

As a superintendent in the rural Lincoln Consolidated Schools in Southeastern Michigan during the 1980s, the author encountered two pressure groups persistently involved in political decision-making. The groups absorbed a great deal of time and energy. The following discussion of these experiences serves only as an example of the thousands of pressure groups experienced by educational leaders in rural schools everywhere. Skill in coping with these groups is a prerequisite for successful leadership.

"My most vivid memories of politics and the superintendency revolve around two pressure groups: (1) the Citizens Against Taxation, and (2) the Region 8 Education Association (NEA affiliation). The Citizens Against Taxation was a registered organization with elected officers and a following that rallied to the cause whenever the board of education sought operating millage or a bond issue for buildings and grounds. In the twenty years preceding my superintendency, the school district defeated twelve bond issues needed for new buildings. Half of the elementary population attended class in portables.

"As the new leader of the district, it was the superintendent's responsibility to pass the next bond issue, and with the help of staff and positive voters, it happened. The Citizens Against Taxation was a bit complacent, and the membership began late the process of distorting the facts, questioning my birthright, and rallying the no voters. The yea's prevailed. So, the membership of the Citizens Against Taxation appeared at the next few board meetings asking the board to abort the unfair election. The board stood tough, so the citizens approached the County Elections Board and told them that the superintendent rigged the voting machines. This resulted in an hour test of the machines where the membership of the anti-tax group pulled the levers over and over. The machines worked perfectly, but the press had a field day. The harassment never ceased and in every future election the Citizens Against Taxation had their say.

"The second group, the Region 8 Education Association, was the bargaining group for the local NEA group that served my rural school district. During the 1980s, the Michigan Education Association consolidated several EAs into regional affiliations to counter boards of education that contemplated firing teachers who willingly or unwillingly took part in strikes. The local association was not my enemy; in fact, we went to great lengths to work cooperatively together. As a principal earlier in my career, I had experienced two major, nasty strikes, and I had no intention of allowing a labor dispute to disrupt the district's mission. Besides, the leaders of the union were teachers I liked professionally. Nevertheless, the NEA served teachers—not students or parents. The NEA was a political interest group.

"While a strike never occurred, the disruption was interfering with my life and my time on task as a superintendent. Negotiations required hours and days of my time, and the union could tie up my hours regularly with grievances and hearings. Since negotiations occurred after working hours and during the summer months, my personal life was also disrupted.

"The constant pursuit of operating and building funds and the attention required to meet union demands shortened my career as a superintendent. I would guess that both situations cause a disturbance in the lives of all administrators who must deal with these situations. On a positive note, I now teach a graduate education class on politics, and my past experiences weave their way into many class discussions."

As mentioned, thousands of pressure groups exist in the United States ready to influence educational decision-making. In rural America these groups are more likely to be local and unconnected to national organizations or national movements. Their methods are usually more informal such as accessing the superintendent or principal directly and personally. School personnel often know the people who comprise interest groups, and organizational expectations are often packaged with a request for personal favor. In this respect the board of education can function as a pressure group. Often other employees of the district are local natives who join with the pressure group and in subtle ways let the administrator know that their first allegiance is to the community power structure. Such individuals and groups can be particularly persuasive with administrators hired from outside the district.

Rural pressure groups that fit the above description could be one of several booster clubs. The football team and marching band characterize small-town America, and their advocates can be vociferous and demanding. Also at the school level, the local PTA can be a political player that is quite helpful, but Wirt and Kirst (1989) report that the organization has become more aggressive, asserting itself as a consumer advocate organization. The Chamber of Commerce in small communities is more locally oriented than nationally oriented and more likely to focus on local education. Service organizations in rural areas such as the Lions Club, Goodfellows, or Grange are more likely to concentrate on schools since schools are the focal point of the community.

Distinct from pressure groups with material interests are those persons whose main interest is moral instruction in schools and the moral condition of teachers and support staff. The days when the townspeople maintained a protective surveillance over teachers' drinking and dating in small, rural towns have not completely disappeared. Do-gooders in small towns can escalate incidents into board confrontations or whispering campaigns. In smaller, homogeneous communities educators often have little recourse but to walk a narrow line with their own morality and also in what they transmit to students (Iannaccone & Lutz, 1970). The small-town church congregation is a political player to be reckoned with also. Local church member can besiege an administrator with questions and comments while he or she walks down the aisle of the local church.

The good news about pressure groups in rural areas is that they are not distant strangers to the administrator, and they are probably not as far out on the fringe of societal mores as similar groups might be in suburban, cosmopolitan areas. Teacher unions, for example, tend to be less effective in rural areas, and similar groups in the business arena, religious sector, and social structure probably are less intense in rural communities. Suggestions for coping with these groups follow.

MICROPOLITICS

A late development in the evolution of educational politics is the growing interest in the micro-politics of schools. Micro-politics is the study of power struggles among educators mainly administrators and teachers, and teachers and students. Boyd (1991) finds micro-politics at the implementation phase of school policy. Educators entrusted with the job of placing policy into action turn out to be the final policymakers. Micro-politics take place, therefore, in the classroom and administrative offices. Armed with a knowledge of micro-politics in his or her own school, the rural educator has a better chance of reconfiguring the school climate simply because the unit is usually smaller and the staff more cohesive.

Effective educational leaders have long recognized the powerful influence of the teacher in the classroom once the classroom door closes. Teachers can ignore directives that interfere with their beliefs and make other directives work if they embrace them. Why not legitimately empower teachers, therefore, since de facto empowerment really triggers their behavior behind closed doors. Ironically, many teachers refuse to empower students if the teacher does not feel empowered. Empowerment of teachers is a two-way street, and educational leaders must provide staff development opportunities that encourage cooperation and collegiality among teachers and students. In Chapter 9, Eleanor Hilty talks about the rural teacher and politics and Anna Hicks does likewise with students in Chapter 10. Teachers and students must always be major players in decision-making.

There is little doubt today that the school principal is a significant figure in the school and that the political orientation of the principal affects all aspects of life in schools. The effective use of power is synonymous with effective leadership. While there are no specific prescriptions for developing principals with a sense of micro-politics, practicing principals must obtain these essential skills and school leaders must receive developmental opportunities in the micro-politics arena (Blase, 1991).

PRINCIPLES FOR THE PRINCIPAL AND OTHER SIGNIFICANT RURAL SCHOOL LEADERS

Educational leaders cannot ignore the political atmosphere that encompasses their very being, but they can cope. The following principles are not restricted to geographical or school-size orientation, but they do have a rural slant. They can make life functional in the dysfunctional world of educational politics.

(1) Develop policy at the district and building level that addresses issues charged with political implications. Start with a personnel policy that forbids hiring preferences for friends or family. Giving preference to local residents for jobs often negates finding the most qualified employee.

(2) Use research and proven practice when making educational decisions. Both are the enemy of political decisions.

(3) Focus intensely on what is good for "kids." Schools do not exist for teachers, merchants, textbook companies, churches, or politicians. Eliminate practices that are political rather than educational such as tracking.

(4) Know your community and its interest groups. Join at least one group with a service orientation and develop a theory for dealing with those groups with a negative orientation.

(5) Be a vocal lobbyist for and/or against legal politics at the federal, state and local levels. Just because rural and small schools are often far away from state or national legislatures, it does not mean school leaders can ignore the politics of legislated learning.

(6) Develop a theory base that helps the leader cope with political decisions as they surface. Theory is often the most practical solution available to leaders faced with instant decision-making.

(7) Understand the power of positive human relations and apply this knowledge to all human relationships.

(8) Practice shared-decision-making.

(9) Be a scholar of rural education and advocate for the advantages it can bring to the schoolhouse.

(10) Be an educator with political skills not a politician with education skills.

REFERENCES

Black, J.A., & F.W. English. 1986. *What They Don't Tell You in Schools of Education About School Administration.* Lancaster, PA: Technomic Publishing Company, Inc.

Blase, J. 1991. "Analysis and Discussion: Some Concluding Remarks," In *The Politics of Life in Schools: Power, Conflict and Cooperation.* J. Blase, ed. Thousand Oaks, CA: Corwin Press, Inc. pp. 237–256.

Boyd, W.L. 1991. "Foreword," In *The Politics of Life in School: Power, Conflict, and Cooperation.* J. Blase, ed. Thousand Oaks, CA: Corwin Press, Inc. pp. vii–ix.

Fargas, S. ed. 1993. *Divided Within, Besieged Without: The Politics of Education in Four American School Districts.* New York: Public Agenda Foundation.

Iannaccone, L., & F.W. Lutz. 1970. *Politics, Powers and Policy: The Governing of Local School Districts.* Columbus, OH: Charles E. Merrill.

Kamii, C., F.B. Clark, & A. Dominick. 1994. "The Six National Goals: A Road to Disappointment," *Phi Delta Kappan.* *75*(9), pp. 672–678.

Kozul, J. 1991. *Savage Inequalities: Children in America's Schools.* New York: Crown Publishers Incorporated.

Lowe, W.L. 1990. "The National Level: Reagan and the Bully Pulpit," In *Education Reform: Making Sense of It All.* A.B. Bacharach, ed. Needham Heights, MA: Allyn and Bacon.

McCarty, D., & C. Ramsey. 1971. *The School Managers: Power and Conflict in American Public Education.* Westport, CT: Greenwood.

Monk, D.H., & E.J. Haller. 1990. "Keeping an Eye on the Reformers: State Education Bureaucrats and the Future of Small, Rural Schools," In *Education Reform: Making Sense of It All.* A.B. Bacharach, ed. Needham Heights, MA: Allyn and Bacon.

Odden, A.R., & L.O. Picus. (1992). *School Finance: A Policy Perspective.* New York: McGraw-Hill, Inc.

Saks, J.B. 1992 "Education Vital Signs," *Executive Educator, 14*(12), 33.

Schmuck, P. and R. Schmuck. 1990. "Democratic Participation in Small Town Schools," *Educational Researcher, 19*(8), 19–21.

Selakovich, D. 1984. *Schooling in America: Social Foundations of Education.* New York: Longman, Inc.

Sergiovanni, T.J., M. Burlingame, F.S. Coombs, & P.W. Thurston. 1992. *Educational Governance and Administration.* 3rd Ed. Boston: Allyn and Bacon.

Sher, J.P., & R.B. Tompkins. 1986. *Heavy Meddle.* Raleigh, NC: North Carolina School Board Association.

Spring, J. 1993. *Conflicts of Interest: The Politics of American Education.* New York: Longman, Inc.

Wilson, H.E. 1987. "Consolidation of Schools and Merger of School Administrative Units," *Education Law in North Carolina.* Chapel Hill: The University of North Carolina, Institute of Government.

Wirt, R.M., & M.W. Kirst 1989. *Schools in Conflict.* Berkeley, CA: McCutchan Publishing Company.

Wise, A.E. (1990). "Student Welfare in the Era of School Reform: Legislated Learning Revisited," In *Education Reform: Making Sense of It All.* S.B. Bacharach, ed. Needham Heights, MA: Allyn and Bacon.

CHAPTER 15

Assessing School District Quality: Contrasting State and Citizens' Perspectives

Regardless of whether the impetus for educational reform stems from the pen of a scribbling academic, an opportunistic politician, or a faceless bureaucrat, a reform movement proceeds in steps, involves many actors playing a wide variety of roles, and can evolve to such a degree that it is difficult to discern the original intent from the ultimate impact.—David Monk and Emil Haller, 1990

An increasing number of state education agencies are either designing, implementing, expanding, or refining methods for holding all schools accountable for educational outcomes. But do the citizens of the school district agree with the state's perspective of school adequacy? This chapter answers this question from the perspective of research conducted by the authors in New York State where school accountability measures have been adopted by the state; and criticized by many residents. Simply put, the chapter reveals that existing state measures do not persuasively demonstrate to ordinary citizens that a problem exists in their schools. The authors offer suggestions designed to bring state agencies and citizens closer together when they judge the quality of their schools.

INTRODUCTION

EDUCATIONAL history abounds with reformers' criticisms of small, rural schools on the grounds of efficiency and equity. By portraying such schools

This study was supported by a grant from the New York State Education Department. The authors would like to thank Alison Ford, Michael Joseph, and Harvey Kaufman for their assistance in earlier stages of the project.

Emil J. Haller, Janie L. Nusser, and David H. Monk, Department of Education, Cornell University.

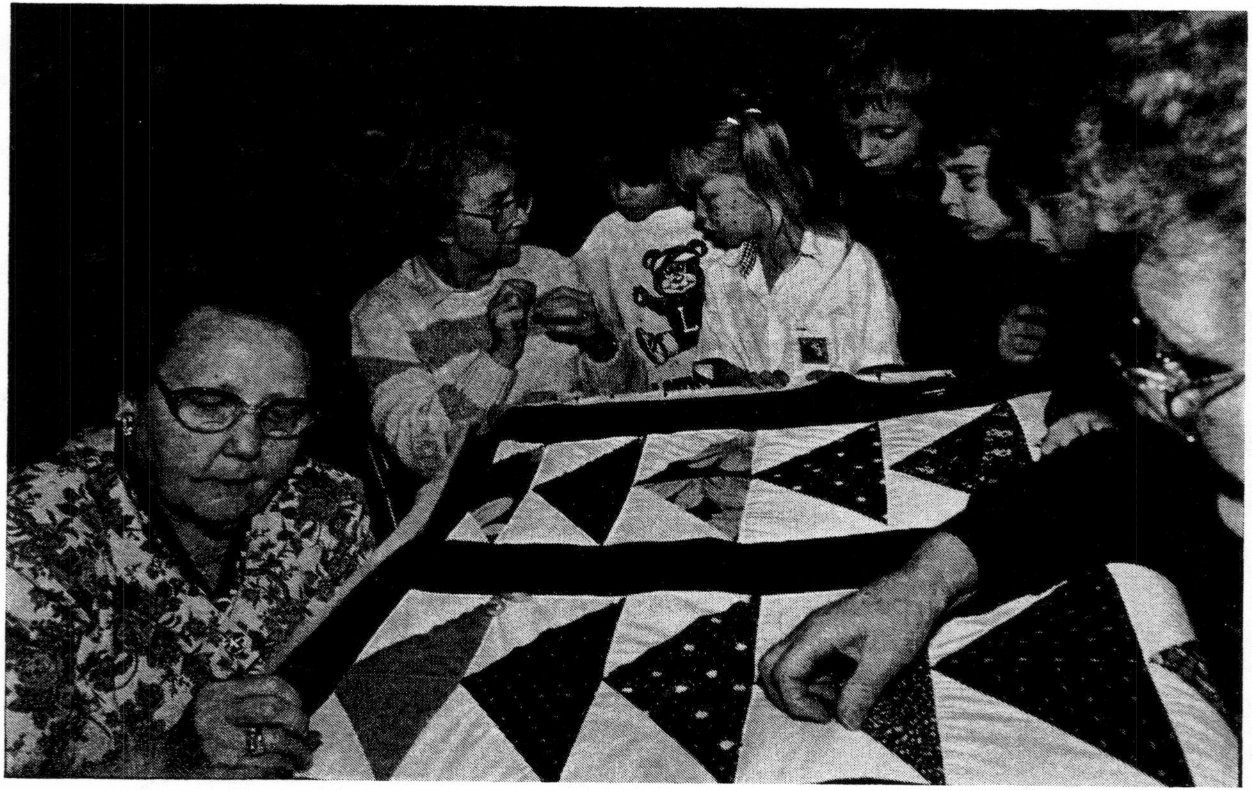

© Photo by Rob Amberg.

as incapable of realizing the economies of scale, the breadth of curricular offerings, and the staffing credentials enjoyed by their larger, less isolated counterparts, reformers have experienced significant success in their move to consolidate large numbers of rural districts. These reformers, most often state education officials, publicized such districts' allegedly dismal performance on selected objective indicators or criteria of school quality (e.g., per-pupil expenditures, average class size, number of different courses offered, percentage of certified teachers, etc.). Officials and legislators promised reductions in tax rates, painted rosy pictures of increased curricular opportunities, and proffered financial sanctions and rewards from state agencies in order to persuade local residents to merge their school district with those of their neighbors.

Were the promises of the consolidation movement realized? Evidence on this question remains ambiguous at best (see, for example, Monk & Haller, 1986; Sher & Thompkins, 1977; Tholkes & Sederberg, 1990). Nonetheless, current reformers have embraced similar tactics in a recent and ongoing agenda aimed at improving the efficiency and productivity of all schools, regardless of size or location.

An increasing number of state education agencies are either designing, implementing, expanding, or refining methods for holding all schools accountable for educational outcomes (Clotfelter & Ladd, 1996; Elmore, Abelmann, & Fuhrman, 1996).[1] The implicit theory behind these efforts is that improvements in productivity and efficiency will result when states: (1) Set educational standards focused on academic achievement; (2) assess and monitor schools' progress on measures of various attributes thought to represent school quality;[2] (3) publicize schools' performance on these measures; and (4) provide other suitable incentives and remove existing barriers to desired change. In essence, accountability system designers hope that stakeholder groups such as taxpayers and parents will bring pressure on local school officials in underperforming districts to make changes that will improve scores on these quality indicators.

Unfortunately, much of the theory framing these widespread reform efforts remains largely untested in educational settings (Hanushek, 1996; Levy, 1994), resulting in numerous unanswered questions. For example, will parents and taxpayers respond as state officials hope they will? An affirmative answer to this question rests on two assumptions. The first is that citizens will concur with the criteria the state utilizes in evaluating school quality, and the second is that

---

[1]A survey of state agencies conducted by the Consortium for Policy Research in 1993 revealed that forty-three states at that time were either planning or implementing certification or accreditation mechanisms that focused more on performance than had previously been the case (see Elmore et al., 1996). Another survey undertaken three years later by the American Federation of Teachers (1996) demonstrated that forty-eight states and the District of Columbia were either formulating or implementing performance-focused accountability features.

[2]Some common examples of such measures or criteria of quality (often referred to as *indicators*) are percentage of students passing state examinations; average class size; teacher-pupil ratio; per-pupil expenditure; and dropout rate.

citizens' perceptions of local school quality will either match the state's rating or will change as a result of the state's rating. In the research reported here, we address these assumptions.

If substantial organizational changes are to result from states' efforts to hold schools accountable through the application of assessment systems founded on objective indicators of performance, then residents must be convinced that their schools are as effective or ineffective, as frugal or wasteful, as state officials claim they are. If citizens routinely use criteria that are significantly different from the state's, or if the standards they apply to the same criteria are widely disparate, conflicting judgments of school quality are inevitable. When judgments differ sharply over a matter of such import as the quality of the education received by a community's children, controversy and resistance become more likely, and the possibility of desired change is apt to decline.

While the current rush to reform schools seems fated to lead states to the collection of more evaluative data, more is not necessarily better. The wrong data, no matter how broad in scope, and complex measures based on the wrong data, no matter how sophisticated the measures, are expensive mistakes worth avoiding. In their rush to implement new monitoring systems, states have most often failed to conceptualize carefully enough the kinds of data they will need if they are to gain citizens as allies in their efforts to reform local educational organizations. A report on a series of studies by the Kettering Foundation on the public's stake in education (Mathews, 1996) found that the public is becoming increasingly estranged from its schools. The report concluded that, because education's objectives are publicly derived (as opposed to being determined by a state education agency's employees), this estrangement may be expected to increase unless and until the public's concerns become central. The Kettering research has serious implications for current reform efforts. If, as indicated in the theory underpinning assessment system design, public support is an essential element, then failure to gather data and construct indicators that are deemed important by a district's citizens may have undesired consequences. Our research inquires into the appropriateness of the criteria utilized in New York for gaining necessary public support.

Before committing additional time and resources to an undertaking based on faulty assumptions, states would benefit from a close examination of citizens' reactions to state officials' assessments of their schools' quality. Here we address this issue by reporting the results of a study of citizens' responses in twenty districts to one effort by the New York State Education Department (hereafter SED) to judge district quality. New York is one state with considerable experience in assessing school adequacy through the use of objective indicators of educational quality. Boasting a lengthy tradition of collecting, compiling, and reporting massive amounts of descriptive school and district data, the state may, in fact, be exceptional in this regard. Because of its extensive background in the use of monitoring systems, New York may well represent a look to the future for other states, most of whom find themselves at the beginning of the system design process. They may benefit from New York's experience.

BACKGROUND

Two strands of research are particularly relevant to the problem we have highlighted. One is a collection of recent empirically derived evaluations of states' indicator-based assessments of school quality, and the other is a body of research known as consolidation studies.

Literature devoted to the evaluation of states' monitoring systems is replete with conclusions that citizens' perceptions are paramount and that, if the promises of theory are to be realized, states' assessments must be perceived by important stakeholders, including local residents, as credible, understandable and fair (American Federation of Teachers, 1996; Clotfelter & Ladd, 1996; Elmore et al., 1996; Meyer, 1996). This strand of research provides no insignificant body of evidence suggestive of states' violation of these standards. In fact, although evaluation studies are in their early stages, there is a disquieting consistency in the findings regarding citizens' lack of comprehension of and trust in states' assessments of school quality.

More pointed findings emerged from a series of studies conducted by researchers in the Consortium for Research on Educational Accountability and Teacher Evaluation (Jaeger, Johnson, & Gorney, 1993; Jaeger, Gorney, Johnson, Putnam, & Williamson, 1994a; Jaeger, Gorney, Johnson, Putnam, & Williamson, 1994b). Focusing solely on "school report cards" (publications disseminated to parents and residents consisting largely of schools' performance on various measures deemed important by report designers), these reports illustrated that, generally, state and/or school officials were not in agreement in their judgments about the criteria and supporting data deemed important in assessing the quality of educational organizations.[3]

As a second relevant strand of research, consolidation studies highlight the circumstances and experiences of small, rural schools. Since the consolidation movement has rested on states' assessments of school quality buttressed with incentives for organizational change, findings from this research strand, while peculiar to small, rural schools, well have increasing relevance as states move to assess a wider variety of school types. A substantial body of consolidation research literature suggests that controversy and resistance to state assessments of district efficiency and productivity and state incentives pushing organizational reforms are common. (See, for example, Peshkin, 1982; Sher, 1977; and in the

[3]For an example of an attempt to make it possible for the public to make evaluative comparisons of specific schools, see the "Report Cards" published on a web site by the New York State Education Department (http://nysed.gov/emsc/repcrd96.html). These provide extensive, results-oriented data on all public schools in the state.

case of New York, specifically, Galvin, 1986; Monk & Haller, 1986; Woodward, 1986.) The history of the consolidation movement is not reassuring: Agency officials and citizens have rarely seen eye to eye when it comes to assessments of the quality of local education organizations. In fact, bitterness and rancor have often resulted from conflicting assessments of district quality emanating from agency officials and from citizens of small, rural districts. Since the success of current reforms relies in no small part on pressure brought to bear by districts' citizens, evidence from consolidation initiatives does not bode well for prevailing efforts to change schools, whatever their location.

While small, rural schools were not the sole focus of our research, the study does concern them: Eleven of the twenty districts we report on are rural. Furthermore, the history of the movement to consolidate small, rural districts is instructive about citizens' reactions to state agency assessments of local schools. It may be tempting to dismiss evidence from merger studies on the grounds that rural citizens are more benighted, more likely to be unreasonably protective of their schools, or more irrationally resistant to state interventions than are their more urban counterparts, as some have suggested (see, for example, Davis, 1986). Our research permitted us to examine citizens' responses in a variety of community settings. If rural residents have a greater tendency to dispute state assessments of their schools, we should be able to detect that tendency.

DATA AND METHODS

In 1991 the SED became concerned about inefficiencies and low performance in New York's schools and thus initiated a study to derive indicators of school quality.[4] As a product of that study, a system was developed that enabled the SED to judge districts' performance on a variety of measures of efficiency and productivity. These measures, a series of indicators of school district quality, were then combined into a composite measure of school district performance. In our study we utilized the SED's measures and subsequent judgments to select a sample of twenty districts. The portion of our study reported here addressed these questions: How do citizens in these districts judge the quality of their local schools? That is, what criteria do they use and how do those criteria relate to the criteria developed by the SED?

We approached these questions from two directions. First, in each of the twenty districts we visited, we asked the superintendent to arrange for a small group of residents to meet with us. We requested that these persons be influential members in the district and knowledgeable about school affairs, but not dis-

---

[4]The Organizational Change Study progressed through two phases. The first phase was conducted by the SED (see New York State Education Department, 1995); the second was conducted by a team of researchers from Cornell University (see Monk, Haller, Nusser, & Ford, 1996).

trict employees.[5] These persons would serve as a focus group in each district. In our discussion with each group we asked members to reflect on the kinds of criteria that they might use in judging the quality of the education a district offered. We then asked them to rank the importance of those criteria. Next, we presented seven global criteria used by the SED to assess quality, and we asked the group to comment on those and to rank them in terms of their importance.

Our second approach to our question was to conduct a telephone survey of a random sample of district residents or, where that was impractical, of district parents, drawn from a telephone book or school records. In these interviews we presented the respondents with the global criteria used by the SED and asked that they rate their school district on them. We also asked them to rank the criteria in importance. These approaches permitted us to elicit the criteria used by citizens when judging school quality and to compare those criteria to those used by the state.

FINDINGS

THE FOCUS GROUPS' CRITERIA.

We turn first to the criteria for judging educational quality that we were able to elicit from our focus groups. Since these criteria differed both among individuals and among groups, they do not lend themselves to tabular presentation. Instead, we will present our findings interpretively, as a series of eight themes that emerged from the discussions among group members. The first two of these concern the quality of groups' responses, while the remaining six were more substantive in nature.

We labeled the first of the qualitative themes as *Personalism*. The focus groups consistently identified criteria, ranked criteria, and rated their own districts by situating their thinking and comments squarely within their personal experience with their current district or with a district from their past—sometimes from their own childhood. For example, one respondent criticized the state's criterion of class size by recalling his own education in a parochial school more than a quarter of a century earlier: "I went to a Catholic school and we had 40, 50, even 55 kids in a class, so I don't understand why there is so much attention on class size. Are the kids different today? I wouldn't look at class size if I was moving to a new district, because I assume that teacher is going to give my child what he or she needs."

Sometimes, when volunteering a criterion, a respondent would recount a par-

---

[5]In one district our request was not followed and the group contained both teachers and administrators (as well as local residents). We cannot be sure what consequences this may have had for the resulting discussion.

ticular incident that illustrated and gave meaning to what otherwise would have been a mere abstraction. For example, one respondent said that an important criterion of school quality is the energy and creativity teachers exhibit in the classroom. To illustrate her point, she recounted her experience with a particular elementary school teacher who had used the same Thanksgiving activity (cutting out construction paper turkeys) with every one of her three children. "Every year it was the same damn turkey." In this respondent's mind, the teacher's repeated use of the identical activity year after year was evidence of laziness and mediocrity among the faculty of this district.

A related but distinct qualitative theme we called *Subjectivity*. Respondents' criteria and comments captured the more personal, subjective, qualitative, and hard-to-measure aspects of a district's performance. This theme most often emerged in a discussion of teachers: What was important was the relationships that teachers were able to establish with individual pupils. (The same quality was valued in principals and other administrators, though it figured much less prominently in the focus groups' discussions.) Teachers were clearly the preeminent figures in our respondents' thinking when they judged the quality of schools, and just as clearly, the attribute of teachers that was most valued had to do with their personality and the quality of their interaction with our respondents' own children and those of their friends and family—not necessarily their capacity to promote the cognitive development of their charges. (Apparently the latter was usually assumed to be a consequence of good pupil-teacher relations.) In every focus group, one or more respondents invariably expressed the need for districts to employ teachers who are caring, sensitive, and available to students and parents. One focus group member described approvingly the staff of the district by saying: "A defining characteristic of this school district, of everyone in it, is [that they are there] to take care of kids. All are in the business of educating. They are cheerleaders for kids. I've always admired that in this district."

The remaining six themes were more substantive in nature; they provided six criteria that focus groups considered important when judging schools. These are discussed in no particular order.

A third theme, *Diversity*, to emerge from the focus group interviews was respondents' insistence that students' differences be respected. Here, the central idea was that a school district must serve many kinds of pupils and adults, and that it must do so equitably. While racial and ethnic diversity was occasionally mentioned, most often our respondents were referring to students with diverse needs and abilities. Said one respondent, "I had four children with very different educational needs. The district meets the needs of all of them." Said another, "I have a daughter who studied makeup artistry at BOCES,[6] and my other daughter is into science and math. It's nice to know that as diverse as my kids

[6]The reference is to a Board of Cooperative Educational Services, an intermediate school district in New York that provides specialized services to member districts. In this example, the BOCES provided a class in cosmetology for students in those districts.

are, their needs were met." Thus, school districts were held accountable for providing courses, teachers, and experiences that would enable all students to lead productive and happy lives after they leave the public education system.

The notion of diversity was sometimes tied to a fourth theme, that of *Achievement*. In every district, focus group members stressed the importance of educational outcomes. Often this fourth theme centered on the usual measures of student success: college-going rates, Regents exam results, PEP scores, and so on.[7] Although respondents generally indicated that these traditional measures of student performance were important, they also emphasized that, because not all students can, should, or will go to college, districts should be assessed according to their ability to prepare students for suitable, satisfying, and productive work positions upon graduation from high school. Presumably preparation for civic responsibilities would be included. Scores on Regents tests are insufficient evidence of the quality of student performance.

A fifth persistent motif running through the focus group interviews was that a district should be judged by the quality of its relationship with parents and other community residents. We termed this theme *Community*. Group members indicated that boards of education, superintendents, and teachers should not only be available, but should listen to parent and community input. Observed one respondent, "There were a lot of tough decisions that had to be made in this district, and they were smart enough to get input from parents and the community." "The school should respect parents and the community," said another.

The notion of community went beyond the idea of educators and board members who would listen to the concerns of parents and the public. It often encompassed the idea of the school as a community, a place where individual students were encouraged to look beyond their personal needs to consider the needs of others. One respondent, in commenting on the virtues of small schools, noted that in their high school, an individual: ". . . could make a difference. In order to promote the general well being, [students] would expose themselves to experiences that, in a different setting, they would be unable or unwilling to commit to. [For example, a girl] gave up cheerleading to play girls' basketball so that the school could field a team." Or, as another put it, "Each school is like its own little community, and they are all friendly places." Sometime this idea of the school as a community was expressed as the idea of a family. "There is a feeling of family in the district," said another respondent.

A sixth theme, not unanticipated, concerned *Discipline*. This topic was mentioned in every focus group as important in judging the quality of a school. In a way this was surprising, since by and large the districts we visited seemed to have few discipline problems to contend with. Most were small school systems

---

[7]New York's two-tiered diploma system is well known. Although it is currently being revised, this system requires students to pass examinations. The more demanding of these are the Regents exams, and successful completion is one requirement for the prestigious Regents diploma. PEP stands for Pupil Evaluation Program and refers to examinations administered to New York's elementary students.

and many were rural or suburban; their "discipline problems" were more likely to consist of students cutting classes rather than dealing drugs or carrying guns. Perhaps the media's attention to crime in general and school crime in particular has made people sensitive to the issue. In part it may derive from previous experiences in other, less civil environments. Discussing safety, one of our respondents said: "This is a wonderful place to live and to raise kids, and the school is part of that. In Buffalo [we] had to have security guards to get from the bus to the school. Safety means a lot. It's such a simple thing, but it means a lot."

A seventh theme centered on *Money*. This aspect of focus groups' discussions was complex. In one sense it would be more accurate to say that money did *not* emerge as a criterion of school quality. For example, on one hand the costs of schools, in the form of taxes, was not frequently mentioned as a matter of significance. We found this surprising, especially when it turned out not to be particularly salient even in high-tax-low-wealth districts, where we expected that school taxes would be prominent in everyone's mind. In some focus groups taxes were not mentioned at all without prompting from the researcher leading the group. In one district, a respondent noted that money had not appeared on their list of criteria, "and I think that is indicative of how much people value education." Perhaps this is merely a consequence of the renowned inevitability of taxes, school taxes included. "Resignation" would accurately describe the tone of some groups' discussion of their annual tax bills. While many in a community were likely to say that their school taxes were "too high," our focus group members did not seem particularly exercised by that perception.

On the other hand, particular costs of school sometimes came in for sharp criticism. The costs referred to were usually salary costs of teachers and administrators. In these cases the phenomenon was clearly one of relative deprivation. In the poorer communities we visited, educators were typically paid somewhat less than they might expect to earn elsewhere in New York. Relative to the local wages paid to residents, however, teachers and administrators were among the highest paid people in the community. One respondent maintained, "It's not right when student programs are cut and teachers continue to get increases." Noted another respondent, "When cuts come through, it is the programs that get cut, but salaries never get cut. Every year they go up."

Also related to this theme of money, community members seldom complained about the costs of providing direct services to children. For example, the cost of special education is a substantial and growing part of most school districts' budgets. Administrators, in particular, can be acutely aware of its drain on a system's resources. Special education, however, seldom cropped up in residents' concerns about money. Similarly, we rarely heard disparaging remarks about "frills" provided to regular students. This was true even in a district that spends an extraordinary sum on its students—approximately $35,000 per pupil each year, about five times the state average.

Finally, an eighth theme centered on the *Extracurriculum* and its importance in evaluating the quality of a school system. Many focus group members recognized the limitations of a school that was too heavily focused on academic matters. They expressed the idea that a good school district would offer a wide variety of activities for students that would supplement the standard academic fare. Several criticized their district, claiming that more should be spent on extracurricular activities, or that the extracurriculum was the first to be cut when money got scarce. One person even suggested that a major distinction between public and (the presumably better) private schools was the latter's "dedication and commitment to the extracurricular." It would be easy to dismiss many of the sentiments we have quoted above as clichés. And ,of course, they are. Nevertheless, we think that it would be a mistake to dismiss them. A cliché is not a false assertion, it is merely an oft-repeated one. However, the emphasis on the personal and the subjective aspects of the criteria we elicited from the focus groups does make laypersons' judgments of school quality difficult to define, highly idiosyncratic, and a consequence of unique events in the lives of individual adults and their children. It follows, then, that any relationship between those judgments and the analogous judgments reached by the SED are likely to be attenuated and problematic. We shall have more to say about that relationship shortly. For the moment let us turn to the reaction of our focus group members to the SED's criteria.

ASSESSING THE STATE'S CRITERIA: FOCUS GROUPS

The themes we have just enumerated as emerging from the free discussion of focus group members influenced their observations of the state's criteria for judging school quality. After we had led the groups in a discussion of the criteria they would use to judge schools, we presented them with a figure similar to Figure 15.1, which summarizes the factors that the SED believed to be important in assessing the merit of districts. Since we had written residents' criteria on a flip chart as they were elicited, members of each focus group were able to compare the results of their deliberations with those of the state. We then asked each group to comment on the state's list and to rank the state's criteria.

Two sorts of reactions to the state's list were common. First, there were the kinds of general remarks having to do with the nature of the criteria reflected in Figure 15.1. A common sentiment expressed by focus group members concerned the contrast between the objective nature of the SED's list and the more subjective nature of their own criteria. "We have a lot of touchy-feely things, while the state's are quantifiable and measurable," was a comment made by one respondent that catches this contrast. Another sort of general reaction was caught by the notion that the state's criteria were required to be general; they had to apply equally well to all districts in New York. However, districts are also distinctive, and sometimes the things that make a district valued reside in this distinctiveness. Typical of such a view was the remark by one person: "I've

(1) **Physical Factors.** For example, percent of classrooms being used; pupils-to-classroom ratio

(2) **Teaching Environment.** For example, class size; certification of teachers; number of classes teachers must prepare for each day; experience level of teachers; teacher-to-pupil ratio; teacher turnover rate.

(3) **Educational Offerings.** For example, number of and kinds of courses offered, including elective courses and advanced placement courses; percent of courses offered at only one time during the day

(4) **Educational Results.** For example, dropout rate; percent graduating with Regents' diploma; percent scoring above average on achievement tests; percent passing Regents' exams; percent going on to college

(5) **Administrative Overhead.** For example, principal-to-teacher ratio; percent of budget allocated for administration

(6) **Expenditures.** For example, per-pupil expenditures for such things as classes; teacher salaries and fringe benefits; administration; transportation; and school plant operation and maintenance

(7) **Tax Burdens.** For example, school tax rate in relation to community wealth

Source: New York State Education Department (1995).

Figure 15.1 Criteria and some examples developed by the New York State Education Department as indicators of school district performance.

heard all of these kinds of things ever since the 1950s [referring to the state's list]. The state's criteria are okay, but the list does not capture the specialness of [district's name]. A lot of the things I value most in a rural school aren't captured in these measures." One respondent even suggested that the state's criteria were "cooked," deliberately selected to make small districts look bad (e.g., measures of course offerings and expenditures for administration). Such comments hint at a deep suspicion of the SED and its actions.

A second set of reactions concerned specific aspects of the state's list. In general, these remarks were mixed. Sometimes a focus group member would note that the group had missed a criterion that was important and was on the state's list. Administrative expenditures was perhaps the item most commonly left out of focus groups' deliberations, and the one most members agreed could be a significant criterion. Another that often went unmentioned in groups' spontaneous discussions was the physical aspects of the school plant (e.g., space utilization). We have already noted that the tax burden created by their schools often went unremarked in focus group discussions. As one person commented: "I can see that the ones the state would be most concerned about would be the ones I'm least concerned about. What it costs to put on the show doesn't bother me. I only care how good the show comes out. But unfortunately they're running a business, so cost has to be there."

On the other side, members noted that items appearing on their list were absent from the state's. "The state's list is missing parental involvement," noted one person. Another commented that student discipline did not seem to be represented. The majority of our respondents, however, conceded that the state's criteria were, for the most part, important. Yet they were also perceived as dangerously narrow and quantitative, and unable to capture some of the features that residents consider paramount when they judge the quality of their school district.

RANKING THE STATE'S CRITERIA: FOCUS GROUPS

After developing their own criteria for judging school quality and commenting on those used by the SED, we asked focus groups to rank order the state's criteria, where a 1 indicated the most important and a 7 the least important. The results of this ranking are displayed in Table 15.1.[8]

Two points should be noticed in Table 15.1. First, there are essentially two groups of criteria, differing sharply in judged importance. Judged most important were Educational Offerings, Teaching Environment, and Educational Results, in that order. It seems clear that these residents would agree with the state's emphasis on the teaching environment and the number and variety of courses a district offers as a criteria of quality. Similarly, there would be agreement that educational results are important.

The second group of criteria, Expenditures, Physical Factors, Administrative Overhead, and Tax Burden (in that order of importance), were considerably less significant to residents. That is, there is not a simple gradation running through individuals' judgments about these seven criteria. Rather, there is a sharp disjuncture between the top three and the remaining four. The first three are centered on students; they can reasonably be described as integral aspects of a quality education. The remainder are ancillary, respondents seemed to say. The last four are best thought of as useful instrumentalities for providing a high-quality educational experience for students, perhaps even as necessary prerequisites, but they should not be confused with the educational experience itself, nor should they be important criteria for judging the quality of that experience. We will return to this point in our discussion below.

The second point to note about Table 15.1 is that even among the top three

---

[8]While this ranking was carried out in only ten of the twenty districts we visited, involving fifty-three respondents, we have reasonable confidence in the results displayed in Table 15.1. In any case, the telephone interviews provide us with another (and more representative) view of the same issue.

TABLE 15.1. Mean Ranking of State Criteria by
All Focus Group Members
(N = 10 Groups, Fifty-Three Individuals).

Educational Offerings	2.15
Teaching Environment	2.49
Educational Results	2.87
Expenditures	4.12
Physical Factors	5.13
Administrative Overhead	5.30
Tax Burdens	5.64

criteria, the agreement between our respondents and the state is more apparent than real. In the free-flowing discussion used to elicit criteria, community members frequently spoke of the importance of teachers. Similarly, they ranked the state's criterion of teaching environment as very important. However, the meaning of their discussions and the state's criterion are quite different. Only rarely did our respondents mention the specific items the state uses to measure teaching environment (e.g., class size, certification, the availability of preparation periods, etc.). As we noted above in our discussion of *Subjectivity*, the qualities prized in the teaching environment had to do with the personal, caring, and nurturing behavior of teachers to students. Similarly, both the focus groups and the state stressed the importance of educational outcomes. However, as we have said, many of the focus groups' conception of these went beyond equating them to Regents tests and college-going rates. We think it is important, then, to recognize that, overall, there was substantial disagreement with the state's criteria among our focus group members.

This finding of disagreement must be viewed cautiously, however. Recall that only ten groups were represented involving just fifty-three individuals. To get another view of any discrepancy between the SED's criteria and those used by school district residents, we turn to our telephone interview.

THE TELEPHONE SURVEY

In our visits to each district we secured the telephone numbers of a random sample of fifty residents or, where that was not feasible, of parents. After returning to the university, we called each of these individuals and conducted a brief interview. Essentially, we presented each person with two tasks. First, we read to them a list of the state's criteria (see Table 15.2), and asked each respondent to name the most and least important of them for judging district quality. This was analogous to the task that we gave to our focus groups, except that we did not ask for a complete ranking of all seven criteria because of the difficulties created by requiring respondents to rank seven items from memory. However, because it involves a much larger sample of residents, who were randomly drawn from either the community or parents, it provides us with a more reliable sense of any differences between public and state criteria. We present the results of this ranking in Table 15.2.

With some modification, and allowing for the differences in method, these results reflect those derived from the focus groups (see Table 15.1). The same three criteria are judged most important: Quality of Teachers, Educational Accomplishments, and Course Options. Clearly, the quality of the teaching staff and the educational accomplishments of students count most heavily with the majority of residents. (Recall also that the quality of teachers is not analogous to the SED's "Teaching Environment," and that Educational Accomplishments was almost certainly more broadly defined by the telephone respondents than by the state's measures.) Notice also that "Course Options," while it is among the top three, garnered only 12.5 percent of the nominations for most important criterion. Clearly, the large majority of respondents viewed having a wide variety of courses available to students as only of moderate importance. Of least significance is central administration expenses and the quality of the school buildings themselves. While the focus group discussions seemed to relegate spending levels and taxes to relatively insignificant roles, we see here that it is probably more accurate to think of them as of modest importance.

As a final way to compare the SED's criteria to those used by district residents, we will examine the overall ratings given to districts by each party. As part of the first phase of this study, the state developed a "Composite Efficiency Rating" (CER) for each school district. This rating played an important role in the selection of school districts for our work. More importantly, it represents a significant new approach to identifying districts that are problematic—districts that seem to have serious problems of effectiveness or efficiency.

Each school district in the state received a score on this index, including the twenty districts drawn into our sample. The measure was constructed to have a mean of fifty and a standard deviation of 10. What this means is that approxi-

TABLE 15.2. Telephone Respondents' Ranking of the Most and Least Important of the State's Criteria, across Nineteen School Districts* ($N = 947$).

Criteria	Most Important	Least Important
School Buildings	1.2%	33.4%
Quality of Teachers	44.1%	1.0%
Course Options	12.5%	3.5%
Educational Accomplishments	36.9%	2.0%
School Taxes	2.5%	14.5%
Spending Levels	1.4%	7.8%
Central Administration Expenses	1.4%	37.7%

*One district declined to participate in the telephone survey.

TABLE 15.3. Comparing the State's and Residents' Judgments of School District Quality (*N* = 19, Table %).

State's Composite Efficiency Rating	Above Average	Average	Below Average	Totals
Above Average	2 (10.5)	2 (10.5)		4 (21.0)
Average	4 (21.0)	3 (15.8)		7 (36.8)
Below Average	2 (10.5)	6 (31.6)		8 (42.1)
Totals	8 (42.1)	11 (57.9)		19 (100)

mately two-thirds of the school districts in New York received scores between 40 and 60 on the index. Districts with scores in this range make up the large middle group of school systems in the state, districts that are neither especially effective or ineffective, efficient or inefficient.

We used the CER to classify all of the districts in our sample. Districts with scores over 60 (i.e., among the top 17 percent of the school systems in the state) were classified as "Above Average." Districts with scores below 40 (i.e., in the bottom 17 percent) were classified as "Below Average," with the remainder falling in the middle or "Average" group. In our telephone surveys, we asked respondents to give us an overall rating of their own school district using the same categories (plus a "Don't Know" option). Using the telephone responses, we classified a district according to the rating given it by the largest proportion of its respondents. That is, if more residents called the district "Average" than any of the other alternatives, it received that rating. This permitted us to directly compare the SED's judgment of a district's quality with the rating awarded it by a majority of a random sample of the same district's residents. We present the results below in Table 15.3.

Several aspects of Table 15.3 are worth comment. First, no district was described as below average by the majority of its residents (though the state's classification results in 42 percent of the districts being so designated). In only two cases did residents rate their district below the rating given it by the state, and in those cases the districts were seen as average, as compared to the state's rating of above average. On the other side of the coin, there was a very obvious tendency among our respondents to judge their school district more favorably than did the state: In well over one-half of the districts (63.2 percent) this occurred, while in only one-fourth of our cases were the state and district citizens in agreement.

DISCUSSION

Essentially, we have been concerned with two questions: What criteria do citizens use to judge the quality of their schools, and how do the criteria they use and the judgments they reach accord with the SED's assessment of the same schools? We can summarize our results in the following points.

First, perhaps our most significant finding has been that residents' judgments of the merit of their schools bear only tangential relationships to the assessments made by the SED. This finding casts doubt upon one of the central assumptions underlying current statewide reform efforts based on monitoring school systems' performance through commonly utilized criteria expressed in quantitative terms. As we have noted, success of these reform efforts depends in no small part on the assumption that the publication of data illustrating schools' performance on various measures will prompt citizens to exert pressure on school officials in deficient districts. If citizens and state officials do not agree on which criteria best capture school quality or on the summative judgment derived from those criteria, then there is little reason to expect that they will conclude that their own assessments are inferior to those of the state. In the districts we studied, even when district patrons recognized that their schools were characterized by objectively undesirable conditions (e.g., very high tax burdens or highly restricted programs), they did not necessarily reach the conclusion that their district was deficient. Certainly, they did not conclude that any sort of massive organizational reform was required to remedy existing defects. While focus groups' discussions would occasionally turn to the virtues of cross-district sharing, a relatively innocuous sort of reform, other sorts of organization reforms were rarely mentioned. Certainly, the consolidation of school districts, when it was discussed at all, was roundly rejected. Perhaps it would be useful to put this in another way. Even when people are in complete agreement on the facts of some matter, it does not follow that they will agree on any particular course of action based on those facts. It is not facts that count, but people's interpretation of those facts. If, for example, residents and state officials are in agreement that a district's course offerings are much more restricted than those of similar districts, it does not follow that there will (or should) be agreement that the district is deficient. Lacking that interpretation of the fact of restricted course offerings, calls for organizational restructuring will be unpersuasive.

Second, in many instances, residents were simply unaware of their district's problems. For example, focus group members in high tax burden districts did not necessarily know that their tax rates would be seen as exorbitant by residents in other New York districts, or that their school system's noninstructional expenditures were out of line with state averages. This is particularly significant because focus group members, while laymen, where deliberately chosen from among those residents who were most active and knowledgeable about school affairs. We are certain that they were more informed about their schools than were ordinary citizens. But, if the impetus for organizational reform is to take root in a community, we think that widespread knowledge that a serious problem exists is a necessary precondition to that reform.

We suggest that local school administrators may successfully prevent such knowledge from becoming commonplace. We need to be clear about this point. We are not suggesting that administrators deliberately hide perturbing information, though undoubtedly some do. Rather, we see this phenomenon as a natural result of restrictions in the upward flow of negative information in any organization. It is not in subordinates' interest to report every problem or defect to a superior, who, after all, is responsible for evaluating the subordinate. Thus, teachers do not report all of their classroom troubles to their principals, and those principals do not report all of their schools' difficulties to their superintendent, and so forth. The net result of this process is that those at the top on the organizational hierarchy, in this case boards of education, and ultimately the public, are less knowledgeable about the inefficiency and ineffectiveness of their schools than they might be. When this restriction in the upward flow of negative information is coupled with superintendents' seeming inborn tendency "to put the best foot forward," and "to emphasize the positive" when presenting the school system to the public, residents are likely to have a rosier view of conditions in their schools than is warranted. Indeed, it would be an extraordinary superintendent who routinely presented and dwelt on a district's most serious defects when making public presentations. It is better to present the district's successes and, when necessary, to discuss problems in the context of the (successful) efforts being made to overcome them.

We think this point is relevant to understanding citizens' seeming resistance to organizational change of their schools. As we noted in the beginning of this chapter, when states publish measures of school district performance and thereby identify school systems with significant problems of effectiveness and efficiency, they hope that citizens will use this information to instigate successful reforms. But even if the measures are entirely accurate, *they are the state's measures*, that is, they are not measures chosen by residents to assess their schools' performance. Hence, if state education department officials appear on the local scene with objective evidence of a district's deficiencies, we think that those deficiencies are likely to be news to many residents. It may well be the first inkling ordinary citizens have that there is a serious problem with their schools. When this is coupled with the prevalent tendency of the public to view their district positively (as we saw from the telephone interviews), it should not surprise us if citizens greet claims of district deficiencies with more than the standard dollop of skepticism reserved for visiting state officials.

Obviously residents do make both positive and negative judgments of the quality of their schools. We found, however, that these judgments were most often based on highly personal and subjective criteria, a result of their own, their children's, and their neighbors' experiences with the schools. This basis, per se, does not make those judgments unreasonable. If, for example, a resident's child has graduated from a small, rural high school and been accepted into a selective university, that too is a "fact" and it provides reasonable grounds for the conclusion that the curriculum of the high school is satisfactory. Thus, a claim that it is not supported by "facts" showing the school's offerings are much more restricted than are those of the state average is likely to be greeted with incredulity.

Our third finding concerned the relative importance of the various criteria used by the state. In general, the quality of the teaching faculty and the educational performance of students were considered most important by citizens. The quality of programs offered by a school district was also a prominent consideration. Of least significance were physical aspects of the building and administrative overhead. The tax burden created by schools and its expenditures were of moderate significance. Of course, these are relative judgments. Undoubtedly, all of these factors are important at one time or another. The critical thing to note, however, is that in the SED's calculations of districts' effectiveness and efficiency, these criteria are treated as of equal weight: Inefficiencies evidenced by high administrative costs are as significant as restricted course offerings. Residents do not see it that way. Hence, if state education officials wish to successfully encourage organizational reform of school systems, they may want to attend to the priorities that the public establishes for these criteria.

Fourth, a comment on the differences between the public's and the state's criteria is in order. We have already noted a few of the remarks of focus group respondents who called attention to the fact that certain of their criteria were not reflected in the state's list. Specifically, what we have termed *Diversity, Community, Discipline*, and *Extracurriculum* were not represented there. Perhaps the most highly rated criterion, *Achievement*, was represented, but in a somewhat truncated way, that is, the SED's version had an emphasis on the success of academically talented students (e.g., the percent passing state examinations and going on to college). There was less recognition of those students who entered the labor force upon high school graduation. We suggest that if a state seeks to secure the support of local citizens in the process of organizational change, the criteria that it uses to claim that a problem exists must reflect the criteria that the community uses when it judges the quality of its schools. This seems especially appropriate because some of the public's criteria are also ones that are commonly supported by decades of educational research. We have in mind the twenty years of "effective schools research," which suggests, among other things, that student discipline, a sense of community, and the extracurriculum are important aspects of quality schools. It was notable that a set of criteria for judging school quality developed by professional educators should be uninformed by that body of work.

We would not claim that the thousands of studies in the effective schools tradition should be an unfettered guide to practice. Clearly, there are problems with this research tradition. (See, for example, Levine & Lezotte, 1990; Purkey & Smith, 1983.) However, we would suggest that a set of criteria designed to identify effective and efficient schools (and their opposites) might reasonably be expected to reflect the accumulated knowledge contained in this research tradition. In some respects (e.g., their understanding that student discipline and a sense of community are important), the residents of the districts we visited seemed to have a better grasp of what should be measured when deciding whether a school system is deficient or not than the professional educators involved. A system of school district evaluation that relies on measuring that which is easily measured, or on using data that are already at hand (e.g., the proportion of teachers who are certified) is not adequate, citizens seemed to say.

Fifth and finally, recall that we were interested in determining whether our data would yield differences between rural and nonrural districts. Specifically, we wanted to know whether our data would support the contention of some researchers that rural patrons might be more apt than nonrural patrons to disagree with state assessments of their schools. Our data revealed no such rural-nonrural distinctions. This finding lends credence to the possibility that the contentiousness and ill will reported in studies of school district consolidations may be likewise experienced in more recent efforts to reform our schools. In fact, one of the districts we studied was quite small (641 pupils in grades kindergarten through twelve) but was located in an urban community. A resident, responding to the state's criteria during a focus group interview, noted: "Although class size is a part of the teaching environment, other important teaching environment characteristics, such as warmth of the organizational climate, were not considered, probably because they cannot be quantified. Small schools may have warmer organizational climates than larger schools, but this was not considered by the state."

We do not wish to make too much of this finding of no differences between rural and urban citizens. After all, splitting our twenty districts into rural and nonrural categories makes for small cell sizes. It is plausible to argue on at least two grounds that rural residents may be more apt to be critical of state efforts to reform their schools than other persons. First, it is often suggested that parents and other citizens are more likely to be involved in rural schools than urban ones (Monk & Haller, 1986; Sher, 1977). If that contention is correct, rural residents may be more familiar with both the strengths and the weaknesses of their schools than are urban dwellers. Thus, they may be better equipped to critically evaluate the state's claims. Second, as a group, rural school districts have a long history of contention with state officials over the issue of school quality, a history that may lead them to begin any discussions with representatives of the state at a higher level of skepticism than residents of urban places.

Irrespective of district size or type, respondents were likely to chastise state officials for failing to take into account the special strengths of their particular districts, and this failure may lead to resistance rather than support of reform efforts. Similarly, officials' failure to recognize unique circumstances that cause a district to exhibit an admitted deficiency may undermine support for reform. These problems point to a true dilemma for state reform efforts that are based on the publication of objective, comparative data about each school within it's borders. In order to be effective, the same data must be collected and the same measures constructed for each. But the degree to which the state is successful in doing this is the degree to which those data and measures may be viewed as invalid for any particular school, precisely because they do no take into account the unique qualities of each. Indeed, we found that local administrators were even more adept than residents at explaining away demonstrated deficiencies in their schools as the result of the unique circumstances in which they must operate.

Widespread calls for systemic reform of America's schools are based, at least in part, on the idea that significant organizational change is essential if schools are to be improved. Clearly, New York officials (and those in most other states) accept this notion. The first phase of this study was an explicit and systematic attempt to explore measures that would permit the state to identify districts that seemed to require reform if they were to adequately serve the children and taxpayers of their communities. However, if such changes are to occur, or at least if they are to occur without substantial community conflict, it will be necessary for the majority of the residents of those communities to recognize that *they* have a problem with their schools, not simply that state officials do. This study suggests that such recognition is not on the immediate horizon. Indeed, we are driven to the conclusion that, even in the those districts that have been "objectively" identified as among the most ineffective and inefficient school systems in New York, residents are, by and large, happy with the education their children are receiving.

The key, we suggest, to gaining community cooperation and support for structural reorganization may lie in understanding the importance of the concept of *problem* in the change process. A problem is a gap. A problem exists when there is a gap between what is and what ought to be—in this case between the way schools currently are and the way they should be. People are much more likely to support changes that they believe will solve one of *their* problems. Demonstrating that a problem exists in a community's schools, then, requires a state to show that there is a discrepancy between what the community desires in its schools and what it currently gets. As we have seen, what communities seem to desire is that schools prepare students for higher education *and* for work, that they be staffed by dedicated, caring teachers, that they listen to the concerns of residents, that they function as small civil communities where pupils respect teachers as well as each other, that they offer many opportunities for students to be involved in extracurricular activities, and so on. It follows, then, that people will see their school district as problematic and support changes in it, if it can be demonstrated that it falls short of these aspirations.

We suggest that if a state seeks to secure the support of local citizens in the process organizational change, the criteria that it uses to claim that a problem exists must reflect the criteria that the community uses when it judges the quality of its schools.

Such a demonstration will not be easy. We have noted the pervasive subjectivity and personalistic qualities of residents' criteria. Constructing convincing measures of some of these will be a formidable task. But we have also noted residents' criticisms of New York's current measures of school adequacy. Simply put, existing measures do not persuasively demonstrate to ordinary citizens that a problem exists in their schools. We suggest, then, that New York—and other states attempting to initiate large-scale reforms—may need to move beyond constructing ever more refined indices based on the data they routinely collect, and begin the process of conceptualizing the kinds of data needed to address the criteria that citizens use when they judge the quality of their schools.

REFERENCES

American Federation of Teachers. 1996. *Making Standards Matter, 1996: An Annual Fifty-State Report on Efforts to Raise Academic Standards.* Washington, DC: The American Federation of Teachers.

Clotfelter, C. T., & H. F. Ladd 1996. "Recognizing and Rewarding Success in Public Schools," In H. F. Ladd (ed.), *Holding Schools Accountable: Performance-Based Reform in Education* (pp. 23–64). Washington, DC: The Brookings Institution.

Cohen, D. K. 1996. "Standards-Based School Reform: Policy, Practice, and Performance," In H. F. Ladd (ed.), *Holding Schools Accountable: Performance-Based Reform in Education* (pp. 99–127). Washington, DC: The Brookings Institution.

Davis, C. E. 1986. *If We Can Haul the Milk, We Can Haul the Kids. A Personalized History of School District Reorganization in New York State.* Department of Education, Cornell University. (ERIC Document Reproduction Service No. ED 287 632).

Elmore, R. F., C. H. Abelmann, & S. H. Fuhrman. 1996. "The New Accountability in State Education Reform: From Process to Performance," In H. F. Ladd (ed.), *Holding Schools Accountable: Performance-Based Reform in Education* (pp. 65–98). Washington, DC: The Brookings Institution.

Galvin, P. 1986. *School District Reorganization: A Case Study of the Community Participation Approach.* Ithaca, NY: Department of Education, Cornell University.

Hanushek, E. A. 1996. "Comments on Chapters Two, Three, and Four," In H. F. Ladd (ed.), *Holding Schools Accountable: Performance-Based Reform in Education* (pp. 128–136). Washington, DC: The Brookings Institution.

Jaeger, R. M., R. Johnson, & B. Gorney. 1993. *The Nation's Schools Report to the Public: An Analysis of School Report Cards.* Kalamazoo, MI: The Evaluation Center, Western Michigan University.

Jaeger, R. M., B. Gorney, R. Johnson, S. E. Putnam, & G.Williamson. 1994a. *A Consumer Report on School Report Cards.* Kalamazoo, MI: The Evaluation Center, Western Michigan University.

———. 1994b. *Designing and Developing Effective School Report Cards: A Research Synthesis.* Kalamazoo, MI: The Evaluation Center, Western Michigan University.

Levy, J. E. 1994. "A Review of Public Policy Studies on the Use of Outcomes," In R. Berne & L. O. Picus, *Outcome Equity in Education* (pp. 45–70). Thousand Oaks, CA: Corwin Press.

Mathews, D. 1996. *Is There a Public for Public Schools?* Dayton, OH: Kettering Foundation Press.

Meyer, R. H. 1996. "Comments on Chapters Two, Three, and Four," In H. F. Ladd (ed.), *Holding Schools Accountable: Performance-Based Reform in Education* (pp. 137–145). Washington, DC: The Brookings Institution.

Monk, D. H., & E. J. Haller. 1986. *Organizational Alternatives for Small Rural Schools: Final Report to the Legislature of the State of New York.* Ithaca, NY: Department of Education, Cornell University.

Monk, D. H., E. J. Haller, J. L. Nusser, & A. Ford. 1996. *The New York State Board of Regents' Study of Organizational Change: Final Report from Phase II.* Albany, NY: The Education Department, Cornell University.

New York State Education Department. 1995. *An Analysis of 139 School Districts Selected for Phase I Study: Final Recommendations and Technical Supplements.* Albany, NY: Author.

Peshkin, A. 1982. *The Imperfect Union: School Consolidation and Community Conflict.* Chicago: University of Chicago Press.

Sher, J. P. (ed.). 1997. *Education in Rural America: A Reassessment of Conventional Wisdom.* Boulder, CO: Westview Press.

Tholkes, R. J., & C. H. Sederberg. 1990. "Economies of Scale and Rural Schools," *Research in Rural Education,* 7(1), 9–15.

Woodward, K. S. 1986. *Reorganization and Rancor: The Atermath of a Troubled Reorganization.* Ithaca, NY: Department of Education, Cornell University.

Curriculum Needs for a Rural Native American Community

Cherokee ways of thinking would be good in school and would help you know who you are, but there isn't much of that at my school.—Bobby Lambert, Cherokee Indian Student

Ideally, education reinforces parental infusion of self-worth and ability, as children progress from the raw material of a kindergartner into the finished product of a competent twelfth grader. That is the ideal. However, many children in our rural communities are left out of this ideal. Chapter 16 explores the demands of diverse rural ethnic groups and the Indian cultural influences that Native Americans find to be positives in the development of curriculum for Native American students. Cultural identity, belief systems, and learning styles should be infused into the development of curriculum for rural communities while following demands of national curriculum guidelines.

THE EASTERN CHEROKEE: A TYPICAL INDIAN SCHOOL, AND INDIAN COMMUNITY

AT the beginning of the nineteenth century, a tribe of people calling themselves YUN-WI-YULT, meaning "Principal people," were the most civilized of all the North American Indians. This tribe, who became known as the Cherokee, negotiated treaties with the United States government and progressively lost more and more land with each treaty (Greene, 1986). At one time Cherokee possessions extended over a territory of 53,000 square miles, which covered half of Tennessee, Alabama, and Georgia and some portions of Kentucky, South Carolina, and North Carolina.

Doris Hipps, Department of Curriculum, Valdosta State University.

Sylvester Walker's granddaughter playing basketball in her front yard, Spivey's Corner, NC. © Photo by Rob Amberg.

In 1838, Congress ordered the removal of the Cherokees to the west under military escort. Those making the "Trail of Tears" march to Oklahoma are called Western Cherokees, and the few who were left behind or refused to go are called the Eastern Band of Cherokee Indians. At the time of the removal, 1838, the Cherokee Indians had one of the most progressive educational systems in America. Since that time the education of Cherokee Indian children has undergone several great significant transitions.

The education system for the Eastern Cherokee Indians was reestablished by Quaker missionaries in the late 1800s. The Indian boarding school was then taken over and administered by the Bureau of Indian Affairs and evolved into the Bureau of Indian Affairs community day schools. In the 1990s a majority of Bureau schools were contracted to the individual tribes to operate. The Cherokee elementary school contains grades K–6 while the high school serves 7th–12th grade students. Indian students have the choice of attending tribal schools or state-supported public schools. Approximately one-fourth of the students on the reservation attend county public schools. The average allocation per Indian student who moves to a public school is $2,400 per year through a federal funding system called Impact Aid.

The rural schools serving American Indian students are unique with considerable challenges for educators and educational leaders. For example, the Cherokee High School, a tribal school, is a small school of less than 200 students in grades 9–12. Middle school students include grades 7–8 and are contained in a separate part of the building. Therefore, there is a school within a school. The middle school consists of about 100 students. The school population is 99 percent Cherokee Indian students. The 1 percent of white students are descendants of Cherokees living on the reservation. Until three years ago the Cherokee Central Schools were funded and administered by the Bureau of Indian Affairs. The teachers were federal government employees, with comprehensive fringe benefits. The school system was not required to follow state curriculum guidelines. Today, the schools are administered by the Eastern Band of Cherokee Indians. The majority of the teachers commute daily from nearby towns. A few teachers have been with the school for years as they began teaching for the Bureau of Indian Affairs. However, there is a high turnover rate among the other teachers. There is no tenure, a minimal retirement system and the annual pay is below the neighboring public systems' pay schedule. There are only four to five Indian teachers in the high school and only two of these teachers are in academic areas. The other teachers are not full-fledged members of the community and may have little understanding of the Indian culture. The start of each school year brings a new faculty with beginning and inexperienced teachers. There are many challenging problems in this educational setting.

CULTURAL INFLUENCE AND EDUCATION IN A DEMOCRATIC SOCIETY

DEMANDS OF DIVERSE ETHNIC GROUPS

There are those who argue that America has no "we," no national culture (Gould, 1981). For some their culture has been lost. For some, the culture was never there, while others feel there should be no common culture. Our society, they say, is nothing more than a collection of distinctive racial and ethnic cul-.tures. Some of the vehement partisans in this camp claim that any effort to teach a "common culture" disparages the role and contributions of minority groups (Gould, 1981). Such critics speak contemptuously of the common culture, as if it were a vehicle of oppression. They claim that public schools must teach children to revere the culture of their parents, grandparents, and ancestors. The goal of the public school, according to the critics, must be to transmit, preserve, and strengthen the separate identities of the nation's many racial and ethnic cultures. By this definition, the culture taught by the schools will vary according to the color or language of children in the school (Ravitch, 1992).

"The schools and curriculum authors must realize it is not necessary to chose between uniqueness and commonality in building a core curriculum. In a democratic society, all cultural groups must be represented" (Hillard, 1992, p. 13). The respect for differences is a characteristic of our democratic society. Since most immigrants to America came seeking freedom, many curriculum critics would be going against a founding principle of our country if they demanded a universal curriculum.

> We say that the search for truth is our highest goal for students. To foster truth, we must facilitate in students the assumption of a critical orientation. Of course, criticism implies an awareness of all cultural alternatives and a thoughtful and honest examination of those alternatives. Students in the mainstream culture need to view themselves in terms of their own culture and with regard to other cultures. No cultural tradition can be regarded as immune to criticism. (Hillard, 1992, p. 13)

According to Hirsh (1987), there are many interests to be served by having a curriculum with a similar focus or method in handling culture for all our children. However, it is not necessary to choose between uniqueness and commonality. Human minds and systems should be flexible enough to handle uniqueness and a curriculum with many things in common. Nevertheless, how a democratic society arrives at a common core is important.

Asante (1992) is greatly disturbed by the lack of direction and confidence that plagues many African-American children and believes it is because they are not culturally centered and empowered in their classrooms. According to Asante, one of the principal concepts of empowerment is to present information so that students come out of their school feeling they have a place in the information they have learned.

White children do not have to be empowered. Everything within the classroom is familiar to them. That is, school subjects and curriculum in most schools are designed around white middle-class values. Information and values from African-Americans, American Indians, Latinos and Asian-Americans are not part of school curriculum in most American schools.

According to Banks (1992), every person becomes centered in a particular culture because of the way the person is raised. We all accept the ideas and culture of the community of our childhood. Children from a white middle-class community will have no problems with this concept. However, it is a problem for minority children. When minority children begin their life in a public school they are forced to question the culture within which they have grown up. For example, American Indian children learn that each human is a multidimensional being made up of a body, a mind, and a spirit. The spirit world and the mental world coexist and intermingle with the physical world. This is not a concept found in the ever-centered curriculum.

Education within a pluralistic society should help students understand their home and community cultures. To maintain a civic community that works for the common good, education in a democratic society should help students add the knowledge, attitudes, and skills they will need to participate and make society more equal for all cultures.

INDIAN CULTURAL INFLUENCE ON EDUCATION

Teachers must consider the psychological, social, and academic needs along with the cultural identity of their students in order to develop an appropriate learning atmosphere. When considering their Indian students, teachers need to care about their children, teach them to care about each other, show them that hatred hurts, show them how to think critically, open up new worlds for them to discover, offer them the tools of change, and create a small caring community in the classroom.

It has already been shown that American Indian society is pluralistic. In fact, "tribal identity" is a more useful way to operationally define cultural identity. The first self-identifier for Indian people is usually membership in or affiliation with a specific tribe or tribes. For many, the next most salient identifier is membership in a clan or society within a tribe.

Within the Cherokee nation are seven clans, and each Cherokee knows which clan he/she belongs to and how their parents affiliations affect them and their children. A great concern for many Indian people is the fear that identification with a non-Indian culture is equivalent to the loss of their Indian culture. For example, total acceptance of the white culture would deny one's place in the clan system, the tribe, and the Indian world, a situation educators need to consider.

A large proportion of the scientific literature concerning the psychosocial issues of American Indians addresses Indian identity. An important contribution to this line of inquiry is the research of Oetting and Beauvais (1990), who tested the theory that identification with different cultures is orthogonal. That is, instead of cultures being placed at opposite ends of a continuum, this theory holds that cultural identification dimensions are independent of each other, thus increasing identification with one culture does not require decreasing identification with another. In short, coexisting with another culture does not mean assimilating into it. For example, Indian children may attend public schools where the majority of the student body is white, but they will not become a member of the white community although they may participate in many school and community activities.

> Teachers must consider the psychological, social, and academic needs along with the cultural identity of their students in order to develop an appropriate learning atmosphere. When considering their Indian students, teachers need to care about their children, teach them to care about each other, show them that hatred hurts, show them how to think critically, open up new worlds for them to discover, offer them the tools of change, and create a small caring community in the classroom.

BELIEF SYSTEMS

Each tribe has had its own unique set of beliefs that have been influenced by contact with both non-Indians and other Indian groups. Therefore, hundreds of belief systems are held by American Indians and Alaska Natives, but most tribes seem to have some basic beliefs in common (Locust, 1988). The following set of beliefs is meant to serve as a guide for further study and should not be universally ascribed to every tribe.

(1) There is a Supreme Creator, and there are lesser beings also.

(2) Each human is a multidimensional being made up of a body, a mind, and a spirit.

(3) Plants and animals, like humans, are part of the spirit world.

(4) The spirit world coexists and intermingles with the physical world.

(5) The spirit existed before it came into a physical body and will exist after the body dies.

(6) Illness affects the mind and spirit as well as the body.

(7) Wellness is harmony in body, mind, and spirit.

(8) Unwellness is disharmony in body, mind, and spirit. Natural unwellness is caused by the violation of a sacred or tribal taboo.

(9) Unnatural unwellness is caused by witchcraft.

(10) We are all responsible for our own wellness.

Another set of beliefs is related to Indian sacred ways and practices. These common beliefs reflect the desire for harmony among all parts of the cosmos: the Creator, individuals, families, communities, tribes, and all peoples of the world (Simonelli, 1993).

(1) There are unseen powers, what some people call the Great Mystery.

(2) All things in the universe are dependent on each other.

(3) Personal worship reinforces the bond among the individual, the community and the great powers. Worship is a personal commitment to the sources of life.

(4) Sacred traditions and persons knowledgeable about sacred traditions are responsible for teaching morals and ethics.

(5) Most communities and tribes have trained practitioners such as medicine men, priests, shamans, and caciques. These individuals, who may also have titles that are specific to each tribe, are responsible for specialized, perhaps secret knowledge. They help pass along knowledge and sacred practices from generation to generation, storing what they know in their memories.

(6) Humor is a necessary part of the sacred. Human beings are often weak—we are not gods—and our weaknesses lead us to do foolish things; therefore, clowns and similar figures are needed to show us how we act and why.

Native American ideas and beliefs must be considered if the people outside the Native American world are to begin to understand the needs of Native American children in the classrooms of America. The strengths and the weaknesses of Native Americans must be considered as curriculum is designed if the curriculum is to be meaningful to Indian children. Also, the value systems of the Native American individual and the community should be considered when education programs are being designed.

VALUE SYSTEMS

Several studies exist that contrast the white value system to the Indian value system (Kleinfeld, 1974). For example, it is asserted that Anglos value individuality, whereas Indians value the group collective. The listing of contrasts between the two groups has some merit, but it also creates dualities where such do not necessarily exist. There are many Indian value systems, just as there are many white value systems. Different tribes have different beliefs just as white communities in America have different values and beliefs, such as beliefs about the creator or great spirit. With that caveat in mind, some commonly espoused values across tribes include the importance of sharing and generosity, allegiance to one's family and community, respect for elders, noninterference, orientation to present time, and harmony with nature.

LEARNING STYLES

The task of identifying both traditional and contemporary Indian learning styles has been given little attention. The cognitive styles of the American Indian and their relationship to acculturation stress have not received the attention of the researcher or the practitioner that they deserve (Yates, 1987). As it is for people in other parts of the world whose survival depends upon learning the signs of nature, the principle of observation has been central to American Indians for centuries. As with most young children, Indian children learn by watching and listening; trial and error is likewise an honored process for learning. Additionally, societal norms have been passed down through the generations in the telling of stories. The oral tradition was the primary method of teaching values and attitudes in the traditional Indian society. Legends and stories often had highly specific meaning and involved intricate relationships. The use of symbolism, anthropomorphism (giving human characteristics to animals, gods, and objects), animism (giving life and soul to natural phenomena such as rocks, trees, and wind), and metaphors appear to have been extremely effective methods of teaching very complex concepts (Yates, 1987).

Using these traditions was especially helpful when I taught technical writing skills and math concepts. Math concepts were much more easily understood, given concrete, hands-on examples. For example, teaching fractions is better understood using concrete methods. All in all, many scholars in this area agree that modern Indian children demonstrate strengths in their abilities to memorize visual patterns, to visualize spatial concepts, and to produce descriptions rich in visual detail and graphic metaphors (Kleinfeld, 1974).

Unfortunately, the skills described above are not consistently valued in the white school system. Instead, auditory processing, abstract conceptualization, and language skills are emphasized. Although Indian children are capable of shifting to the cognitive styles promoted in formal education, other factors compromise their achievement. Having taught Cherokee Indian children for seventeen years, I have found that starting in fifth or sixth grade, Indian children typically do not achieve academically as well as their Anglo peers. It is likely that, for some, the dissonance between Indian and non-Indian cognitive styles, the attendant negative feelings and other psychosocial stressors plague the Indian child in school and other arenas of life as he or she matures into adulthood.

Cherokees do not expect one student to stand out; success of the whole group is more important than one student's outstanding performance. The conflicting cooperation and competition variables in traditional Cherokee culture and white culture have long been thought to play an important part in the academic achievement of Cherokee Indians (Garrison, 1970; Sanders, 1972).

Several studies have looked at Cherokee educational attainment, all of them finding similar results. For example, Garrison (1970) found that Cherokee children lagged behind their Anglo peers in math, language, and reading achievement. Although at the first-grade level the Cherokee children equaled or exceeded the school achievement of their Anglo peers, as they continued on in school the Cherokee children fell further and further behind.

In order to understand how cooperation and competition affect school achievement, it is necessary to examine how the two forms of behavior develop in Cherokee children. Low academic achievement of Cherokee children has been attributed to their disadvantaged home environments, to negative stereotyping by teachers, and to the disparity of different cultural backgrounds among the teachers and their students (Garrison, 1970), although Sanders (1972) writes that there are "numerous problems regarding discipline, motivation, attitudes, and values that are different from that of the school and its personnel" (p. 76).

Gulick (1960) found one overriding issue and developed the term "harmony ethic" to describe a general rule that guides Cherokee conduct of interpersonal behavior. Cherokees are taught as children to be concerned for a harmonious and peaceable relationship with others and to be sensitive to others' desires. Extending the work of Cherokee anthropologist Robert K. Thomas, Gulick (1960) described the ethic this way: "In living from day to day according to the Harmony Ethic the conservative Cherokee tries to avoid giving offense to others and in so doing, he must always wait and see what others' likes and dislikes are, and . . . perceive what demands are likely to be made of him" (p. 131). Gulick characterizes this demeanor as being particularly sensitive to subliminal cues in overt behavior . . . whereas one actively maintains harmony by giving of one's time and goods, one can passively maintain it by "minding one's own business" (p. 137).

Competition is a common form of interpersonal conflict, so the Cherokee child avoids competition in order to maintain harmony. Maintaining harmony with others could require going along with the achievement norms of friends. For instance, in class when a child cannot answer a question that several Cherokee children know the answer to, all the children remain silent (Fuchs & Havighurst, 1972). The individual Cherokee child that seeks to outdo his/her peers is creating disharmony; is not "going along" or cooperating with the aspirations and abilities of his/her friends.

As a result of the way they are reared, Cherokee children are reluctant to exhibit ineptitude (Sanders, 1972). Cherokee children will not ask questions because the question might disturb someone, or reflect a lack of knowledge. At the same time, Cherokee children are frequently reluctant to be singled out for public praise by a teacher. Such praise in front of the other children, with its emphasis on individual rather than group effort, is likely to produce embarrassment because it disrupts group harmony.

As Cherokee children mature, they fall more and more under the influence of their peer group. A number of writers have pointed out that peer group influence has an especially strong leveling effect on individual aspirations among Cherokees (Dumont & Wax, 1969; Sanders, 1972). Cherokee children work within an interdependent and cooperative framework that is nearly diametrically opposite to the individualistic and competitive atmosphere of middle-class white society.

The Indian culture stresses togetherness; it is group-dominated and emphasizes strong family and communal ties. Examples of strong family ties are the knowledge of an Indian individual's family tree and who one's relatives are. Another example is the strong community club organization and the role these clubs play in the lives of Indians at all age levels. Also, when a conference is called for an Indian student in the school setting, it is not unusual for many family members to attend the meeting. Mother, father, grandmother, cousin, aunt or uncle might be in attendance at the meeting.

The studies cited were completed twenty years ago. For the last seventeen years I have taught Cherokee Indian children. I find the ideas of Sanders, Dumont and Wax are as timely today as when originally written. Cherokee children still do not like to outdo their peers. They are extremely reluctant to ask questions; they are uncomfortable with praise and being singled out. Cherokee children do not, even today, want to produce embarrassment because it disrupts group harmony. Cherokee adolescents fall under a very strong influence of their peer group. It is my experience that the peer group has a great influence on how the student performs in school and how much importance is placed on schooling.

Today's public educational systems do not consider the Cherokee's harmony ethic. Much of today's education is based on competition with an emphasis on individual achievement. These concepts are in direct opposition to the ways and thoughts of Cherokee culture. When a school ignores such basic beliefs of a culture, it is not surprising that students of the culture tend to have problems in school.

Historically, American Indian youngsters were educated, for the most part, in federal and mission schools, where the purpose of schooling was much the same as for Anglo young people attending public schools during the nineteenth century: to provide vocational training for semi-skilled work (Spring, 1989). In addition, the purpose of educating young American Indian people was to civilize, Christianize, and hasten assimilation into the dominant white society. Public schooling became available to American Indian youth in some regions of the country in the early 1900s.

A government task force on Indian education (Cooper, 1991) urged schools serving Native American students to provide "a multicultural environment" that would promote tribal languages and cultures. The fourteen-member panel of educational and tribal leaders reported some progress in Indian education during the past two decades but noted continuing problems, such as a high school dropout rate of 36 percent, the highest of any racial or ethnic group. Contrary to popular assumptions, most Indian students do not attend Bureau of Indian Affairs schools on reservations.

Rumberger (1987) notes that African-American, Hispanic and American Indian populations, disproportionately represented among dropouts, are increasing at a faster rate than the white majority. This is a critical problem when one considers that in many areas of America, these populations represent the majority of school-age children. Increased academic requirements are likely to have severe repercussions for the population of at-risk students. The importance placed upon educational achievement to gain entry into the work force leaves the dropout with only opportunities for menial jobs.

Dropping out has myriad individual and social consequences. Individual consequences include low academic skills, lack of employment opportunities, limited advanced educational and training opportunities, and an adverse effect on the dropout's psychological well-being and health. The social consequences include foregoing income, increased demand for social services, increased crime, reduced political participation, reduced intergenerational mobility, and fragile levels of community stability and security.

America's dropout problem is a result of a changing society and education systems that have not grown to meet the needs of their diverse clients. Although, according to Spring (1989), education systems were never meant to meet the needs of children but were meant to meet the needs of industry and despite a greater awareness of at-risk students, few alternatives exist to combat the statistics. Schools and classes remain large; tracking is still widely acceptable; standardized tests are misused; higher graduation requirements without remediation for low-achieving students is a trend; the emphasis is on credits earned rather than on competencies; and there is a lack of support for minorities. All of these factors contribute to the downward academic fall of this special at-risk population.

Greene (1986) offers an example of how Indian education was handled. Because the Eastern Cherokees were wards of the federal government, the state of North Carolina accepted no responsibility for an educational system for Cherokee children. Thus, the schools on the Qualla Boundary were maintained by the federal government, and federal policies on Indian education were the controlling force in the Cherokee schools. As a result of the passage of the Dawes Allotment Act in 1887, the government's goal in Indian education became "education for citizenship." During this period federal policies concentrated on eradicating all vestiges of Indian culture as Indian children were taught the white man's language, history, and way of life.

The 1920s, however, gave rise to new philosophies with regard to the formal education of Native American youth. The government's Indian educational system came under attack by reform groups who became increasingly more influential and who denounced the federal policies in Indian schools. By the closing years of the 1920s the government's Indian educational system was responding to the demands for change, and with the appointment of John Collier as Commissioner of Indian Affairs in 1933, the Indian New Deal was instituted. Through Collier's belief in self-determination appeared the beginnings of a promise—the promise of a time when an Indian child would be regarded as an individual with his own heritage and his own contribution to make to society. The "education for citizenship" policies of the early federal period were abandoned, and an era emerged in which there was a recognition of and respect for Indian culture. The Bureau of Indian Affairs established community day schools; children were allowed to attend school in their own community and go home at night.

World War II had a great influence on the Cherokee educational system and the Cherokee community. As in many areas of federal government, the Indian educational programs were not of major importance. All young men who were of age went into the military, and many young men lied about their age in order to enter the military before they were eighteen. Eastern Cherokees have always had a strong interest in the military and feel that it is their duty to serve in the American armed forces. The military further acculturated Eastern Cherokees into white society and also served as a means of further education and job training. Since the World War II experience, the military continues to be a major educator of the Cherokee Indians.

After World War II, the Bureau of Indian Affairs continued to fund and administer the Cherokee Indian schools. Reservation schools were patterned after surrounding state public schools, although they schools did not have a set curriculum that teachers were required to follow. The Bureau of Indian Affairs funding far exceeded what was spent within North Carolina public schools during the same period, a trend that continued through the 1960s when Indian schools remained heavily funded, and children were provided for in a substantial manner.

During the Carter and Reagan years, funding began to dwindle, and rumors started that the Bureau of Indian Affairs wanted out of the education business. Within eight years, the Bureau schools were, in fact, contracted to the tribal government. The Eastern Band of Cherokees chose to have the school system administered by the Cherokee Boys' Club, Inc. The schools receive federal funding in the form of block grants, and are governed by an elected school board with representatives from each community. The school board develops school policy while the schools follow the North Carolina Basic Education Plan and the North Carolina state curriculum. All the Cherokee tribal schools have earned Southern Association accreditation.

To some degree, formal education is a continuation of the enculturative process. Formal education imparts, at the very least, a number of special skills, which themselves are part of the culture. The extent to which formal education should also include processes of character formation is now, and has been for some time, a matter of controversy in American culture generally. This controversy can be argued at one level when the context is one in which the pupils have much in common culturally with their teachers who are predominantly of middle-class backgrounds. In this case, both teachers and pupils participate in a value system that includes emphasis on cleanliness, promptness, perseverance in the completion of tasks, and positive responses to individualized rewards for competitive success. Thus, the teaching of specialized skills almost automatically reinforces the general value system, and the controversy about character formation tends to revolve around the question of what more, over and beyond basic skills, should be imparted in school.

But suppose the cultural background of the teachers is not the same as that of their pupils, or at least a large proportion of them. This is the situation faced by teachers and many parents and children among the Eastern Cherokees. The educational system, the curriculum, and the personalities of the educational personnel are all part of the value system of white middle-class America. The children of conservative (traditional) parents, however, come to school with a value system in formation that is either contrary to, or does not include, the items mentioned above. The teachers have no choice but to present their material in conformity with educational policies and in a manner compatible with their own value system. Despite the fact that the federal Indian education system has, for a quarter of a century, abandoned its former policy of attempting, forcibly if necessary, to eradicate the expression of Indian cultural patterns, it still remains difficult for many of the educational personnel to conceal their personal distaste for certain practices and attitudes that are incompatible with their own. Some of these attitudes prevail today in the tribal school system.

Among adult conservative Eastern Cherokees, it is obvious that this regime has not resulted in a change in values. It has, however, communicated to them the strong impression that certain conservative patterns of behavior are undesirable from the point of view of middle-class non-Indian Americans. For the conservative child, therefore, the formal education phase of his enculturation puts him in a situation in which he learns certain technical skills but in which he also learns that there are those who believe that many of the practices and attitudes in his home and in his own personality should be changed. Those of the Eastern Cherokees who are the most successful in school are not the conservatives but those whose family patterns and attitudes are already consistent with those of the white middle-class educational system.

SUMMARY AND RECOMMENDATIONS FOR CURRICULUM DEVELOPMENT IN RURAL INDIAN COMMUNITIES

Based on the perceptions of Indian parents and their students on education, the phenomenon of dropping out, and the importance of culture in the curriculum, the following suggestions are offered for the development of appropriate curriculum for Indian students.

The curriculum should allow students to legitimize their ideas, voices, experiences, and histories. This is the way students give meaning to their world. Schools should be places for struggle so that students are allowed to and guided toward expanding their capabilities as active participants in the community. Students should be guided toward all of the possibilities of a democratic society. When students are shown or educated to all of their possibilities, then they are becoming socially empowered.

(1) Cherokee students feel these possibilities would be fostered by culture in the curriculum.

(2) Programs for American Indian dropouts should be closely examined by the local school system so that an action plan to improve the dropout situation for the students of the Eastern Band of Cherokees can be initiated.

(3) There should be early identification and intervention with at-risk children with increased attention to the self-esteem and counseling needs of students and an increase in school counseling staff.

(4) Teachers should be aware of students' cultural characteristics. Educational leaders should consider cultural characteristics such as group achievement rather than competitiveness when creating an educational plan.

(5) Culture in the curriculum would help to improve or create self-esteem in Indian students. Indian students cannot be expected to be successful in school or in life if first they do not know who they are. Indian students should be given the opportunity to develop a strong identity and a healthy self-esteem to know where they want to go with their lives and to be able to travel through life as an Indian rather than an imitation of a white person.

(6) Parents want an education that will enable their children to take control of their lives and fulfill a meaningful role in their society, whether it be as a council member, a teacher, or a mechanic. Parents should be allowed to be a part of their child's education. We need to give children empowerment for ever-increasing possibilities in their futures.

(7) A training model should be designed for cultural sensitivity or cultural awareness for teachers who are not Cherokee but who work with American Indian students. Many of the teaching ideas of More (1987) and Yates (1987), such as cognitive styles and learning techniques, should be focused upon and incorporated into teaching with the use of metaphors, legends, and symbolism.

(8) Cherokee students should have the experience of a multiculturalism debate within their classrooms. Students must be given a voice, and education within a pluralistic society should help students understand their home and community cultures and help them understand and debate the prejudices within their world.

REFERENCES

Asante, M. K. (1992). "Afro-Centric Curriculum," *Educational Leadership, 49*(4), 28–31.

Banks, J. A. (1979). *Teaching Strategies for Ethnic Studies* (2nd ed.). Needham Heights, MA: Allyn and Bacon.

Banks, J. A. (1981). *Education in the 80's: Multiethnic Education* (Report No. 81–1504). Washington, DC: National Education Association.

Banks, J. A. (1988). *Multiethnic Education: Theory and Practice* (2nd ed.). Newton, MA: Allyn and Bacon.

Banks, J. A. (1989). *Multicultural Education: Issues and Perspectives.* Needham Heights, MA: Allyn and Bacon.

Banks, J. A. (1992). "Multicultural Education: For Freedom's Sake," *Educational Leadership, 49*(4), 32–36.

Brown, A. (1980). "Cherokee Culture and School Achievement," *American Indian Culture and Research Journal, 4*(3), 55–74.

Bullivant, B. (1989). *Culture: Its Nature and Meaning for Educators.* Needham Heights, MA: Allyn and Bacon.

Cardenas, R. (1990). *Parenting in a Multicultural Society.* New York: Longman.

Cooper, K. (1991, December 27). "Multicutural Focus Recommended for Education of Native Americans," *The Washington Post,* A19.

DePalma, A. (1991, May 19). "Ethnic Diversity Brings Separate World," *Montgomery Advertiser,* 4.

Deyhle, D. (1989). "Pushouts and Pullouts: Navajo and Ute School Leavers," *Journal of Navajo Education, 6*(2), 36–51.

Dumont, R., & M. Wax. (1969). *The Cherokee School Society and Intercultural Classroom.* Subcommittee on Indian Education. Washington, DC: U.S. Congress. Senate Hearings on Indian Education, Part 2.

Fuchs, E., & R. Havighurst. (1972). *To Live on This Earth; American Indian Education.* Garden City: Doubleday.

Garrison, C. (1970). *1001 Media Ideas for Teachers.* Berkeley, CA: McCutchan Publishing.

Giroux, H., A. Penna, & W. Pinar. (1981). *Curriculum and Instruction.* Berkeley, CA: McCuthchan Publishing Co.

Grant, C. (1979). *Participation in Education.* Boston: Allyn and Bacon.

Grant, C., & C. Sleeter. (1989). *Race, Class, Gender, Exceptionality and Education Reform.* Needham Heights, MA: Allyn and Bacon.

Greene, J. (1986). *Federal Policies in the Schools of the Eastern Cherokees, 1892–1932.* Unpublished master's thesis, Western Carolina University, Cullowhee, NC.

Greene, M. (1988). *The Dialectic of Freedom.* New York: Teachers College Press.

Gripp, G., & S. Fox. (1991). "Promoting Cultural Relevance in American Indian Education," *The Education Digest, 57*(4), 58–61.

Guba, E., & Y. Lincoln. (1982). "Epistemological and Methodological Bases of Naturalistic Inquiry," *Educational Communication and Technology Journal, 30*(4), 233–252.

Gulick, W. (1960). *Human Stereopsis; A Psychophysical Analysis.* New York: Oxford University Press.

Havighurst, R. (1972). *Leaders in American Education.* Chicago: University of Chicago Press.

Hillard, A. G. III. (1976). *Alternatives to IQ: Testing an Approach to the Identification of Gifted Minority Children.* Morristown, NJ: Aaron Press.

Hillard, A. G. III. (1992). "Why We Must Pluralize the Curriculum," *Educational Leadership, 49*(4), 12–16.

Hillard, A. G., L. Payton-Stewart, & L. Obadele. (1990). *The Influence of African and African American Content in the School Curriculum.* Morristown, NJ: Aaron Press.

Hirsh, E. D. (1987). *Cultural Literacy: What Every American Needs to Know.* Boston: Houghton Mifflin.

Indian Nations at Risk Task Force. (1991). *Indian Nations at Risk: An Educational Strategy or Action.* U.S. Department of Education. Washington, DC: U.S. Government Printing Office.

Kleinfield, S. (1974). *The Hidden Minority: A Profile of Handicapped Americans.* Boston: Little, Brown.

Lincoln, Y., & E. Guba. (1985). *Understanding and Doing Naturalistic Inquiry.* Beverly Hills, CA: Sage Publishers.

Locust, C. (1988). "Wounding the Spirit: Discrimination and Traditional American Indian Belief Systems," *Harvard Educational Review, 58*(3), 315–328.

National Advisory Council on Indian Education. (1989). *Education the American Indian/Alaska Native Family* (17th Annual Report to the U.S. Congress). Washington, DC: U.S. Government Printing Office.

Oetting, E., & F. Beauvais. (1990). "Orthogonal Cultural Identification Theory: The Cultural Identification of Minority Adolescents," *International Journal of the Addictions, 15*(3), 449–455.

Ravitch, D. (1992). "A Culture in Common," *Educational Leadership, 49*(3), 8–11.

Rumberger, R. W. (1987). "High School Dropouts: A Review of Issues and Evidence," *Review of Educational Research, 57*(2), 101–121.

Sanders, A. (1972). *Perspectives on Perception and Action.* Hillsdale, NJ: L. Erlbaum Associates.

Schumacher, D. (1992). "Indian Task Force Calls for Multiculturalism in Classrooms," *Education USA,* 117, 120.

Simonelli, R. (1993). "Seeds of Diversity," *Winds of Change, 8*(1), Boulder, CO: Aises Publishing, Inc.

Spring, J. (1989). *The Sorting Machine Revisted.* New York: Longman. Mexico Press.

Yates, A. (1987). *The Organization of Schooling: A Study of Educational Grouping Practices.* London: Routledge and Kegan Paul.

Index

303

About the Authors

Rob Amberg (photography) specializes in photography that portrays social issues. His stock subject is photography that depicts the rural lifestyle, and many of the photos selected for this book show teaching and learning at its best in rural America. His photos are copyrighted and nationally accepted and displayed. Rob Amberg can be reached at Rob Amberg Photography, 600 Anderson Branch Road, Marshall, North Carolina 28753.

Donald M. Chalker (editor, Chapter 1, Chapter 14) is a Professor in the Department of Educational Leadership and Foundations at Western Carolina University. Dr. Chalker is a former teacher, assistant principal, principal, assistant superintendent, and superintendent. He is co-author of two books on world-class schools and co-founder of World Class Schools Consulting. Dr. Chalker is a graduate of Kent State University and Wayne State University.

Edward W. Chance (Chapter 5, Chapter 13) is a Professor of Educational Leadership at the University of Nevada, Las Vegas. He is Chair of the Research Forum for the National Rural Education Association and Co-Chair of the American Association of School Administrators Annual Conference Within a Conference. He has contributed extensive research on visioning and leadership in rural America. Prior to coming to UNLV, Dr. Chance was on the faculty of the University of Oklahoma and was Director of the Center for the Study of Small/Rural Schools.

William Clauss (Chapter 12) is Director of the Office of Rural Education at Western Carolina University and a member of the Department of Educational Leadership and Foundations. The office collaborates with rural public schools in the western half of North Carolina. Dr. Clauss is a long-time member of the National Rural Education Association.

Alan DeYoung (Foreword) is one of the most prolific writers in the field of rural education. Dr. DeYoung is a Professor and Chair of the Department of Educational Policy Studies and Evaluation at the University of Kentucky.

Marilyn L. Grady (Chapter 4) is an Associate Professor of Educational Administration at the University of Nebraska-Lincoln. She has been an administrator in K–12 schools. She has published often in the area of rural superintendent/school board relationships and educational leadership. Dr. Grady coordinates an annual conference on Women in Educational Leadership.

Emil J. Haller (Chapter 15), who earned his Ph.D. at the University of Chicago, is Professor Emeritus of Educational Administration at Cornell University. He is co-author of *An Introduction to Educational Administration: Social, Legal and Ethical Perspectives*, and of *The Ethics of School Administration*. In addition, he has conducted research and written extensively for professional journals, most recently on political and sociological issues surrounding public schools.

Richard Haynes (Chapter 7) is an Associate Professor of education at Western Carolina University and the Director of Field Services. He previously served as a teacher, supervisor, and assistant superintendent in the North Carolina public schools. Dr. Haynes is a graduate of Duke University. He has written several children's books, is co-author of two books on world-class schools and co-founder of World Class Schools Consulting.

Mary Jean Ronan Herzog (Chapter 2) is one of the movers and shakers behind the rural research effort in the Department of Educational Leadership and Foundations at Western Carolina University. She co-authored a feature article on rural schools for *Phi Delta Kappan*. Dr. Herzog, a graduate of the University of Tennessee, is an Associate Professor of educational foundation, curriculum, and research.

Anna T. Hicks (Chapter 10) is an Assistant Professor in the Department of Educational Leadership and Foundations at Western Carolina University. She taught high school, served as an assistant principal and language arts coordinator and then as her district's first female high school principal. She holds a Ph.D. in Educational Administration from the University of South Carolina (1992).

Eleanor Blair Hilty (Chapter 9) is an Assistant Professor at Western Carolina University, where she specializes in foundation of education and philosophy of education. Her chapter proposing that teachers are educational leaders is representative of her mission to promote the teaching profession. Dr. Hilty is a graduate of the University of Tennessee.

Doris Hipps (Chapter 16) is an Assistant Professor of Curriculum at Valdosta State University and a former public school teacher and researcher for Foxfire. She has researched the educational needs of Native Americans.

Robert Houghton (Chapter 11) has special interests in curriculum development, especially with new systems for interaction. He serves as editor of the college's *Web Journal* at Western Carolina University and teaches courses on computer integration, distance learning, and multimedia. He received his Ph.D. from the University of Wisconsin-Madison.

J. Casey Hurley (Chapter 8) was a teacher, assistant principal and principal in Wisconsin before joining the faculty at Western Carolina University. Dr. Hurley earned his Ph.D. in Educational Administration at the University of Wisconsin-Madison. He is an Associate Professor in the Department of Educational Leadership and Foundations specializing in educational leadership.

Bernita L. Krumm (Chapter 4) is an Assistant Professor of Educational Administration at Texas A & M University-Commerce. She has held teaching and administrative positions in K–12 schools. She has researched the areas of superintendent-board relationships, education law, and Native American leadership.

David H. Monk (Chapter 15) is Professor of Educational Administration and Chair of the Department of Education at Cornell University. He earned his Ph.D. at the University of Chicago. Monk is the author of *Educational Finance: An Economic Approach* as well as numerous articles in scholarly journals. He serves on the editorial boards of the *The Economics of Education Review, Journal of Educational Finance, Educational Policy*, and the *Journal of Research in Rural Education*. He is past president of the American Education Finance Association.

Robert Morris (Chapter 6) is a Professor in the Department of Educational Leadership and Foundations at the State University of West Georgia. He has published four books and numerous articles on at-risk students for public school practitioners, and he yearly directs a workshop on teacher evaluation at ASCD.

Janie Nusser (Chapter 15) is completing her doctoral studies in Educational Administration at Cornell University. Nusser is currently employed as the Director of Curriculum and Instruction in the South Seneca Central School District, a rural district in central New York.

Robert Pittman (Chapter 2) is a Professor of Research and Statistics at Western Carolina University. He has received numerous awards for teaching excellence. He has published several articles on rural education and is a leading proponent of rural education research. Dr. Pittman is a graduate of the University of North Carolina at Chapel Hill. He coauthored a feature article on rural schools for *Phi Delta Kappan.*

Les Potter (Chapter 6) has been a public school teacher, coach, guidance, counselor, assistant principal, principal, and assistant superintendent. He served as principal in five schools in three different states. He is an Assistant Professor at two universities and is currently a principal in Charlotte, North Carolina. He holds a doctorate from The University of South Carolina.

Penny Smith (Chapter 3) chairs the Department of Educational Leadership and Foundations at Western Carolina University. She holds a Ph.D. in History from Rice University and an Ed.D. in Educational Leadership from the University of North Carolina-Greensboro. Dr. Smith is a former public school teacher, principal, and associate superintendent.